ISRAEL
The View from Masada

RONALD SANDERS

ISRAEL

The View from Masada

Harper & Row, Publishers, New York, Evanston, and London

FIRST EDITION

LIBRARY OF CONGRESS CATALOG CARD NUMBER: 66-20745

I-Q

To My Mother and Father

Acknowledgments

Most of the Prologue and large parts of Chapters 1 and 5 originally appeared in *Midstream* magazine, and I am grateful to its editor, Mr. Shlomo Katz, for permission to reprint that material in this book. In addition, I owe Mr. Katz a greater debt of thanks, not only for his advice at various stages in the writing of this work but also for the general climate, created by his friendship and professional help, within which the idea for this book was largely generated and developed.

I also want to thank Dr. Uriel Tal of the Hebrew University for his counsel and his criticism of many of the ideas taken up here. Dr. Ariyeh Goren of the Hebrew University and Mr. Moshe Kohn of the *Jerusalem Post* also were most helpful.

I received valuable advice from two gifted writers, Mr. Albert Fried and Mr. Richard M. Elman. My thanks further go to Mr. Roger Klein of Harper & Row for his help in producing this work.

R.S.

CONTENTS

PROLOGUE:

The View from Masada

I

MASADA is a great brown rock that rises abruptly some twelve hundred feet above the Dead Sea floor, separated from the water's edge by two and a half miles of desert, this latter being an expanse scarred with ravines and parched whitish mounds that many observers have likened to the craters of the moon. Such is the image they present when viewed from the top of Masada itself, especially in the light of the unearthly dawn that rises over the steep cliffs of Moab across the water and contrasts the shadowed white on the western sides of the mounds with sudden illuminations of dazzling yellow-brown where they face the sun. One can make out the village of Ein Gedi to the north, ten miles away by rational measure, but really separated on a more primitive level of perception by "deserts of vast eternity," by the blistered and disfigured calm that ensues some millions of years after an unspeakable conflagration. As the hot dawn breaches the chill night air, the Dead Sea seems to issue steam, suggesting that Miltonic slime in which Satan and his cohorts had found themselves lying, stunned and fallen, after their apostasy. Indeed, no small part of it is salt and brimstone, as if water itself had become an abstraction in the course of its vertiginous descent from the snows of Hermon into this, the nether issue of the Jordan Valley, "this deep, this colossal ditch."[1]

[1] George Adam Smith, *Historical Geography of the Holy Land*, p. 469.

1

The historian Josephus tells us that the High Priest Jonathan, the Hasmonaean, was the first to establish an outpost at Masada, in the second century B.C.E.[2] The name of the place originally meant simply "fortress," but the word came in time to be applied solely to this one, this most unassailable of Masadas. Its natural advantages were later recognized by King Herod, the detested Idumaean ruler of the Jews who murdered his wife and sons and was a sycophant to Roman emperors, but who was also the restorer of the Temple and the greatest builder Israel had known since King Solomon. His paranoia was not the only trait served by this highly defensible rock, which also had the advantage of being, although separated from Jerusalem by only a day's journey, pleasantly remote from the strongholds of Roman influence down on the Mediterranean coast. Even today one can stand atop the ruined shelf of Herod's palace jutting out to the north over a terrifying and beautiful abyss, and readily feel like the unchallenged ruler of a dead universe. Such a state of mind is buttressed by the unique distortion of perspective that takes place in this region: the rises, falls, and contrasts of the surface are so abrupt that to Western eyes they seem to constitute distances greater than they really are. As a result, human figures seem enormous from afar, and a man standing on a mountaintop can easily reckon himself to be a giant. For a small king, it is an ideal spot in which to indulge his imperial fancies. It is also a setting in which a tiny people can know and be obsessed by greatness of vision.

Time here undergoes the same foreshortening. Where are two thousand years of intervening history—where, indeed, is that bad dream, the Diaspora—when one can reach down into the earth at one's feet and pick up a fragment of some Herodian wine jug? Those huge, silent ravens floating in the thickness of the heat must also have been circling here over Herod's pseudo-Roman splendor almost two thousand years ago, over these same mosaic floors, Grecian columns, plaster-covered walls made to look like marble, cheap frescoes, Roman baths, great storehouses filled with grain, pulse, dates and jugs of oil and wine. It is still possible to see the great cisterns cut down below into the western face of Masada, opposite to the Dead Sea side; here the wadis carried the waters of an occasional cloudburst in sufficient quantities to supply the residents above with

[2] "B.C.E." ("Before the Common Era") and "C.E." are the standard Jewish terms for "B.C." and "A.D.," respectively, and will be used throughout these pages.

more than enough water for their needs. Slaves and mules carried the water in jugs up the steep path to smaller cisterns on top. Fresh vegetables were obtained through cultivation of the relatively fertile ground on the summit, where even today flowers spontaneously grow, contrasting with the spare browns of the foothills. There was no lack of civilized comforts here for Herod and his company, whose talk, laughter, belches and yawns broke the air of this otherwise desolate spot until the king's death in 4 B.C.E., whereupon eternity momentarily resumed its interrupted reign.

In the year 6 C.E. Masada was made into a small garrison for Roman soldiers, and it remained so for the next sixty years. These were times of trouble: a memory of its rough and visionary pastoral beginnings was arising in the Jewish conscience and beginning to chafe against the overlordship of a decadent and elegantly polytheistic civilization. Depending upon whether their chief concerns were national or religious, the growing Jewish radical parties were alternately treating Roman power or Hellenistic culture as the focus of their hostility. The foremost nationalist party were the Zealots, whose hopes for ultimate independence were founded upon the knowledge that the people of Israel had already seen great powers come and go throughout their long history, and upon memory of the success that Maccabaean resistance had enjoyed some two centuries before (although the Syria of the Antiochii had been much less formidable an adversary than Imperial Rome). The Pharisees, on the other hand, were the most prominent of those parties whose primary concern was with religious matters; their task was to impart a fresh spirituality to a now worldly and Hellenized Jewry by reinterpreting and adapting to contemporary needs the precepts contained in the wilderness vision of Moses. For the urban upper classes whose ease was challenged by its teachings, Pharisaism was radical enough; and yet the religious fervor of this school was even exceeded by a wave of apocalyptic zeal that was rising up at this time and flourishing in rural and desert places. Jesus and his disciples, simple workingmen, came down to the cities from provincial Galilee, while other men retreated like John the Baptist into the harsh silence of desert and rock to search for lost primeval truths. The Essenes, who had taken to something like monasticism in their settlement at Ein Gedi, could there blink at the purity of God's light through their hot windows. And perhaps, as their eyes cleared and focused upon the Roman garrison at Masada a few miles to the north, their sense of divine mission sometimes also took on a more worldly form. The nationalism of the Dead Sea Valley proved to have the same rock-bound zeal as the religious manifestations to be found there.

For some of the Essenes at least, the ideas of religious revival and of armed national rebellion went together, for there was apparently a group of them among the band of Jews who captured Masada in 66 C.E. and slaughtered the soldiers there, in one of the first acts of the Jewish revolt against the Romans. But the band was made up primarily of Zealots, or rather of that radical wing of the Zealots known to the Romans as the "Sicarii" or "dagger-men," the most warlike of all the Jewish factions at that time. These marauders brought their wives and children to Masada and made it their home for the next seven years. Since even the spacious accommodations of Herod's royal retreat were not enough for nearly a thousand persons, many of the families made homes for themselves within the hollows of the casemate wall that encircles the entire rim of the fortress. As for supplies, Josephus claimed that the desert air had kept the wine, grains and other relatively imperishable foods stored there in Herod's time still usable after nearly a hundred years, but this was perhaps an exaggeration. The band certainly had to obtain at least some of its food elsewhere, and they did so, terrorizing the surrounding countryside with their frequent plundering expeditions. In this way, Masada served as the headquarters for the Sicarii during the entire period of the revolt; many of them sought refuge there, and it was used once as the starting point for an expedition into Jerusalem, in an unsuccessful attempt by the Sicarii to seize power from among the warring factions in the capital.

In 70 C.E., as history and religious tradition have indelibly recorded upon the Jewish imagination, Jerusalem and the Temple were captured and utterly destroyed by the Romans. This in effect put an end to the revolt and to the Jewish commonwealth; but it was only after another two years of fighting to clear out the various remaining pockets of rebellion throughout the country that the Romans sent a legion, commanded by the governor Flavus Silva, to the foot of Masada. Then the long siege began. It is not altogether surprising that the ill-equipped band on top was able to hold off an entire Roman legion for several months, since the approaches to the summit were few and extremely difficult. Josephus, who lived for a time in his youth among the Essenes at Ein Gedi, was able to perceive only one means of access to the fortress: this was the so-called "Snake Path," still known by that name today, which winds dizzyingly up the eastern face, the side that looks toward the Dead Sea. Exercising his talent for occasional exaggeration, Josephus says of the Snake Path that "walking along it is like balancing on a tightrope. The least slip means death; for on either side yawns an abyss so terrifying that it could make the boldest tremble."[3] Though its hazards were not really so extreme—Josephus had never himself made the trip to the summit—Silva, the Roman commander, nevertheless perceived that the Snake Path was no viable approach against the rocks that would be sent tumbling down by the defenders above. Instead, he chose to make his base of operations on the western side of Masada, where the plateau that links it with the surrounding hills forms a floor that is a good deal closer to the summit than the ground on the eastern side. Here he built his main camp; but he also erected a large supply post on the other side, since the desert floor there was much more accessible to routes from Ein Gedi and farther north. These campsites are still visible today, as is the siege wall which the Romans then built from one camp to the other and back again, a circumvallation sealing off the entire base of the rock. Then the erection of a rampart was begun.

Every day for months the men and women on top could look down over the fortress walls and see the Roman soldiers below piling up rocks and dirt, laboriously giving shape to a mound that crept up the steep and otherwise inaccessible western slope. No doubt they scattered the Romans from time to time with volleys of stones, but this could only delay rather than halt the undertaking. When, at long last, this man-made rampart had reached a height of about three hundred feet, the Romans proceeded to build a huge stone platform on top of it, and on this, in turn, an ironclad tower that reached to another hundred feet above the stone base. From the top of the tower, which now stood higher than the walls of the fortress, the Romans began shooting stones and arrows, so that it soon became impossible for any of the Jewish defenders to stand out in the open. The Romans then constructed a great battering ram, and its huge

[3] Josephus, *The Jewish War*, translated by G. A. Williamson (Penguin Books), p. 399.

stone ball was swung and slammed against the fortress walls until they began to break.

The Sicarii devised an ingenious way of nullifying the work of this apparatus. As the outer wall was being broken through by the battering ram, they built a second wall just behind it, made of two rows of wooden beams separated by a space that was filled in with dirt. When the ram struck against the outer layer of wood, which withstood the impact by yielding a little, the earth between the partitions was compressed and the wall was thereby strengthened. The Romans found that they had to seek a new means of attacking the wall. Silva ordered his men to fire a volley of burning torches at the wooden partition; they did so, and the wall caught fire. Then suddenly, according to Josephus, the wind turned and blew the flames back into the faces of the attackers; it seemed for a moment that the Roman fortifications would catch fire, and that the Jewish defenders would thus be saved by a miracle, but the wind changed again and the besieged wall was eventually destroyed in the flames. The Romans returned victorious to their camp, ready to make their entry into the fortress itself the next morning.

During the night the doomed men on top conceived of an unusual manner of reception for the enemy. Eleazar ben Yair, the commander of the camp, addressed a long speech to his men, in which he urged them to take their own lives as well as those of their wives and children sooner than be slaughtered or taken into slavery by the Romans. In the tradition of Thucydides, Josephus reconstructed this speech as Eleazar might have delivered it; it is, indeed, probably more Josephus than Eleazar, an occasion taken by the historian to render some expiation for his own surrender and treasonable cooperation with the Romans a few years prior to the siege of Masada. The Eleazar described by Josephus is perhaps the man that the latter would like to have been. The Zealot commander not only prefers death to being captured, but also apparently would rather see the Jews become extinct than watch them turned into a landless and subjugated people. Surveying the destruction that the Jews have suffered throughout the land, he says in his speech: "those who died in battle we may well congratulate: they died defending their freedom, not betraying it. But the masses who are now under the thumb of Rome who would not pity? Who would not hasten to die rather than share their fate? . . . Old men with streaming eyes sit by the ashes of the Shrine, with a few women kept by the enemy as victims of their lust."[4]

At first Eleazar's men hesitated to do what he urged; but by the time he had finished his moving plea, they rushed away even eagerly to their task. "For at the very moment when with streaming eyes they embraced and caressed their wives, and taking their children into their arms they pressed their last, lingering kisses, hands other than their own seemed to assist them and they carried out their purposes."[5] Hastily, after murdering their wives and children, they gathered up all their possessions and set them on fire; only the supplies in the great storerooms were left untouched, according to Josephus' account, because Eleazar wanted to show the Romans that he had not chosen death out of want. Then the men convened again and drew lots, selecting ten from their midst who would kill the rest of them. When these ten had done their awful work, they in turn drew lots, selecting one who would kill the nine others and then himself. "So finally the nine presented their throats, and the one man left till last, first surveyed the serried ranks of the dead, in case amidst all the slaughter someone was still left in need of his hand; then finding that all had been dispatched set the palace blazing fiercely, and summoning all his strength drove his sword right through his body and fell dead by the side of his family."[6] Only two old women and five children, who had managed to hide away in one of the water tunnels, survived to tell the story to the stunned Roman troops as they entered upon the scene of death the next morning.

II

Palestine is a very small country, a narrow fertile corridor pressed up against the eastern shore of the Mediterranean by mountains that rise suddenly and steeply, though not to great heights, out of the desert to the east. The principal mountain mass of the region is formed by two parallel north-south ranges which straddle the long, deep cut made by the Jordan and the three lakes of increasing magnitude through which it passes in its precipitate southward course, Huleh (now extinct), Tiberias (or the Sea of Galilee) and the Dead

4 *Ibid.*, p. 364.
5 *Ibid.*, p. 366.
6 *Ibid.*, p. 366.

Sea, in which it ends some 1,200 feet below sea level. Two additional ranges or groups of ranges in the north, the Galilee and the Carmel, stretch out like pincers westward to the coast. All these mountains are quite small by Alpine standards, but to the senses they suggest immensity; for they form a restless and varied surface, harsh and jagged, which now leaps skyward and now plummets to earth again in sudden changes of direction that are as firm as they are contradictory. The peaks are neither very high nor very far apart, but the eyes, like the spirit, are taxed to the utmost in the effort to encompass them.

But Palestine is also a part of the Mediterranean littoral; these mountains taper off into valleys and into a coastal plain which, in contrast, are soft and readily made fertile. The ancient Israelites, however, were only rarely able to make a home for themselves in these valleys. The coastal plain was the stronghold of the Philistines, and later usually served as a corridor for passing empires; it was at all times a warm breeding ground of Baal worship and decadence. Wherever this fertile plain turned inland, as in the Valley of Jezreel, the civilized blight followed it inland too, often cutting off one tribe of mountain-dwelling Israelites from another. It was under these conditions, gazing scornfully down their mottled slopes at the pagans below, that the rough and puritan Hebrews shaped their own religion. Essentially, their vision of God always belonged to those mountains. There were occasions when austerity relaxed a little, and then, in the ensuing moment of tension between the spirituality of the hills and the sensuality of the plain—a tension in which the Jewish spirit has always been at its best—such outbursts of lyricism as the Song of Songs came forth. But if the Jewish spirit was to maintain its identity and not disintegrate into merely a rich and pungent fertilizer for the culture of the idolaters, it needed always to be rooted in the hills. So when the Jews were at last pushed entirely into the plains and into the pagan world of the Romans, Judaism had to shore itself up with rocks of the spirit, as it were, to build an abstract and hence all the more austere Judaea of doctrine.

While the Zealots of Masada were bringing their fight to an end in an act of self-immolation, choosing to die rather than be uprooted from the soil which had produced them, a group of scholars was at work in the town of Jabneh on the Mediterranean coastal plain, establishing a new basis for the continuity of Jewish traditions. Johanan ben Zakkai, the leader of the group, was a Pharisee and a disciple of the great teacher Hillel. He had escaped from Jerusalem during the siege: according to the traditional account, he had concealed himself in a coffin, which the Roman troops allowed to pass through the city for burial. He subsequently requested permission of the Roman authorities to found an academy dedicated to the study of Torah. The permission was granted, no doubt with the stipulation that he choose a site far from all the old scenes of strife and the hotbeds of national resistance. Johanan chose well: Jabneh (or Jamnia, from the Greek form of its name) had been built by the Philistines and populated in recent times mainly by Syrians. Although only some fifty miles northwest of Masada and closer still to Jerusalem, it was in the very different world of the plains, temperate in climate and in mood, politically and spiritually just another dot on the rim of the Roman *mare nostrum*. Here in Jabneh, Johanan ben Zakkai and his disciples, to whom the Romans gave legal authority over the remnants of the Jewish community in Palestine, preserved what remained of Jewish nationhood by strengthening the walls of religious doctrine within which it had always been contained. Laying the foundations for what subsequently became Talmudic and rabbinical Judaism, this surviving group of Pharisees enabled a nation-in-exile to continue to exist by giving it an identity as a religious community which would remain firm, no matter how widely dispersed the community was to become.

Pharisaism, which was far from being the narrow and rigid legalism that subsequent Christian tradition made it seem, was the product of one of the most powerful religious currents of the era, a current which originated at least as far back as the Babylonian Exile in the sixth century B.C.E. In the era prior to the Babylonian Exile, the establishment of a Kingdom under Saul and David and the building of a Temple by Solomon had signaled the end of the predominance of the old nomadic elements in the Israelite tradition, and a religion that had been founded in tents became centered upon the priestly rites performed at the national shrine in Jerusalem. But the destruction of the Temple by the Babylonians in 586 B.C.E. and the ensuing experience of some three generations in exile, brought the Israelites back to certain elements of the old nomadic vision. Having neither a shrine nor the opportunity to make pilgrimages to the place where it had stood, the Jews of Babylonia discovered that they were in possession of a religious heritage which needed neither an exclusive sanctuary nor a set of priestly rites in order to validate itself. More so than any other religion of antiquity, the Jewish one—and it is from the Babylonian period onward that one can properly begin to use the term "Judaism" for the Israelite religion—resided in the spirit and could be carried to any place in which pious Jews found themselves.

In Babylonia it became customary for Jews to gather regularly in groups in order to recite the sacred texts together—to pray—and to listen to the most learned men in their midst provide interpretations of the religious doctrine. Even after the return from the exile, this regular assemblage continued as a practice, both in areas in Palestine far away from the rebuilt Temple in Jerusalem and in Babylonia, where a segment of the Jewish people remained permanently settled. Later, during the period of Hellenistic ascendancy in Palestine, this assemblage came to be referred to in Greek as a synagogue—a term which was only subsequently used for the building in which the gathering was held. One of the most important bridges between ancient and modern Judaism, the synagogue also served as the model from which Paul derived the church of Christianity.

An essential element of this newly forming religious institution was the learned interpreter of doctrine, a man who performed in the synagogue a function of pious leadership roughly equivalent to that of the priest in the Temple, but who was profoundly different from the priest in ways that were to prove significant. Whereas the priest was a member of a caste, a man born into his title and functions, this new type of leader—the prototype of the rabbi—was a man who attained his position simply on the basis of his learning. The more democratic aspects of this latter type of religious leadership were further manifested by its function of providing, for the less learned public, clarifications of the meaning of religious doctrine. The priest-hood, a vested interest, gained strength from a certain obscurantism, from the unquestioning awe in which the Temple rites were held by the community at large. From the end of the Babylonian Exile in 538 B.C.E., then, there were two major and conflicting currents in ancient Judaism: the religion of the rebuilt Temple in Jerusalem, whose traditional rites were presided over, as always, by the priests, and the new religious practices of the synagogues (which, like many religious innovations in history, was really a return to primeval sources—to the spirit of Moses and his followers in the tents of Sinai), presided over by a democratically constituted class of learned men.

This synagogue leadership makes its first appearance in recorded history as a special group belonging to the class of *scribes*. Technically, a scribe was a man whose profession it was to make copies of the sacred writings; but such a function, merely a mechanical one in later eras, was usually accompanied by great learning in antiquity. The scribes were therefore often also teachers. The first such teacher known to us is Ezra, who read and interpreted the Mosaic Law before the populace in Jerusalem after the return from the Babylonian Exile. Ezra happened to be a priest as well as a scribe, and it was no doubt his priestly status that gave authority to his pronouncements, even though he was now performing a function very different from the traditional one of the priesthood. The new spirit represented by Ezra and the scribes can be seen to manifest itself in much of the Hebrew literature written after the return from Babylonia, in the unprecedented inclination toward philosophical argument found in Job and Ecclesiastes, as well as the various works of "Wisdom" literature from the biblical Proverbs to the apocryphal Ecclesiasticus of Ben Sirah. All these works were written in the era of Greek and Hellenistic preponderance, and the Greek philosophical spirit is clearly present in them.

The Pharisees were the principal descendants in their own time of the tradition represented by the scribes and the authors of the Wisdom literature. Like their predecessors, they sought, through the interpretation and clarification of traditional doctrine, to invigorate Judaism by recovering the spirit of its sources; and also, like their predecessors, they represented a permanent challenge to the authority of the priestly establishment. This conflict became quite pronounced in the last century prior to the destruction of the Second Temple, the period of Roman domination over a still-existing Jewish commonwealth. In this epoch of extreme spiritual volatility, which produced the ministry of Jesus among many other remarkable manifestations, there was a strong tendency on the part of the various doctrinal schools to form themselves into quasi-political parties. The Zealots, as we have seen, were the most outspokenly nationalist party, although this more or less secular emphasis on their part did not mean that they were in any way strangers to religious piety. The Essenes were in some respects the most extreme pietistic party, but their inclinations were too unworldly to allow them to become greatly involved in the central affairs of the day. The two most prominent parties placing religious questions at the center of their concerns were the Pharisees and their principal rivals, the Sadducees, this latter being the party of the priesthood and its supporters.

The doctrinal conflict between these two parties focused upon the question of the extent to which the tradition of interpreting religious law could stand as authoritative alongside a literal construction of the text of the Pentateuch. Many of the teachings of the Pentateuch were couched in a form appropriate only to the nomadic society to which they had originally been addressed, and were no longer literally applicable to the society of the Second Commonwealth. The Pharisees, holding to a tradition that had been represented at least in part by Ezra and the Wisdom writers, held to the principle that the laws of Judaism could be interpreted, extended and adapted to the era in which they were living. It was precisely this flexibility, combined with an unwavering adherence to the spiritual essentials of Judaism, that enabled the Pharisees to create a body of doctrine with which Jewish identity could survive in exile. The Sadducees, on the other hand, were not attached so much to principle as to outmoded external forms and practices. Opposing the Pharisaic tradition of interpreting Jewish law, they maintained that only the text of the Pentateuch, literally understood, was authoritative in religious matters. In practice, this view meant not only a reaffirmation of the priestly cult to which the Pentateuch gives pre-eminence, but a certain relaxation of Jewish traditions outside of the precincts of the Temple itself. Since many of the precepts of the Pentateuch were no longer literally applicable, the Sadducees felt freer than their Pharisaic opponents to adapt themselves to the prevailing modes of the Hellenistic civilization of the day. Indeed, the natural tendency of their specific brand of dogmatic religious conservatism was toward a pronounced assimilationism which sometimes entered the Temple itself. In the second century B.C.E., when the Syrian king Antiochus Epiphanes tried to enforce paganization upon the Jews of Palestine, it was the Jewish High Priest Menelaus who was foremost in helping to impose this policy.

The Pharisees were thus the only one of the major parties of their day equipped to deal with the crisis of exile. They represented the portable traditions, independent of the Temple, which had been founded as far back as the Babylonian Exile: the synagogue, the stress upon personal and family ritual and conduct, and the more or less "constitutional" tradition of passing down and extending interpretations of Jewish law from one generation to the next. This latter tradition, carried on by Johanan ben Zakkai and his academy, now became central to Judaism. At the same time it began to undergo a change of character. In ancient times, this developing body of legal interpretation—called the *Mishna*—was passed on orally, and was never written down. It was not until about the end of the second century c.e. that the Mishna was committed to writing. This step, which was taken only with great reluctance, was deemed necessary because of the wide dispersion of the Jewish people and the threat of doctrinal confusion among them because of the spread of Christianity. It was a necessary further application of the purpose embodied by the academy of Johanan ben Zakkai: the perpetuation, even in dispersion, of the religious nation of the Jews. But it was also a step away from the spirit of its originators. Pharisaism had given new life to the Jewish tradition with a vision that transcended mere dogma and all that could be swept away by Roman power. But now that same task of perpetuation initiated by the Pharisees could only be implemented by a certain hardening of doctrine. The living arguments of the *Tannaim*—the first generations of interpreters of the Mishna following the destruction of the Second Commonwealth—came to be set down as codified doctrine. To be sure, this was a doctrine so intricate and rich that there was still much room for reinterpretation: in the fifth and sixth centuries c.e. another line of commentators, known as the *Amoraim*, added their own observations to the Mishnaic text. It was all these commentaries together that subsequently came to form the main body of the Talmud. But inevitably the weight of these layers upon layers of discussion became oppressive, and the vision within them grew murky. In time it would be the overweening authority of a rigid Talmudism against which new generations of visionaries would rebel. But until such rebellion was focused upon the Jewish ancestral soil itself, in other words, until modern Zionism came into being, there was ultimately no other source but the Talmud for the continuing identity of the Jewish people from generation to generation.

What Pharisaism had done, in other words, was to establish a portable foundation, as it were, for a nation-in-exile, built out of the material of religious doctrine. It is this fact that represents one of the pre-eminent ways in which Jewish history is unique. In modern times no other civilized people is both a nationality and a religion unto itself, each of these qualities coterminous with and largely dependent upon the other. In antiquity the phenomenon of exclusively national religions was more widespread, but even in that epoch Judaism rapidly became something else: a religious nation, whose sacred rites—which were, on one level, simply those of a cult among others—were also informed with a universalist vision of surpassing power: the notion of a single, omnipotent God, governing the entire universe. This universalist spirit is what ultimately enabled the Jewish nation to abstract itself from a national territory and remain alive; but this is not all it achieved. For in the era of the Pharisees and of the Zealots of Masada—an era of great tensions for the Jewish nation both from without and from within—this mood of prophetic universalism was straining at the boundaries of Jewish nationality itself. Ultimately these bounds were broken through, not by Jesus himself, who was as committed to the national religious tradition as the Pharisees were, but by Paul, who abrogated the Mosaic Law. Once this was done, in effect creating the distinct religion of Christianity out of what had hitherto been a Jewish sect, the new doctrine based on the life and sayings of Jesus became a proselytizing religion without parallel. Released from the national restrictions imposed by Mosaic Law, the spiritual universalism that Christianity inherited from Judaism could now also manifest itself as a practical universalism, and Christianity became the most cosmopolitan and ultimately the most widespread of world religions. Judaism, on the other hand, which had also proselytized, and which was to do so again from time to time, adhered to the national principle contained in its tradition. Thus occurred the historic divergence between these two religions which, having the same origins, were also destined to maintain an intimate and often tragic relationship down to the present day.

Two of the recurring grounds for antagonism in this relationship have to do with the very nature of Jewish history. One is the ambivalence that Christian nations often feel toward a landless nation in their midst, a "rootless and cosmopolitan" people. The other is a recurring feeling of resentment on the part of cosmopolitan Christianity toward a religion which contains elements of the Christian vision—which, indeed, is its ancestor—but which persists in retaining this vision within the trappings of a nationalist particularism. These problems are not easily solved, for the qualities of Judaism that they point to—that of being a nation-in-exile and that of being a religious nation paradoxically harboring a universalist vision—are at the very heart of the Jewish tradition. The first of these problems, for example, that of the nation-in-exile, seems to suggest a solution in a total return of the Jews to Zion, in the extinction of the Diaspora. But exile, or *galut* in Hebrew, is not the mere accidental product of the Roman conquest of Palestine. The Jewish nation and the Jewish religion were both created in exile, first in a covenant with Abraham, a stranger and restless wanderer in the Land, and then in a revelation to Moses, leading his people through the wilderness and never himself to set foot in Canaan. Now, it is not essential here whether we are speaking of actual events or of creations of the Jewish folk imagination. The important thing is the folk memory, which recognizes itself as antecedent to the fact of living in the Land. It is manifestly clear that, from Abraham onward, the Canaan of the Bible is the Promised Land with which the Jewish people is ever afterwards to identify its historic aspirations, but it is equally clear in the Bible that this Land is not to be the sole repository of Jewish historic activity—at least not until the End of Days. Thus the Babylonian Exile of the sixth century B.C.E., which was in some respects a rehearsal for the great dispersion that was to follow upon the Roman conquest, and in which the groundwork for the institutions of the Diaspora first was laid, was also in part a reversion to first principles. When Cyrus permitted the Jews to return to Jerusalem and rebuild the Temple in 538 B.C.E., a part of them remained in Babylonia, and there has been a continuous Diaspora from that day to this.

In other words, the existence of a Jewish political commonwealth in Palestine, in antiquity as well as at the present time, is a fact which, though it has always proved to be essential to the safety and spiritual health of the Jewish people as a whole, does not signify the end or imminent end of the historic Jewish condition of exile. For exile, or *galut*, is—to revert to the religious folk memory once again— not merely the physical condition of the Jewish people but the spiritual condition of all of mankind until the day the Messiah comes and brings universal redemption. Here lies the central paradox of the Jewish condition: a universalist sense of mission which refuses to be identified *exclusively* with a political state, combined with the par-

ticularism of a national identity in dispersion, this national identity
being the very condition for maintaining the sense of mission in the
first place. But a sense of nationhood cannot last for very long
without a political-territorial focus for its identity. The result is a
continuing dialectic in Jewish history: periods of heavy stress upon
political nationhood followed by restless leaps of the spirit beyond
political bounds to the universalist conception of Jewish destiny—for
example, the era of Kings David and Solomon followed by the era of
the great prophets. And then—to describe the return cycle in terms
of the secular religiosity of modern times—a period in which the
Jewish intellectuals of Europe were largely drawn to the political
universalism of liberalism and socialism was followed by a revival of
the Jewish national spirit in Zionism. At all times there is an
unrelenting struggle between these two irreconcilable and yet equally
indispensable conceptions of creative human community: nation and
universalist religion—a struggle that must continue until all of mankind comes home.

III

Masada has, in the years since the re-establishment of a large
Jewish community in Palestine, and especially since the founding of
the state, increasingly become a place of Jewish pilgrimage, a kind of
secular national shrine. Much of Herod's fortress had remained
visible through the centuries, so that there always had been ruins
among which to walk and set up one's tents, shapeless mounds of
stones to invoke in the mind dim images of ancient heroism and
catastrophe. All this had been enough for the romantic imagination
of a bygone era, but the more scientific curiosity of our own day came
to know ways of cracking into secrets that had been buried for centuries in Masada's dust. In the years 1963 to 1965, a large-scale
archaeological expedition was conducted on the summit by Professor
Yigael Yadin of the Hebrew University (General Yadin had also
been Chief of Operations in Israel's War of Independence), which
uncovered vast portions of the citadel and rebuilt many of the ruined
walls. Scrolls, shards, bones, and bits of charcoal from Zealot cooking
fires have all been dug up to serve as source material for future
historians' reconstructions of what happened in that era and in that
place. The expedition, which consisted of some two hundred workers

at any given time, was organized out of groups of volunteers who came to work in two-week cycles, many of them signing up again for further cycles that took them through an entire season of excavations. Students, teachers, kibbutzniks, clerks, men and women, Christians as well as Jews, coming not only from every part of Israel but from all over the world, joined eagerly together in a task of digging that often took on the atmosphere of a kind of religious undertaking.

I was a volunteer at Masada, and I, like many others, found digging there to be an act that unexpectedly turned into something like a religious communion. Let us say that you begin your day's work by tugging at a pile of rocks on a ledge that juts precariously over a drop of some five hundred feet or more. As you strain in the hot sun to send each stone crashing down the slope, loudly disturbing the bimillennial repose of that abyss, it might occur to you to yearn for the few sticks of dynamite that some less pious roadbuilder would use for a task of this sort. But the fact is that in pulling out even the weightiest of these dolomite chunks you are doing work which is ultimately as delicate as the spirit that conceived of such a thing as archaeology. This fact becomes evident even in the sifting of the first layers of broken rubble, from which a dirt-logged shard, coin or broken arrowhead will suddenly shake itself clear. But it becomes truly impressive (for even the most striking of fragments do not yet conjure up the presence of a way of life) when you suddenly observe that two adjacent rocks which you were about to pull down seem to suggest a pattern, possibly that of a wall. You dig deeper into the dirt surrounding them, perhaps still using your pickax from force of habit, only to discover that by this indelicacy you are now chopping away plaster from what is, indeed, a wall. Switching to a small pick hammer and even to brush and bare hand, you begin tenderly to shape every scar and convexity of that battered old surface, sometimes giving form to some more marked variation, such as a door, a window, or an at first inexplicable but exquisitely shaped projection that turns out to be a water conduit. Under your hands and those of your companions around you a 2,000-year-old room begins to emerge, and suddenly there comes to mind the image of one of those unfinished sculptures of Michelangelo, a mighty shape that was once mere rock but is now porous and alive, struggling to extricate itself from the rigid primeval stuff out of which it has achieved the miracle of differentiation.

During my stay at Masada, one of the members of our group of volunteers was a lively man with a great, gray-streaked beard, who spoke with intelligence and relish in thirteen languages, and who turned out to be a Carmelite monk. This fact was not evident during the day, when he wore soiled work clothes like the rest of us, but each evening at sunset he could be seen a short distance from the camp, saying a Mass at which one or two communicants might be present, and wearing a glistening white robe and golden surplice which clashed with the twilight colorlessness around him. His altar was a huge, brown-gray mound which sloped away from him to a height of some thirty feet or more above his head. As he swung his intricately ornamented censer through the air, one could not but be struck by the contrast between that dull mound and the altar of any Catholic church. This was indeed a Jewish altar he was facing, not some rich and graceful fabrication of the Gothic spirit but the kind of stark place at which Abraham had been called upon to lay Isaac on the wood. What had brought him here? This was not even one of the Christian holy places, where, often enough, the erection of a church or a shrine had transformed the harsh Judaean landscape into something more resembling the prettier Holy Land that Renaissance painters had conjured up through their observations of Tuscany. This was simply a place where many Jews had died in the name of their own uniqueness nearly two thousand years ago.

It is clearly also the restored Jewishness of the Holy Land, and not the presence of the holy places alone, that draws many Christians to it, especially from Europe, and imparts a feeling that is often religious in quality for even the most secular-minded among them. Only a little more than twenty years ago they stood helplessly by while the worst elements in their civilization rose up and destroyed most of European Jewry. And today this same ravaged people is reborn in its own ancestral land, in the very place where it gave Christianity to the world. Now, the pattern of awful sacrifice followed by regeneration and general salvation lies deeply within the Christian spirit, at least among Catholics and some Protestant sects, and it is hard for the European, in the pain of his memory, not to see this pattern working itself out among the Jews and the state of Israel. Under the guise of a simple holiday tour, a pilgrimage to Israel often becomes a kind of penitential act; this is the reason, for example, that the presence of young Germans, usually under thirty years old, has become quite noticeable in Israel in recent years. In the course of this development the entire Jewish state has become a holy place as it were, sanctified wherever Jews have rebuilt their land and regenerated themselves, wherever they once fought and died against their enemies, as at Masada. Groups of Christians digging into the Jewish ground at Masada, or spending the months working the land in kibbutzim, form a kind of communion throughout the country. If, after all, the return to Israel represents for many Jews a secular version of messianic redemption, why should Christians be any less inclined to see in it an intimation of the Second Coming?

Digging is a form of prayer in Israel, for Christian as well as Jew, and for farmer as well as archaeologist. In the hands of many of the Zionist pioneers, digging was the ritual of a rather anticlerical cult, which claimed to reject religion on the grounds that, as a priestly creation it had enslaved mankind in general and as a rabbinical creation it had made the Jew into only half a human being, alienated from the soil and from physical labor. But in practice there is really no form of communicant so pious as the Jewish farmer engaging the soil of Israel. His motions are superficially those of farmers anywhere, but the passion that attends them is that of a heart recovering a living relationship that had been interrupted for a period of nearly two thousand years. The French peasant also cultivates his plot of land, but he need not endow this act with any more religious or philosophical significance than he gives to the act of putting on his shoes in the morning. But the Jewish farmer will need many generations before he can achieve this tranquil state of mind; he must come to forget what a marvelous thing it is for a Jew to be farming at all, and that this or that green patch of land was desert or swamp only a few years ago. Above all, he must come to feel rooted (which is a feeling that is not to be felt at all, since it implies an absence of self-consciousness) in this soil which, for two millennia, has only been an abstraction to him, no matter how passionately he has longed for it. The zeal of recovery, and the energy of re-creation, that have made the Jewish state are things that have come naturally out of the Jewish spirit; a lack of self-consciousness is something far more difficult for that spirit to achieve. But in the case of archaeology, as compared with that of agriculture, the problem is somewhat more easily resolved. For here is a way of negotiating the land that glories in its own self-consciousness, striking an ideal balance between the intellectual inclination that is hard for many Jews to suppress and the Zionist urge to burrow one's hands, in spirit at least, into the soil of Israel.

The Israeli seeks through archaeology what the Frenchman seeks, let us say, when he travels to a nearby cathedral or château to feel the presence of his history. There is perhaps an even greater sense of presence in the Israeli's experience, at the same time that there is more mystery; for, as any Israeli farmer knows, his plow could turn up a fragment of some ancient village or altar at any time, as has happened on numerous occasions in the past. But in cases such as these, the Israeli often cannot know what he is looking at until it has been subjected to scientific analysis. This suggests what seems to be a peculiarly Jewish fate: that not merely the nation's normal scientific researches into its past, but even the quest for its myths, can only be undertaken through concentrated intellectual effort. Archaeology is a national passion in Israel; it is discussed everywhere in the country, with the kind of readiness and knowledgeability that most nations reserve for political discussions. A conversation about archaeology in an Israeli home often has the feeling of some sort of rite; it is an earnest and refined effort to recover life, a life that has somehow found a way of defying the laws of nature and of not becoming a fossil through centuries of slumber, just as in the cool dryness of the caves at Qumran the organic papyrus kept its mystery fresh for two millennia. Through the combined power of action and reflection, the once moribund organ of Jewish national life in Palestine is being resuscitated and, what is more, made youthful again. And in this way a new body of tradition and interpretation—a kind of counter-Talmud in the making—is being built up from the moment at which Jewish national history in the land had last left off, and Johanan ben Zakkai had gone down into the valley to create the Diaspora. The new religion of digging is like a call down to Johanan ben Zakkai from the top of Masada, a demand that he come back, as it were, and that Jewish history be planted in these mountains once again, for all time.

CHAPTER 1

The Rise of Political Zionism
in Western Europe:
Theodor Herzl

I

THROUGHOUT the first three quarters of the nineteenth century, the Jews of Central and Western Europe placed their hopes for the social and political advancement of their lot primarily in the ideology of liberalism. It was the liberal ideal that had already produced the two major revolutionary steps bringing the Jews of Western Europe out of the Middle Ages: Enlightenment and Emancipation. The Enlightenment, represented to the Jews of Europe primarily by the figure of the German-Jewish philosopher Moses Mendelssohn, stood for the possibility that a pious Jew could legitimately study and profit by the thought and literature of Gentile Europe without losing his own traditional Jewish values. Emancipation was introduced by the French Revolution in 1791, when, for the first time in the history of Modern Europe, a law was passed granting the Jews full civil equality with all other citizens of the country. Prior to that time, the Jews of any European state had been treated as a corporate entity before the law, to whom special and usually disabling regulations accrued. But the liberal ideology of the French Revolution was above all opposed to any form of the corporate conception

23

of society that had prevailed in Medieval Europe. Liberalism, in its most zealous form, would not tolerate the intervention of any juridical entity between the individual and the state. This is why the French revolutionaries abolished the craft and mercantile guilds and sought even to nationalize the Catholic Church in France if not to do away with it altogether. By the same token, the authors of the law emancipating the Jews of France hoped that it would bring about the eventual disappearance of Judaism in the country.

Liberalism was therefore in some ways only a mixed blessing for the Jews of Europe. To the extent that it disdained to identify the Jews as a distinct group within society—an attitude that was not always founded upon tolerance—it threatened to undermine an identity which they had struggled to maintain through almost two thousand years of dispersion and suffering. Indeed, the intoxicating taste of Enlightenment and Emancipation together led many Jews to renounce that identity with zeal. In France, where the more radical wing of the liberal movement was characterized by an anticlericalism whose intensity of feeling was often no less religious than the Catholicism it opposed, a left-wing intellectual of Jewish origin was as likely as a Christian-born one to want to throw off the religious affiliations of his forebears. In Germany, where liberalism was less successfully realized than in France, the desire on the part of many "Enlightened" Jews to become fully identified with the surrounding culture led them to take an additional step and be baptized. The German-Jewish poet Heinrich Heine, who himself underwent conversion, said that a baptismal certificate was "the entrance-ticket to European civilization."

But a religious conversion naturally often provoked a crisis of the conscience, particularly in Germany, where an undercurrent of racialism often made it impossible even for a Jewish convert to be considered anything but a Jew by society at large. Heine cynically accepted baptism for the sake of expediency, and then found that the government bureaucratic career he had sought was not open to him anyway. He never lost a feeling of guilt about his conversion, and eventually returned to Jewish lore for the subject matter of some of his finest works. In general, a certain retrenchment began setting in among the Jews of Germany by the middle of the nineteenth century. Intellectuals like Heine and the socialist writer Moses Hess recovered a nostalgia for their Jewish origins in reaction to the inadequacies of liberalism and to the smug bourgeois civilization that it produced, while the middle-class Jews of Germany found in the development of Reform Judaism a way of reconciling their ancestral traditions with the more or less liberal Protestant ideals of their generation.

Germany seemed for a time to provide the best soil in Europe for a reconciliation between Jewish traditions and the Western civilization of the nineteenth century. Tsarist Russia contained a Jewish population that was nearly as ancient as the German one, and that was also far larger and far more deeply bound to Jewish traditions; but the medieval atmosphere which still prevailed in its life, and the oppressively reactionary regime under which it lived, made Russian Jewry an unlikely prospect for modernization at that time. French Jewry, on the other hand, tended to be absorbed too easily into the intense cosmopolitanism, whether liberal or Catholic, of the civilization which surrounded it. German conservatism put a brake upon the assimilation of German Jewry into the surrounding population, while the Protestantism which prevailed in Germany provided Jews there with an atmosphere of pietism which favored the continuance of their religious traditions, and with a climate of sectarianism that favored the proliferation of religious sects. Indeed, in its most extreme form, German Reform Judaism virtually sought to identify "the Mosaic religion" as simply another Protestant sect.

Reform Judaism in Germany represented the pinnacle of Jewish liberal hopes. But by the last quarter of the nineteenth century liberalism was suffering a rapid decline all over Western Europe. The advancement of large-scale monopoly capitalism was undermining the old ideal of free enterprise, and a vigorous anticapitalist revolt began to emerge on both the left and the right of the political spectrum. The revolt from the right came with particular strength from the lower middle classes and peasantry, those old yeoman classes whose traditional place in society was being upset by the Industrial Revolution. This revolt was conservative and even reactionary in character because it was opposed to the progress of the Industrial Revolution, but, being also anticapitalist, it had its roots in certain of the currents of early nineteenth-century socialism, particularly as expressed in the writings of Pierre Joseph Proudhon. The socialism of Proudhon was a protest not so much against private property in general as against the kind of abstract ownership represented by industrial and financial

capitalism. A peasant by birth and a printer by trade, Proudhon was
the ardent spokesman of an ideal world in which every man would
have his own plot of land or his own shop, and would work it
himself.

But this way of life was being destroyed by the advance of large-
scale capitalism, and in casting about for some specific locus of blame
for this fact Proudhon, like the leaders of the late nineteenth-century
lower-middle-class revolt, was inclined to look toward the Jews. The
moral structure of Medieval Europe, which barred the practice of
usury to most Christians and barred the Jews from most other
economic pursuits, along with the special need for economic mobility
that had always been imposed upon the Jews by their plight, had led
to a long-standing predominance of capitalist occupations among
them. Most of the Jews of Europe were not capitalists in the
nineteenth century, but popular myth was still strong enough at that
time for Proudhon and others to consider a few wealthy financiers,
like the Rothschilds and the Pereires, to be more or less representative of all Jewry. Indeed, many young Jewish intellectuals were prone
to accept this myth, and they sought vigorously to prevent any
application of it to themselves. By the turn of the century, it came to
seem as characteristic for a young, middle-class Western European
Jew to be an intellectual and a Socialist as it had seemed for his
father to be a capitalist and a Liberal. In the meantime, the anticapitalist feelings of those lower middle classes which Proudhon had
represented earlier in the century had become antisocialist as well.
Socialism, too, now seemed to be part of the technological onrush
which threatened to destroy the old yeoman way of life, along with
capitalism; and just as there had been a strong tendency to blame
capitalism upon the Jews, so now there was a tendency to blame
socialism upon them.

This latter change had been brought about primarily by the
emergence of Marxian socialism. Socialists of the stamp of Proudhon
were as opposed to the Industrial Revolution itself as they were to
any of the exploitations that came with it. Marx was equally opposed
to the exploitation that took place within the framework of the
emerging industrial system, but as for the system itself, he favored it,
recognizing its capacity to bring untold wealth to mankind. In fact,
he honored the historic role played by the capitalists—even as he
hurled invectives at them and sought their demise—in having

brought such a system about. They had after all conjured into being the very class—the proletariat—that was to be the instrument of the socialist revolution. Proudhon, in his early days, had been somewhat reluctant to look upon an organized industrial proletariat with any-thing but scorn, since it, too, was a class more or less abstracted from the traditional yeoman relationships that he stood for, a class pro-duced by and representative of the industrial system. This is why the conflict that arose between Marx and Proudhon in the 1840's was of historic significance. It was a revolutionary point of departure, at which the representative of a worthy and obsolescent social order came into conflict with the creator of one of the main social philosophies of the new economic order being created by the Industrial Revolu-tion. This latter social philosophy, unlike its rival, was founded upon a conception of economic relationships which gave validity to all the nontraditional classes created by capitalism. A true product of liberal-ism, the Marxian world view acknowledged none of the social distinc-tions established by a precapitalist corporate order. Jews instinctively recognized that, despite Marx's own anti-Semitism (which must always be qualified in the light of the fact that Marx himself had been born a Jew), this was a world view which was essentially not prejudicial against them. In fact, it was in many ways a continuation of the liberal idea. Therefore, as liberalism declined toward the end of the nineteenth century, the passion felt by many Jews in favor of self-emancipation and general social reform found its new vehicle of expression in Marxian social democracy.

The last two decades or so of the nineteenth century brought an utter decline in the rationalist faith bequeathed by the Enlighten-ment. A certain despair came over the European bourgeoisie; two or three generations after playing its role as the most revolutionary force in European history, this class suddenly suffered a loss of direction, a decline of faith in its own ideals. The confident rupture with the past that had been made by the parents and grandparents of the late nineteenth-century bourgeois now left many of them with a legacy of a sense of loss, of alienation and despair. But then a mood of re-trenchment began setting in. In literature, an era of assiduous decadence suddenly gave way to a passionate seeking of the heroic mold. Not Baudelaire, but Nietzsche, came to be the representative type of literary figure. Gabriele D'Annunzio passed from decadence to heroic posturing in the course of a single lifetime, and his capture

and eighteen-month-long domination of Fiume at the head of an
illegal army presented to the world the first so-called "corporate"
constitution of the twentieth century, which was to provide ideological baggage for fascism a few years later. The medieval ideal of the
corporate society came into being once again, only what it meant this
time was not so much a series of corporate entities within a larger
social grouping (though Italian fascism paid lip service to this idea),
as a large, enclosed religious and national—and even racial—community, from which alien elements were to be excluded.

This outburst of pseudo-medieval idealism directed a large part of
its hostility both at socialism and at the Jew. The two were identified
with one another and equally despised as major instruments of
abstract cosmopolitanism, the antithesis of the new ideal of enclosed
community. To the lower middle classes in particular, who were now
making a last bid not to have their way of life swept away, Marxian
socialism was a Jewish conspiracy to destroy the old Christian social
order—just as finance capitalism had been and continued to be in
their eyes. This hostility from the right reinforced the growing
alliance between the Jewish intellectuals and the social democratic
parties. These parties were now taking up a position not only as the
vehicles of the working-class movement but also as corporate bodies
in their various home countries, functioning as the chief means of
defense for all the elements that were being threatened by the
growing corporate structure of the right. In this atmosphere the
individual stance represented by the old liberalism was becoming
increasingly untenable to Jews, whereas the corporate identification
with social democracy was the most natural means of self-defense for
them. In France, for example, a lasting alliance between the Socialists
and a large segment of French Jewry was brought into being in the
struggle against the right-wing anti-Dreyfus bloc.

But this alliance with socialism seemed unsatisfactory to many
Jews, and not merely to those wealthy individuals to whom a socialist
philosophy was a personal threat. Some Jewish intellectuals, having
learned the lesson from the recent decline of liberal attitudes that a
"Jewish Question" continued to exist in Western Europe in spite of
the Emancipation, were skeptical about the ability of socialism to
provide a solution. In some respects, socialism was simply a continuation of liberal hopes. Having decided that the bourgeoisie was not
capable of liberating itself from prejudice, Socialists had turned to

the workers' movement as the sole true liberal brotherhood, the only society in which group distinctions did not exist between men. But anti-Semitism could be found among workers and Socialists too.

Zionism came into being in Western Europe as a way of seeking a solution to the Jewish Question in precisely the corporate and nationalist terms that were then being used as a means of threatening the Jews. It was conceived as an alternative to socialism, a better vehicle for Jewish hopes. The Zionist and the Jewish Socialist of Europe at the turn of the century were alike in being motivated by a certain contempt for the attitudes of the Jewish middle classes. Both of them sought a way of life that would be different from their Jewish middle-class heritage. There were even affinities between the tactics of the Zionist and the Socialist. Theodor Herzl recognized that the Jews scattered throughout Europe could be conceived as a single political entity in the same sense as was the international working class, and that their economic power, like that of the workers, could be used as a political lever. In other words, political Zionism, for all its apparent affinities with the language and aspirations of the nationalism of a previous era, came primarily out of the corporatist atmosphere of the late nineteenth century, and was influenced largely by both the form and the spirit of the socialist movement.

II

Zionism came into being as a modern, secular form of the traditional Jewish messianic idea. In a sense, the messianic vision of return had to await its epoch, since the historicism implicit in the world view of ancient Judaism did not come into its own as a general cultural attitude until the nineteenth century. Only then could this idea, held in a state of suspended animation within the bosom of the Jewish people for two thousand years, come to life again through contact with the surrounding culture. Theodor Herzl was caught up in the mood of historical messianism that prevailed in nineteenth-century Europe, but being a somewhat assimilated Jew, he was only dimly aware of the connection between this mood and the world view of his ancestors. Rather, this connection was best understood and expressed in a book written and published more than thirty years before Herzl had even conceived his own Zionist idea, a work that must be considered the first major expression of modern Zionism, and which appeared a generation before its time.

Rome and Jerusalem was published in 1862 by the socialist writer Moses Hess, who was a unique and anomalous figure in many ways. Born in the Rhineland in 1812, six years before the birth of Karl Marx, Hess was an authentic member of that generation of German radicals who, in the course of the 1830's and 1840's, had made their way through German philosophy and through the framework of pallid German liberalism into a revolutionary socialist conception of human liberty. Gripped by a high sense of social universalism, these men were almost all anticlerical and opposed equally to any religious establishment. Marx had been born a Jew and was converted to Lutheranism by his father while still a child, but he denounced Judaism and Christianity with equal vehemence. As a young liberal journalist, Marx had rallied to the cause of the Jews when they were discriminated against, since the Jewish Question was a test of liberal principles. But in 1843, five years before the publication of the *Communist Manifesto*, he had made his last extended observations on the Jewish Question in a pair of articles in which he defined the Jews as an economic category—the financial arm of industrial capitalism—which would disappear with capitalism. This view, which clearly foreshadows the sociology of Marx's later writings, is simply a *reductio ad absurdum* of classical liberalism. The Jews, like any other social category in the capitalist system, are here depicted abstractly as simply another part of an unjust economic construct, which will disappear in a more human world.

Hess was not so inclined to liberal abstractions. He had been born and raised, unlike Marx, in a thoroughly traditional Jewish atmosphere; his family had come to Germany from Poland, and as a boy Hess spoke Yiddish before he learned to speak German. In his twenties and thirties, when he was caught up in the excited formulations of the circle of young German revolutionaries in which both he and Marx participated, he paid lip service to the requisite anticlericalism of the group, and even delivered his share of correctly anti-Semitic remarks. But he apparently never convinced his associates that he was wholehearted about this; they called him the "communistic rabbi." He always did harbor reservations about this anticlericalism where Judaism was concerned, for it never seemed to him quite the same thing to oppose the established church of a Protestant or Catholic country and to oppose the religious and cultural institutions of an oppressed people. In fact Hess came to view the situation of the Jews of Europe in much the same light as that in which Marx came to view the situation of the proletariat. Hess's knowledge of the character and traditions of Eastern European Jewry, unusual among the "Enlightened" Jews of Germany, had a great deal to do with this. In the West the Jews were widely regarded as being universally wealthy, and superficial observation there did not offer too much refutation to this notion. But in the East, as Hess well knew, the vast majority of the Jews were living in great poverty; in fact, a conception of an affinity between the Jews and the proletariat was readily arrived at by the Eastern European Jewish intellectuals of a later generation. To a large extent, Marxism achieved great influence among these latter because its conception of an oppressed people, clearly definable though scattered among the nations, bearing a historical and even apocalyptic mission of redemption for all mankind—a conception applied by Marx to the worldwide proletariat—reflected their sense of their own lot as Jews. Perhaps Marx himself had arrived at this vision out of something Jewish that had remained in the depths of his spirit despite a formal act of conversion.

Such an affinity was strongly felt by Hess. This is indicated by a passage in *Rome and Jerusalem* that reads like an emendation upon the *Communist Manifesto*: "All of past history," Hess writes, "was concerned with the struggle of races[1] and classes. Race struggle is primary; class struggle is secondary. When racial antagonism ceases, class struggle also ceases."[2] In the context of this passage Hess is pointing to the uprisings of oppressed nationalities taking place all over Europe at that time as an example of "race struggle": the Italians have just thrown off Austrian hegemony and become a unified nation-state (this national revival of an ancient people is the "Rome" of the title), the Poles are to make another thwarted attempt the following year in their perennial struggle for independence against the Russian tsars. This concern with the cause of oppressed nationalities was a characteristic attitude of Socialists then as well as now. But

[1] Hess is not using the word "race" here in the pseudo-biological sense that arose in the twentieth century. In his own era, when it was widely and respectably used, it had a broader meaning that would have to be expressed today, depending on the context, either by the term "ethnic group" or by the word "(a) people."

[2] *Rome and Jerusalem*, translated by Maurice J. Bloom (New York, 1958), p. 10.

for Hess the Jews are unique among oppressed nationalities. For Jewish history, like the history of the proletariat (or of the oppressed toiling classes that preceded it), is contained in the history of all the other nations of the West. To Hess, whose philosophical conception of history was as sweeping as that of Marx, the shifting role of the Jews throughout the different eras and nations in history became a paradigm of a great moral struggle on the part of mankind in general, much as the shifting economic substructure built upon the toiling classes served as such a paradigm for Marx.

These philosophical views on the part of both Hess and Marx were generated in the atmosphere of Hegelianism that dominated German thought in their youth. The problem that both men were grappling with was the Hegelian one of alienation, the resolution of which was to restore wholeness and freedom to mankind. As Hegel had understood it, the reason man was not free was that Spirit and Nature were alienated from each other, or, as the problem expressed itself in more concrete terms, the cultural, social and political institutions that man had created for himself had not yet achieved perfect harmony with his aspirations. But, in Hegel's view, human history was moving steadily toward such a realization, and he considered the political states of Western Europe to be the vehicles for such an outcome, representing, as they did, the highest development of cultural and political freedom that had ever yet been achieved. Oddly enough, Hegel thought that the most advanced representative of this ideal among the European states of his day was not France or England but his own Prussia. In the eyes of a younger generation of political radicals this was an unsatisfactory resolution of a compelling idea, particularly in the atmosphere of frustrated liberalism that prevailed in the Germany of the 1830's and 1840's. In their own theoretical formulations, the young "Left Hegelians" concerned themselves particularly with the gap that seemed to exist in Hegel's philosophy between a lofty conception of human freedom in the mind and its rather puny objectification in the world of practical activity. This problem of the gap between thought and action—in effect, the very problem of the gap between Spirit and Nature that the Hegelian philosophy purported to have solved—was becoming a central one in German thought and literature (it is the underlying theme of Goethe's *Faust*), and it was the question to which the young Hegelians of the left directed themselves.

Hess made a tentative stab at a solution in an early work, a pamphlet-size essay entitled *The Philosophy of the Act*, which he published in 1843. Here he asserted that a power-seeking political, social and religious establishment had conspired to present man with a false dichotomy between his identity and the products of his actions, a dichotomy which presented itself in philosophy as a distinction between subject and object, in religion as a distinction between the sacred and the profane, and in economic life as a distinction between man's work and his property. This last formulation was very close to the point that Marx was to take up the following year in his *Economic and Philosophical Manuscripts*; as Hess had done, Marx here applies the concept of alienation to the problem of work and property, but he refines the point and makes the first cogent formulation of his incipient idea of the exploitation of labor power by capital. This was soon to be developed into Marx's powerful theory of *class* conflict, something that Hess had bordered upon but not quite arrived at. Hess broadly accepted Marx's formulation, though with some reservations about its rather strongly materialistic philosophical orientation, and let the matter go at that. Marx went on into a wholesale study of economics, and Hess consigned the airier questions of the human spirit that continued to intrigue him to the recesses of his mind.

Hess remained a Socialist, but he eventually came to seek a solution to the problem of alienation in another vein. For Marx, the link between thought and action, which he had sought in his youth, was located in the entire class of the proletariat, the one class whose subjective consciousness and concrete objective situation were united in a revolutionary moment. Hess sought a social group that would have similar properties, but to which larger spiritual questions would accrue—on the level, for example, of philosophy and religion as well as of economic relations. In this regard Hess, from the time of his earliest published writings, had considered Spinoza to be the great prophet of the modern era, the man who had achieved a philosophical reconciliation between Spirit and Nature. The fact that Spinoza was a Jew had no doubt always intrigued Hess, but it does not seem to have become of major significance to him until middle life when, for reasons that are still not perfectly clear to his biographers, Hess made a passionate return to Judaism. This new religiosity was not precisely a return to the orthodoxy of his youth, but a more or less secularized vision of the Jewish spirit and Jewish history, viewed through the prism of his lifelong study of philosophy.

As he describes it in *Rome and Jerusalem*, the Jewish tradition is one in which, by its very nature, thought and action are united, in which the alienation of Spirit and Nature does not exist. At least it does not exist when the Jewish spirit is in a condition whereby it can realize its own proper character. But the Jewish spirit has not been in such a condition for nearly two thousand years. According to Hess, Christianity arose out of a double crisis in the ancient world: the decline of pagan civilization and the destruction of the Jewish commonwealth. Paganism had been founded upon a primitive confidence in man's spiritual relationship to nature—a state of mind which is able to preclude a sense of alienation only by an excessively materialistic sense of life, one in which a genuine spirituality has no place. When this confidence declined, the pagan world turned for consolation to the spiritual elements in messianic Judaism. But this was a leap to another extreme: the kind of overly spiritualized Judaism that the pagan world extracted—the strain represented by the Essenes, for example—was itself a product of crisis, and did not belong to the mainstream of Jewish tradition. The result was that the unilateral spiritualism of Essenism and of Pauline Christianity was what became dominant in the Western world, instead of the balanced grasp of both Spirit and Nature that had characterized ancient Judaism. This spiritual alienation of Western man has lasted for just as long as Judaism itself has remained in a weak and alienated condition as a result of its national crisis in antiquity. But a prophetic vision of a new era that is to come has been provided by a Jewish philosopher, Spinoza, whose career Hess regards as the moment that begins the modern era.

What Spinoza had done in the world of thought was now to be done in the world of political action. The messianic implications of the French Revolution were very important for Hess, as they were for Marx, and in his earlier writings he had described that event as the beginning point of the practical redemption of mankind. But, just as Marx gave up the liberal vision of the French Revolution for the socialist one of the revolution of the proletariat, so also Hess renounced it in favor of the Zionist hope. For Hess, the return of the Jews to Zion would not only bring about their own redemption, restoring them to the wholeness that they had lost in antiquity, but it would mark the beginning of an era of general redemption, of spiritual wholeness and freedom, for all mankind.

III

THEODOR HERZL

Theodor Herzl was a true successor to Moses Hess in more ways than in their common Zionist vision. Like Hess, he had an acute sense of the problem of the gap between thought and action, and sought its solution through the identification of the human will with history. But he did not have Hess's ardently philosophical turn of mind: when he first came across *Rome and Jerusalem* some years after he had arrived independently at his own Zionist conception (Hess had died in relative obscurity in 1875), he found his predecessor's Hegelian terminology to be too much for his taste, although he otherwise greatly admired the book. Furthermore, his sense of history was not such as to lead him to range spiritually through the centuries in search of the rhythms of historical evolution, as Hess had done. The focus of his concerns was, rather, utterly contemporary, and he only rarely gazed beyond an immediate past and an immediate future. His passion for technological planning, stimulated by an almost childlike enthusiasm for such advances of the age as electricity, telephones and the dirigible, makes him, indeed, a precursor of the mid-twentieth century. Once he had formulated his Zionist vision, his life, in a manner suggestive of a later era, yielded to a kind of religion of constant movement, to a principle of incessant and ultimately self-destructive drive for its own sake—Herzl himself used the metaphor of the dirigible, with its constant state of motion and suspension in space, to characterize his own life. But even his technological dreams were filled with an aura of mysticism that comes from an earlier time, and that in particular suggests a kinship with the Saint-Simonians. His mind, like theirs, was a remarkable union of unworldly visions with a sober sense of practical affairs. Such men have the capacity to realize great projects, but they are driven to do so only because they are motivated by a dream of something still greater and, in truth, unrealizable. They are technological poets, for whom, say, a blueprint for an urban electrification system harbors a beauty not unrelated to that of a work by Goethe or Shakespeare. For

them, practical activity is itself a work of art. A conception of this
sort is the very fulfillment of the ideal of the unity of thought and
action sought after by the generation of Moses Hess. It also represents, as Hess understood, an attitude deeply ingrained in the Jewish
spirit, part of the very essence of the Talmudic outlook. But Herzl
was hardly a Talmudist by rearing. It was only through a long and
painful struggle that he arrived at his vision.

Born in Pest (later Budapest) in 1860, Theodor Herzl did not
settle in Vienna until he was eighteen years of age; nevertheless, it
was the latter city that most decisively placed its stamp upon him.
His early life was filled with the hopes and frustrations of that
generation of Viennese Jewish intellectuals. They were young men
caught between the romantic fantasies instilled in them by the
postures of an Austrian nobility that was then rapidly in decline and
the dull and often craven imperatives of a middle-class way of life
that was made even more oppressive for them by the fact that they
were Jews in a thoroughly anti-Semitic society. Technically, the Jews
of Austria-Hungary had been accorded full civil equality in 1867, but
in fact large sectors of the social and economic life of the country
remained closed to them. For the generation of Jews who had already
reached maturity by the time of the Emancipation, this situation was
not necessarily irksome; they simply went on pursuing the occupations, mainly centered upon the world of commerce and the Stock
Exchange, that had long been open to them. It was rather their sons
who were vexed by the hidden restriction that Austrian society
placed upon them. University graduates, professional men, intellectuals, they were inclined to be as scornful of the Stock Exchange as
any Catholic baron; and yet it was precisely the world of Jewish
finance that young Jewish lawyers like Theodor Herzl were forced to
serve, for want of any other outlet for their talents.

The persistence of these social and economic barriers to assimilation
forced the continuance of a thoroughly Jewish identity in a generation
that might otherwise have been inclined to give it up. In Herzl's day the
Jewish population of Vienna was a whole world in itself, large and
lively if not quite spiritually robust. It was as rich in artists and
intellectuals, especially in the younger generation, as it was in businessmen. In fact, the Jewish intelligentsia of Vienna were at the
forefront of the European spirit in that era, and, among them,
Jewishness simply became an element—an added touch of piquancy

—in the definition of a certain type of Central European man of the spirit. However, in a period in which decadence was not only a literary posture but also a widely felt and corrosive experience of the soul, a Jewishness defined in this way could only come to seem like some kind of disease. A young man like Herzl was Jewish in every way in which the exclusiveness imposed by anti-Semitism could make him; but his early life was largely or even wholly lacking in any real content of Jewish values. If anything, the cultural content of his life was defined by a Germanness more ardent than that of other Austrians. Other than this, the major positive way in which Central European Jewish intellectuals identified themselves at this time was through secular political movements which, in the circumstances of the epoch, came to have a quasi-Jewish character. Liberalism had been the predominant political philosophy of the generation of Jews who sought and achieved their own Emancipation, and who combined a deeply felt passion for liberty with a practical sense of the values of a free-trade policy. In Herzl's generation liberalism was giving way to socialism as the predominant political ideology of the Jewish intelligentsia.

But, for all the socialist fervor that he might muster, even the most politically radical of the Viennese Jewish intelligentsia was still likely to be a member of the Jewish middle class of the period, and to bear its stamp. The Central European middle classes of the late nineteenth century were in some ways the quintessence of bourgeois civilization; their style of life provides us with the very meaning of the concept. A man born in the same year as Herzl was only ten years old at the time of the Franco-Prussian War; he then lived to the age of fifty-four before he came to experience war in any other way than through the reading of news dispatches from remote and less civilized parts of the world. He could thus have reached middle age secure in the belief that European social life had come, for better or for worse, to be permanently dominated by rationality. This is the outlook implicit in the writings of Sigmund Freud—another Viennese Jew of Herzl's generation—who sought to ease the sufferings of a human psyche whose irrational drives clashed with the perhaps excessively rationalized demands of civilization. Ironically, it was the very classes who had done the most to create this rationalized order who were now suffering the most from its demands. Reading Freud's works one can dimly perceive the social paradigm upon which his life's activity was played: a middle- or more often upper-middle-class world, made up of the sons and daughters of industrial and financial conquerors, who now suddenly find themselves at a loss to deal emotionally with their double and conflicting legacy of ease and nervous energy. For want of greater wars to fight, their restless spirit turns inward and the great morass of the Unconscious itself becomes a battlefield, parents and siblings a lineup of allies or foes. We see in Freud's writings a society powerfully ruled by the inner emotional tensions of middle-class family relationships, one that is above all—perhaps even more so among the Jews than among the Gentiles—strongly matriarchal in character.

But men in general cannot be long content with this kind of emotional indwelling. Perhaps inevitably, a reaction against the self-indulgent and unheroic postures of their way of life began setting in among the European bourgeoisie even before Freud had begun to write. Signaled by such writers as Friedrich Nietzsche, a new search for transcendence got under way, founded upon the sort of yearning for the primitive that can only come from a sophisticated mind. With a self-consciousness characteristic of the age, great stress was placed upon the power of the Will to lift men out of the craven situation in which self-consciousness had placed them. This mood established the emotional groundwork for the encounter with war as a poetic experience that so many European intellectuals underwent from 1914 to 1918. It provoked that search to test the civilized will against a primitive environment that produced both Albert Schweitzer and the Zionist pioneers of Palestine. It also gave rise to dark and perverse passions, which in their most extreme form found expression ultimately in nazism, with its stress upon the "triumph of the Will." For this state of mind was bound to produce, among other things, a new wave of anti-Semitism. Centuries of social and economic restrictions had made the Jews the most utterly middle class of peoples; they had become the very symbol of bourgeois life. Anti-Semitism was therefore a psychologically convenient way for a man of middle-class origin to hate bourgeois civilization without having to be excessively contemptuous of himself. But this easy kind of solution made the problem of self-identification all the more vexing for a romantic Jewish intellectual like the young Herzl, who was as prone as his Christian counterpart to see the Jews of his own milieu as the symbol of the middle-class way of life against which he was rebelling.

Self-hatred was hardly the way out of his plight, and so he had to seek further for a solution.

The pre-eminent way out was always, of course, the path of conversion to Christianity; but this often only resulted in a double alienation in the life of the convert, who continued to be seen as a kind of Jew by Christian society even after he had, by his act of apostasy, earned the scorn of his fellow Jews. Another possible solution was to become a Social Democrat, as so many Jews did in that era. But in order to do this one had to make peace with two opposing contentions about Jews: on the one side, a persisting undercurrent of socialist rhetoric against Jewry in general for being an alleged spawning ground of finance capital, and on the other, the widespread feeling among conservatives that the Jews, with their persistent inclination toward socialist and revolutionary movements, were instinctual enemies of society and the state. One could perhaps find the solution to one's personal plight as a Jew by emigrating to America; but this would mean frustrating the very passion for European civilization that was the source of one's spiritual crisis to begin with. It was the Eastern European Jews, less a part of European civilization than their coreligionists in the West and hence less addicted to it, who were more amenable to an American solution to their problem. One could also find a solution through suicide, as did Herzl's friend Heinrich Kana in 1891. Or perhaps, under the influence of the same Wagnerian mood of regeneration that was causing many German "Aryans" to reach back for their heroic origins, the Jew also could begin reverting to memories of his people as a people like any other, with its warriors, nobles and peasants, as well as its merchants, and above all, with a land of its own, as it had been in biblical times. It was this last resolution that slowly began to dawn on Theodor Herzl, who also knew something about all the others.

Herzl's first mature experience of anti-Semitism took place in his student days in Vienna. Like so many Jews of his generation, his own inclination was to plunge without any reservations into the romantic life of the German university, with its German song, beer drinking, and dueling fraternities. But Vienna was at that very moment becoming one of the main centers, along with Berlin and Paris, of a new kind of phenomenon in European history: political anti-Semitism. In the still rather new world of popular suffrage, anti-

Semitic rabble-rousing was proving to have vote-getting power, particularly among those lower-middle-class elements who found their social and economic position threatened by the advance of large-scale capitalism, and who sought an emotional release for their resentment at this development by placing the blame for it upon the Jews. The ultimate success of Karl Lüger and his Christian Social party in gaining control of the Viennese municipality through tactics of this sort later served as a source of inspiration to Adolf Hitler. But the appeal of Lüger's program was not restricted to the mob. Anti-Semitism enjoyed a certain fashion among some of the intelligentsia at that time, in Germany and France as well as in Austria. Young Herzl resigned in chagrin from the dueling fraternity that he had joined at the University of Vienna, when he learned that one of his fellow members had given support to Lüger's program in a public speech. A few years later, while working for his doctorate in law, Herzl came across Eugen Dühring's book, *The Jewish Problem as a Problem of Race, Morals and Culture*. This work, which became one of the handbooks of the anti-Semitism of that period, advocated a complete segregation of the Jewish elements from the rest of society. It had a profoundly disturbing effect upon the young Herzl, who never ceased to refer to it later in life, and who claimed it was influential in giving rise to his Zionist vision. Herzl was, in fact, far from being the only Zionist whose views were at least partially shaped by anti-Semitism. It is significant that much of the Gentile support that he later received for his Zionist program came from men who were wrestling with anti-Semitic feelings within themselves. One important element in common, after all, between the Zionist and the anti-Semite was the realization that a "Jewish Question" still existed, despite the protestations of the older liberalism that all citizens were alike.

In spite of these early signs of disturbance to the liberal euphoria, Herzl managed to ignore the problems raised by anti-Semitism for a good part of his young manhood. Superficially at least, he continued throughout this period to adhere to the moribund liberal milieu, the proper path of respectability for a son of the Jewish middle classes. But Herzl was no mere conformist. After a brief spell of practicing law, he undertook to become a writer, concentrating his talents as a playwright and feuilletonist. It was in the latter capacity that he became a regular contributor to the *Neue Freie Presse* of Vienna, and eventually a member of its staff. Owned and edited by Jews, the *Neue Freie Presse* was the most distinguished liberal newspaper in Austria.

In these years as a rising young literary talent Herzl lived what seems to have been a rather pleasant and carefree life, despite the fashionable posture of melancholy that pervades his writings. Much of his time was spent traveling, whiling away days at elegant resorts, carefully observing the social life and landscape of *fin-de-siècle* Europe, and recording his fleeting impressions of it all in sophisticated feuilletons. The art of the feuilleton, which was at the peak of its development in Herzl's day and which utterly characterized the mood of that era, has been largely lost in our own time, especially in America, where—with the exception of the immigrant foreign-language press—it perhaps never really existed. Brief, usually witty, the most intimate and seemingly casual of literary forms, the feuilleton is ideally suited to the needs of a newspaper-reading audience that is at once clever, worldly and hurried. Highly impressionistic, it usually centers upon the description of some scene or vignette, but characteristically takes off from there into some kind of philosophical reflection. In one of Herzl's finer pieces, for example, a description of himself coming home to his children's empty nursery while they are out at play leads to reflections about fleeting time, and death. The mood is established so lucidly and convincingly that the quick juxtaposition of small and large themes is not jarring. It is precisely this kind of agile use of ironic transition that epitomizes the form. Perhaps Herzl's most celebrated feuilleton—the one that earned him the post of Paris correspondent for the *Neue Freie Presse*—is a description of the Spanish village of Saint-Jean-de-Luz, where, plunged into deep reflection at viewing the beautiful springs for which the town is famous, he suddenly hears a woman's voice behind him, saying in English: "Isn't it pretty?" to which the woman with her replies, "Really very nice!"

This kind of scintillating play of sensibility not only indicates the French origins of the feuilleton form but also serves to suggest the reason why, when it made its way into Central and Eastern Europe, the art of the feuilleton was taken up with particular mastery by Jewish writers. Heinrich Heine, many of whose greatest prose works are really extended feuilletons, was the very quintessence of the spirit that gave life to the genre—ironically contemplating a European civilization that would not entirely take him in though he loved it passionately, speaking of it with a mockery that came from despair. It was Heine who set the tone that one can see in Herzl's feuilletons: a French refinement of spirit, infused into a rough-grained German language, the very coarseness of which is the element most often called upon by the writer to give an additional quality of tension to the piece. Such a formula suggests precisely the tension of elements that resided in the spirit of the Europeanized Jew in the nineteenth century, caught up as he was between that ingrained moral and religious fundamentalism which always drew European Jews to German culture and an inherited lucidity of thought and wit that had far greater affinities with the French sensibility.

There is yet another characteristic of the feuilleton genre that particularly suited it to Herzl's personality. It is a restless genre; indeed, one is tempted to say that it is the retreat of men of literary talent who lack the patience to sit through any longer form of composition. It was, at any rate, the characteristic literary expression of a certain type of Jewish aesthete-man-of-action at about the turn of the century, of men whose restless engagement in life itself usually left them little more than scattered moments in which to write about it. There is in a sense a truly revolutionary spirit at work here, an apparent fulfillment of the ideal that Marx had in mind when he said that in the postrevolutionary society there would no longer be that clear distinction between art and life which is so characteristic of bourgeois society. Such a spirit represents yet another attempt to formulate a solution to that problem of the gap between thought and action with which both Marx and Moses Hess had struggled.

Herzl's spirit was of precisely this sort, although it was a number of years before Herzl discovered this fact about himself. It is noteworthy that his plays were generally quite inferior to his feuilletons, even though he always quite naturally looked upon the former as the more serious endeavor. His plot and construction were usually stilted, his characters unconvincing artifacts. Despite his desire to be a kind of Viennese Georges Feydeau, and despite occasional touches of brilliance in his plays, he was simply not at his best in an extended imaginative construct whose only end was art. Later he would discover that the extended workings of his imagination—such as a highly detailed blueprint for a Jewish state that was, in many of its particulars, more imaginative than workable—took on their greatest power when they served as stimuli for practical activity. But so far as his writings themselves were concerned, it was the drama of everyday life, the immediate experience of his own fine sensibility, that provided the material for his talent at its best. It was only with the eventual discovery of his Zionist vision that he also found for himself, at the same moment, a literary genre which would reconcile his talent for the description of actual experience with his aspiration to transcend everyday life—and the worldly melancholy that seemed an inseparable part of it—through a construct of the imagination: his diaries, which he often referred to as "my political novel." But this latter achievement consisted in placing the transcendent act of the imagination not in the work of art, as he had once aspired to do, but in life itself; the literary work then simply became the record of such a life. This formulation was the outcome of a revolutionary development in Herzl's spirit.

During the course of the period from about 1890 to 1895, Herzl underwent an emotional and spiritual crisis that found its focus both in his personal life and in historic events that he witnessed. Herzl had married in 1889, but though he and his wife had become the parents of two children by 1891, their marriage had not found stability. His wife, the daughter of a wealthy Jewish businessman, apparently had tastes that were burdensomely expensive for the struggling young writer. The external difficulties of this relationship were compounded by the fact that Herzl's own emotional capacity for marriage was not yet fully developed. He was still ardently attached to his parents, and particularly to his mother, in a way that was perhaps not wholly compatible with emotional maturity. His private, poetic ideal of women apparently centered around the memories of two girls who had died early in life: one, a girl he had known at school; the other, his sister Pauline, who had been a year older than himself, and who had died at the age of eighteen. His sense of love tended to formulate itself as a tragic and unrealizable vision. In 1891 Herzl's marriage difficulties reached the point at which he and his wife underwent a brief separation.

There were other major crises in Herzl's personal life that same year. On February 6 his good friend Heinrich Kana shot himself. Kana was a melancholy young man who also had been struggling to become a writer, and who had been grappling unsuccessfully with an inability to produce any work at the time he decided to take his life. His suicide note was addressed to Herzl. "My dear, good Theodor," it said, "your old friend sends you this farewell before he dies! I thank you for all the friendship and the goodness you have shown me. All earthly happiness to you and yours. I kiss you. Your Heinrich."[3] Some months later, another close friend of Herzl's, Oswald Boxer— he, Kana and Herzl had been a "circle" in their student days in Vienna—died of yellow fever in Rio de Janeiro, where he had gone on a mission to see about the possible settlement of Russian Jews in South America. Herzl came to see the deaths of both these men as being due to the fact that they were Jews, each seeking in his own way a solution to his personal "Jewish Question."

A sense of the problem of his Jewishness that was now reviving in Herzl was given further stimulus by his assignment, begun in March, 1892, as Paris correspondent of the *Neue Freie Presse*. He had hardly begun in his new job when the Panama Scandal broke. The fact that the French undertaking to build a canal through the Isthmus of Panama was an utter failure had been shielded from the public for years by a large and ever-growing system of bribery, which in the end implicated many members of the French parliament. The affair was a huge blot on the fledgling Republic, and it gave new strength to the antirepublican movement. What is more, it gave French antirepublicanism a new and insidious weapon: anti-Semitism. Among the names of the men who had actually been handling the exchange of bribes were those of two Jews prominent in the French financial world—a world that had come to seem, in the hostile eyes of many a French *petit bourgeois*, to abound too richly with Jewish names in the first place. This fact gave ammunition to a French variety of anti-Semitism that had hitherto rested under the tutelage of German and Austrian models, but which now was to become, for the next few years, the most eminent anti-Semitic movement in Europe. Edouard Drumont, a Paris journalist who had published a two-volume screed against the Jews, called *La France Juive*, in 1886, was catapulted into fame by the Panama Scandal; his book, after several years of obscurity, became a sudden best seller, and his anti-Semitic newspaper, *La Libre Parole*, leaped high in circulation. In this way the scene was set for the Dreyfus Affair, beginning at the end of 1894, in which Drumont and his newspaper played a major part. The fact that

[3] Alex Bein, *Theodore Herzl*, translated by Maurice Samuel (New York, 1962), p. 68.

developments of this sort were taking place not in reactionary Germany or Austria but in the land of the very Revolution that had brought Emancipation to the Jews of Europe in the first place had a sobering effect upon the outlook of Jewish Liberals everywhere.

These political events acted in such a way upon the mood of personal crisis within Herzl as to drive his mind back to old and still unresolved problems concerning his Jewish identity. Men like Drumont were giving an objective meaning to personal despair; they led Herzl to perceive that such things as his wife's excessive interest in money and the death of his two best friends were at least partly due to the fact of being Jewish. The scattered encounters with anti-Semitism that he had experienced in his life, and had sought to ignore at the time they took place, now accumulated in his memory and began to take on meaning. This was the state of mind he had reached even before the Dreyfus Affair broke out. The events of the affair itself, then, could thus have seemed to him like the fulfillment of a prophetic vision—sufficient ground for undertaking great actions that would ultimately transform his life.

His first concerted effort at dealing with the Jewish Question—at least within himself—took place in a three-week period which ended only a matter of days before the treason trial of a certain Captain Alfred Dreyfus began to gain public attention. During this period he wrote a play, which he called The New Ghetto. Its central character, Dr. Jacob Samuel, is a young Viennese-Jewish lawyer who resembles Herzl himself. He is married to a young woman, the daughter of a wealthy business family, who appreciates neither her husband's frequent inability to meet the bill for her expensive tastes nor his strangely idealistic turn of mind. Jacob is engaged by his wife's brother-in-law—a man who has enjoyed great success on the Stock Exchange—to handle the legal affairs of a business in which he owns a large share, a mining enterprise run by a German nobleman. Jacob eventually discovers that the mine is run in such a way that the miners are placed in constant danger of their lives. When a workers' delegate from the mine comes to him for aid, Jacob agrees to become the miners' representative in their fight for better working conditions. In the end the mine goes bankrupt, Jacob's hitherto smug brother-in-law is ruined, and the German nobleman who owns the mine blames all Jews for his misfortunes. He challenges Jacob to a duel, and the young lawyer is shot and killed.

Throughout the play the venality of the Viennese-Jewish middle classes is stressed as a central theme. Jacob's friends constantly seek to convince him that his solidarity with his own people demands, among other things, that he protect their financial interests. But for Jacob this is too craven a conception of his Jewishness. At one point in the play someone tells him the story of a certain Moses of Mainz, who lived in the fifteenth century, and who one night heard a man crying for help outside the ghetto wall. It was after the curfew hour, but Moses wished to go out and help the man, whoever he was. His family and his friends pleaded with him not to do so, warning him of the danger, but he ignored them. He went out and was killed. When Jacob hears this story he replies that he, too, would answer a cry from outside the ghetto walls regardless of the danger. At the very end of the play, as he is dying, his last words are: "Jews, my brothers, there will come a time when they will let you live again—when you know how to die. . . . I want to get out! Out—of—the—ghetto!"

In Jacob's case the ghetto is, of course, the world of Jewish finance, and the cry for help from the outside is that which is made to him by the workers in the very business in which Jewish interests are at stake. Clearly, Herzl, when writing this play, was standing on the brink of the kind of personal decision that made many of the Jewish intellectuals of his generation into Social Democrats. Later his Zionist conception was to be filled with elements borrowed from the socialist world view: the Eastern European Jewish masses became his proletariat, whose regeneration would also be the salvation of the spoiled Jewish bourgeoisie of Western Europe (this was, basically, Moses Hess's view as well), and at times he even seemed to be consciously trying to outdo the Socialists, as in his proposal for a seven-hour working day in the Jewish state (the Socialists were still demanding only eight hours!). Why Herzl never took the one additional step into actually becoming a Socialist remains a mystery. Chances are he was restrained by the filial piety that was one of the overwhelming sentiments in his life—a piety that projected itself not only upon his own father but upon an entire liberal older generation, and that ultimately found mature fulfillment in Herzl's spirit when he himself sought to become a universal father to his people. The rationale that he found to explain his hesitations about socialism is given in *The New Ghetto*. "I'm certainly not in favor of uprooting capital," Jacob says. "Too much would go by the board—too many cultural values. I don't want to see thrift and incentive banished. And useful enterprise is entitled to handsome rewards—up to a certain limit!" Ultimately, when he arrived at his Zionist vision, Herzl resolved this socioeconomic question in his own mind by conceiving of the Jewish state as a *mutualistic* society—an ideal of cooperative but free entrepreneurship that was widely discussed in the latter half of the nineteenth century. But Herzl always remained aware of some connection between socialism and the Zionist idea that lay within the Jewish spirit, one that remained even when these two ideologies were most in conflict with each other. One of the arguments he most often presented later on in favor of his Zionist program to such conservative eminences as the German Kaiser, was that it would draw Jews away from social democracy. The Kaiser saw the point.

The aspiration to "get out of the ghetto," to which Herzl had given expression through the character of Jacob Samuel, was at this time growing into an obsession on his part. But this never took the form of a mere personal ambition. Herzl had a large historical appetite, a profound sense of honor and an epic vision of fatherhood, all of which led him to cast his hopes at all times in the form of a vision of himself leading a flock to salvation. For most of his early life, such a vision could hardly have seemed more than a daydream. But it persisted, and in time Herzl came to entertain the idea that this dream could perhaps be fulfilled through literature, at the very least by his somehow describing such a process of salvation in a novel or a play or, best of all, by his writing a book that would actually lead men to perform great acts. At times he even stood on the brink of dispensing with literature altogether and giving more direct and practical expression to his dreams. Most probably, when his friend, Oswald Boxer, left for South America on the Jewish mission that ended in his death, Herzl would have seriously considered going too, but for his marriage. The idea of Jewish colonization—and even, specifically, of Jewish colonization in South America—remained in his mind.

But his romantic spirit also toyed with bolder schemes for solving the Jewish Question. In 1893 he conceived, with no small degree of seriousness, a project for the mass conversion of the Jews to Christianity. Even in this rash conception his filial piety and sense of honor held sway. For, said Herzl, "the leaders of this movement—myself in particular—would remain Jews. . . . We, the steadfast men, would have constituted the last generation. We would still have adhered to the faith of our fathers. But we would have made Christians of our young sons before they reached the age of independent decision, after which conversion looks like an act of cowardice or careerism."[4] This concern with honor is mingled with a spirit of theatricality that is equally important to the conception: "The conversion was to take place in broad daylight, Sundays at noon, in St. Stephen's Cathedral, with festive processions and amidst the pealing of bells. Not in shame, as individuals have converted up to now, but with proud gestures."[5] This conception is not at all far from Herzl's later Zionist idea. All the elements are there: the sense of the dramatic, the passionate search for honor, the belief in the possibility of transforming the Jews through a sudden and sweeping act—and, above all, Herzl's sense of his own central importance in bringing such a thing about.

But in 1893 such schemes were still arrived at by Herzl in a spirit something like that of an earnest boy, utterly convinced of the seriousness of his dreams, yet also vaguely aware of the luxury of still not having to be taken too seriously by the adult world. Actually, such a frame of mind never wholly departed from Herzl, who always remained able to derive a certain sense of freedom from reserving at least a part of his imagination to a somewhat childlike self-indulgence. Perhaps most people do this to some extent, but in Herzl's case it was this very area of his imagination which also came to serve, after a certain point in his life, as the source of his major activities. From then on, the world rapidly usurped his imagination—and his youth. This was the outcome of a fulfillment Herzl had strenuously sought, but it exhausted him.

The New Ghetto was Herzl's farewell to the adolescence of his visions; the leap into manhood began only a few months later. In the intervening period, the trial and sentence of Dreyfus—whom Herzl had watched being publicly dishonored in the courtyard of the Ecole Militaire, crying "I am innocent!" while the sinister shout came back from the crowd, "Death to the Jews!"—had transformed his idle speculations about the Jewish Question into a frenzy of schemes. In the course of his reflections, two ideas appear to have struck him with particular force, and more or less simultaneously. One was the idea that the financial resources of the great Jewish millionaires—the chief targets of the wrath of anti-Semites—could be used as a lever for

[4] The Complete Diaries of Theodor Herzl, edited by Raphael Patai, translated by Harry Zohn (New York, 1960), Vol. I, p. 7.
[5] Ibid., p. 7.

achieving a revolutionary solution to the Jewish Question. At this time Jewish financiers like Baron Edmond de Rothschild and Baron Maurice de Hirsch were prominently engaged in Jewish philanthropies, and it was this fact that made Herzl think of turning to them; but he regarded his own scheme to be as different from their Jewish philanthropic projects as socialism was from charity in general. Like the Socialists, Herzl believed that economic self-interest could be played upon as a revolutionary instrument. In the Marxist conception of things, the proletariat was to bring a socialist society, not because it was more idealistic than other classes but because its own interest demanded such an outcome. By the same token, it would be in the interest of the Jewish financiers to bring about a genuine solution to the Jewish Question, such as Herzl felt he had conceived, instead of merely ameliorating the lot of some Jews, as philanthropy did. One can perceive in this notion a touch of the influence that anti-Semitism often exerted upon Herzl: in the view that finance capital was as fundamental an economic trait of the Jews as labor power was of the proletariat.

The other idea that came to Herzl at this time was based upon the programs of Jewish colonization that were then current. This period was, after all, the classic age of imperialism, when the European mind was caught up in a euphoria of visions of wastelands and jungles in various remote parts of the world, waiting for European intelligence and initiative to tame them. It was natural for Jewish philanthropists to think of alleviating the lot of some of their more impoverished coreligionists by establishing Jewish settlements in a few of these remote places; Hirsch was sponsoring such settlements in Argentina, Rothschild in Palestine. But Herzl's imagination now exercised the same kind of transformation upon these projects of colonization that Jewish philanthropy in general had undergone in his mind when he reformulated it in terms of economic self-interest. He sought not charity but revolutionary solutions. What he envisioned was not scattered colonies ameliorating the lot of a few settlers but the rapid mass colonization of a Jewish commonwealth. As he saw it, once such a commonwealth had been legally established—he hoped to use Jewish wealth to buy a "charter" to some territory—virtually the entire Jewish population of Europe would then settle in it. A genuine solution to the Jewish Question—a *political* one—would then have been achieved.

This vision was founded upon the sudden emergence within

Herzl's spirit of a transcendent sense of personal destiny, a sublime egotism that was henceforth to drive him with an increasing and self-consuming fury and that was to imbue his presence with charismatic force. For, simultaneously with the emergence of his vision, he sensed that its realization was to be the product of his own self-immersion—and even self-immolation—in Jewish history. This outlook is reflected even in the political theory that he formulated at this time to explain the principles of his program for founding a Jewish commonwealth. For it was essential to his aim that he conceive of the Jewish people as a single and even quasi-sovereign entity, which he could present as such in his dealings with the powers of the world; but how could such a thing be possible? Herzl asserted its possibility by rejecting Rousseau's conception of the social contract as something founded upon the common consent—the "general will"—of an entire body politic. If Rousseau were correct, then Herzl would be unable to construe the existence of a *political* body comprising all of world Jewry; he had to work out a formula that could dispense with the element of explicit common consent. What he did was to invoke a classic principle of Roman law, that of the *negotiorum gestio*—a conducting of the affairs of some body by a power that has not necessarily been given the authority to do so by that body. According to Herzl's theory, it is to such a power—the *gestor*—that the body owes its very existence, and not the other way around, as Rousseau would have it. On the basis of this theory, Herzl forthwith proceeded to consider himself the *gestor* for the Jewish people. Such an autocratic notion bears the earmarks of Herzl's Central European background; it is infused with a certain scorn for democracy that was always to manifest itself in his outlook. It also betrays the profound and somewhat mystical drive in Herzl's spirit toward a vision of universal fatherhood for himself; there ever was to remain at the bottom of his thoughts the temptation to feel that he had somehow *sired* not merely the Jewish state but an entire Jewish people as nation.

In May, 1895, however, when Herzl wrote the letter to Baron de Hirsch that was to be in effect the beginning of his Zionist career, he was still a young man of thirty-five with only a moderate literary and journalistic reputation. He still had to undergo a period of consider-able struggle to establish not only his name in the world but a fully realized conception of himself. His letter to Hirsch was audacious and had an authoritative ring: "I . . . wish to have a discussion with you about Jewish political matters, a discussion that may have an effect on times that neither you nor I will live to see";[6] but there was no reason to be certain that the Baron would grant him an audience. After two exchanges of letters, Hirsch did agree to see Herzl—the Baron was perhaps intrigued by so unliberal a use of terms as "Jewish *political* matters" coming from a correspondent of the *Neue Freie Presse*—but one afternoon's conversation was enough to enable him to dismiss the young man as an impractical, if interesting, visionary. Nevertheless, Herzl was encouraged by having had this first chance to air his views before an eminent man, and he began to try elsewhere. He wrote to Bismarck (who was then in retirement), but never received an answer. He spoke to other men, some of them prominent members of the Jewish communities of Paris and Vienna, with whom his journalistic connections brought him into contact, and often found that he was at least provoking interest. He began "to notice that I have the power to stir people."[7] Following through his initial interest in great Jewish financiers, he tried the Rothschilds, presenting to them a long memorandum expounding his idea. When this brought no results (it was only years after Herzl's death that Baron Edmond de Rothschild was converted from purely philanthropic enterprises to a more Zionist commitment), he decided to aim for a larger audience, and reformulated the memorandum into a book. *Der Judenstaat* was published in February, 1896.

Throughout this entire first year of his Zionist enterprise, Herzl, still rather unsure of himself, was aware of the fact that he was walking a hazardous borderline between dream and reality. He constantly braced himself for the possibility that he might be dealing with the merest delusion on his part. The device that he used to cushion himself from the shock of a possible breakdown of his entire vision was to entertain the notion that, in the end, he was perhaps undergoing nothing more than a rather vivid period of gestation for some novel that he was to write. The early pages of the diary that he began keeping simultaneously with the birth of this vision are filled with a constant playing with this notion, a constant vacillation between two commitments: the idea as a novel and the idea as a

---

[6] *Ibid.*, Vol. I, p. 14.
[7] *Ibid.*, Vol. I, p. 228.

program for action. In fact, the notion of the novel dies hard, even as
the practical activity begins to manifest itself as his destined purpose.
The idea of formulating his vision as a novel did not really disappear
completely until it had borne fruit in the completion, in 1902, of
Old–New Land, his utopian novel about the state he was then fully at
work trying to realize.

Until then his conception of himself and of his own activity always
remained, in a sense, novelistic. For, as Herzl fully understood, the
diary, which was being written by life itself rather than mere imagination, had now became his novel. He was always aware of it as a
work of literary significance. There are many fine descriptive passages
in it, such as those dealing with all the pomp, color and pathos of his
several visits to the Sultan in Constantinople. There are many great
moments of self-revelation in it. But, as time goes on, the diary
increasingly becomes a mere record of the day's transactions, often
interspersed with Herzl's own annoyed observation that, as his activities are becoming more demanding, the diary is becoming inferior in
literary quality. This observation is quite significant, for the diary was
indeed the representative of that preserve of his imagination which
was steadily used up by his Zionist activity. As his work gained in
power, his spirit was drained of its power. Herzl was fully aware of
this tragic aspect of his choice to become a man of action. On May
13, 1901, while sitting in a hotel room in Constantinople during his
third sojourn there, and reflecting upon the more youthful mood of
his previous visits, he writes: "I look out the windows, a changed
man, and see the unchanged Golden Horn. Beauty no longer moves
me. For the world is no longer Representation (Vorstellung), but
Will."[8] This reference to Schopenhauer (Die Welt als Wille und
Vorstellung, sometimes rendered "The World as Will and Idea") in
part constitutes a triumphant reflection upon that old philosophical
problem of the relationship between thought and action with which
Moses Hess had struggled; it is also a sad recognition of the price that
has been paid for its resolution.

The publication of Der Judenstaat caused Herzl's name to become
known to the small Zionist groups scattered throughout Central and
Eastern Europe at that time. Actually, it was only in the period
which now ensued that Herzl's idea for a Jewish commonwealth
became, strictly speaking, a "Zionist" one. Until this time he had

[8] Ibid., Vol. III, p. 1105.

never been exclusively committed to Palestine as the locus of the commonwealth, and he seems rather to have been more inclined toward the South America of Oswald Boxer and Baron de Hirsch. For the Zionists, on the other hand, as their very name indicates, Palestine was the sole *raison d'être* of their aspirations. The *Hovevei Zion* (Lovers of Zion) of Odessa, for example, the most important of the Zionist organizations at that time, concentrated primarily upon sending small groups of colonists to Palestine—even as it then existed, under Turkish rule—with the intention simply of building a Jewish community there, and without, for the moment, focusing upon some kind of political outcome. Herzl, who came in from the outside as it were, and who was converted to Zionism properly so called by these Palestine colonization groups as they rallied to him, introduced an alien but stimulating element into their scattered activities with his cavalier ideal of suddenly and dramatically proclaiming a commonwealth. But the elements of the Hovevei Zion and the similar groups who threw in their lot with Herzl and became part of the political Zionist movement that he created at the Basel Congress in August–September, 1897, always retained a certain skepticism toward Herzl's stress upon seeking a "charter" that would grant a sovereign or quasi-sovereign territory to the Zionists. They did not expect the Jewish barons to open wide their coffers for such a scheme, nor did they anticipate that the Great Powers would rush to grant a charter; above all, they did not imagine that, even if such a charter were obtained, the bulk of middle-class European Jewry would be eager to be promptly resettled in some area that was then still either a desert or a swamp. Their first loyalty continued to be to the task of gradual colonization by determined young pioneers.

These two approaches—the Herzlian, or "political," Zionist approach and the "practical" Zionism of the Hovevei Zion tradition—marked a good deal of the subsequent history of the Zionist movement, even after Herzl's death. To a large extent, these two approaches also marked the difference between the Western European Zionists, who tended to be Herzlian, and the Eastern Europeans, who leaned more toward "practical" Zionism (this line of distinction tended to disappear after the First World War and the Balfour Declaration). The distinction was largely founded upon the cultural differences between, on the one hand, a bourgeois, Europeanized Jewry that had little attachment to authentic Jewish traditions and

saw Zionism almost exclusively as a solution to anti-Semitism and, on
the other hand, a Jewish community that remained deeply attached
to Jewish moral and cultural traditions even when it was modernist in
religious outlook, and that hoped therefore to create a true Jewish
national culture in Palestine.

Yet, in spite of whatever skepticism the Eastern European Zionists
felt toward Herzl and the type of Western Jew that he represented
(Herzl, in fact, became much more susceptible to the Eastern European way of looking at things than did many of his Western colleagues in the movement), his personality exerted a magnetic pull
upon them. His charm, his imagination, and the will in him that was
now growing into an overwhelming force would have been enough to
attract followers, but there were other, less spiritual, traits that also
made him attractive to the Eastern Europeans. For, despite the
presence of many learned and distinguished men among their leaders
(Herzl, betraying a certain ingrained Western prejudice, was sur-
prised and delighted when he first discovered how many such men
there were among them), the Jews of Russia and Poland still
harbored feelings of inferiority toward the culture of Western Europe. And Herzl, after all, was a correspondent for one of the most
distinguished newspapers in Europe, a man whose connections in
Paris, Vienna and elsewhere were most impressive. Furthermore, by
the time of the First Zionist Congress, he had come to treat on rather
intimate terms with the Grand Duke of Baden, and had been
received at the palace of the Turkish Sultan. He lent an unquestioned
air of high dignity to the Zionist movement, a claim to walk in the
solemn corridors of European diplomacy that the sons of Yiddish-
speaking Eastern Europe did not yet feel they had acquired for
themselves. In fact, they maintained a certain attitude of irony
toward such things even as they acknowledged the necessity of them.
Herzl's passion for dignified splendor was perhaps a little excessive,
and not, after all, entirely free of the Jewish sense of inferiority that
beset his Russian and Polish colleagues. But his presence unquestionably gave form and weight to the Zionist movement, and impressed it
upon the imagination of the world as the quasi-sovereignty he wanted
it to be. He was the founder of Jewish diplomacy, a new phenomenon in history.

The sudden appearance before Herzl's eyes, as a result of the
publication of Der Judenstaat, of a network of Zionist organizations

all over Central and Eastern Europe gave to his growing passion precisely the stimulus it needed. The exultation of this discovery quite possibly impressed itself upon the more mystical depths of his imagination in the form of a feeling that, despite all rational evidence to the contrary, he had somehow *conjured* the Zionist movement into being. Shortly after the publication of *Der Judenstaat*, Herzl was given a copy of Leo Pinsker's *Auto-Emancipation*, a pamphlet expressing a Zionist idea similar to that of Herzl, which had been published by a Russian Jew in 1882. Herzl's comment upon reading it was that, had he come across it earlier, he would probably never have embarked upon his own project. The sense of acting upon an original creation of his own imagination and will was very important for Herzl. It was the very spontaneity of his encounter with Zionism that spurred him on to absolute dedication to it. And this inexhaustible energy and initiative on his part—not to mention his almost reckless expenditure of his personal savings whenever he deemed it necessary to do so—was what was primarily responsible for the creation of the Zionist Congress, the tribunal that gave cohesiveness and political identity to the Zionist movement.

The crisis of Herzl's personal life was thus partially resolved through projection onto a public plane. The young man who had still been struggling with his own immaturity in 1894 had become transformed, by the end of 1897, into a father of his people. This latter role manifested itself in particular in his relationship with the Eastern European Jews in the Zionist movement, whom he treated with an indulgence that was largely accepted by the Yiddish-speaking masses but only served to aggravate the differences between himself and their leaders. But, on the level of his personal life, there was an ironic and even tragic side to this role that he came to play. For, if he genuinely became a kind of father in the larger world that he had created out of his vision, in the small world of his personal relationships he continued to bear some of the earmarks of the young man he had been, treated as even rather immature by some of the people with whom he was associated. He seems to have gone on living in two worlds, in each of which the other world must have looked like a dream.

In his diaries it is particularly the story of his continuing relationship with the *Neue Freie Presse*, where he remained employed until his death at the age of forty-four, that characterizes the private side of his life during his Zionist years. The two editors of the paper, Moritz Benedikt and Eduard Bacher, both older than Herzl, belonged wholeheartedly to the liberal and assimilationist school. When Herzl first presented his Zionist idea to them, they rejected it as the same sort of childish scheme he had come up with two years earlier, when he had proposed the mass conversion of the Jews at St. Stephen's Cathedral. As the Zionist movement grew, the refusal on the part of Benedikt and Bacher to pay any attention to it became tense and even desperate, but Herzl never had the satisfaction in his lifetime of seeing his own newspaper give coverage to Zionism. The whole situation, as one reads of it in the diaries, reminds one of parents trying hard not to accord any seriousness to the aberrant activities of a boy who is growing up in their midst. Herzl was fully aware of the ironies of this predicament. One day, when he had undergone one of his frequent hopeless arguments about Zionism with Bacher only a short time after having had an audience with the Chancellor of the German Empire, he wrote in his diary: "A strange psychological phenomenon that Bacher causes me more anguish than Imperial Chancellor Hohenlohe! In his [Bacher's] presence, strangely enough, I still feel like what I once was: a shy journalistic tyro, although he certainly does not impress me intellectually."[9] At one point in his diary Herzl jokingly refers to Benedikt as "Maledikt"—a kind of behind-the-back name calling that employees traditionally indulge in toward their bosses; but this was from the pen of a man who was, at the time, conferring with the crowned heads of Europe as the political leader of the Jewish people! This job was an invaluable asset to Herzl, who drew no salary from the Zionist movement but rather was spending his own money on it. He was paid quite well by the Neue Freie Presse—he was the glory of its staff, which was why he was retained in spite of everything—and his post as feuilleton editor gave him considerable freedom to come and go as he pleased. Yet, from the standpoint of personal pride and psychological well-being, it seems incredible that he was willing to keep this job right down to the end of his life. Possibly he continued to harbor a certain emotional need for this relationship.

Some elements of what was his private state of mind at the very height of his Zionist career are revealed in his 1902 novel, Old–New

9 Ibid., Vol. II, p. 708.

Land. This book was written during a period of political frustration. Herzl had created a political movement and given it fame, but after three unsuccessful trips to Constantinople in search of a Palestine charter from the Sultan, he still did not have at hand the kind of concrete achievement he had always hoped for. This fact was particularly irksome with respect to his relationship with Benedikt and Bacher, for they had promised to give due coverage to Zionism should it ever really accomplish something. At this impasse with reality, Herzl allowed himself some moments to indulge his old impulse to realize the Zionist idea as a novel. *Old–New Land* is a description of the Palestinian utopia of his dreams. But the technocratic paradise that he describes, utterly free of any character of its own, Jewish or otherwise, is not the most interesting aspect of the book. Rather, the main interest, both for intrinsic reasons and for what it reveals about the author's state of mind, lies in the structure of action and personal relationships that Herzl uses as the vehicle for describing his utopia.

The story begins in that Jewish Vienna which was the spawning ground of Herzl's own experience, full of businessmen and financial speculators, their wives, and their toadies. The protagonist, Friedrich Loewenberg, is a young Jewish lawyer, twenty-three years old, just out of the university, and still not adjusted to the harsh realities of the world in which he must now find his place. He has just lost the two good friends of his university days, "Oswald," who went to Brazil on a mission to found Jewish colonies and died there of yellow fever, and "Heinrich," who has shot himself. It turns out that the reason Friedrich, who is thoroughly discontented with the torpor and lack of idealism that prevail among his contemporaries, did not go along with Oswald to Brazil, is a certain Ernestine, whom he hopes to marry.

But Ernestine, for all her charms, is simply another spoiled daughter of the Viennese-Jewish upper middle class; shortly after the opening of the novel, Friedrich attends a party at Ernestine's home, during which her parents announce her engagement to a successful young businessman. Disgusted with the world, Friedrich answers a newspaper advertisement calling for "an educated, desperate young man willing to make a last experiment with his life." The author of the advertisement turns out to be a certain Kingscourt, born Koenigshoff, a Prussian nobleman who had contemptuously renounced his origins and settled in America, where he became a millionaire. Late

in life, after having struggled in solitude to make his fortune, he had
married a young woman who subsequently was unfaithful to him.
Like Friedrich, who is some thirty years his junior, he has become
disgusted with the world, and now plans to sail his yacht to a certain
remote island in the South Pacific and there live the life of a well-to-
do hermit. His only need will be for a companion in chess and
conversation, and that is why he has sought someone as eager to
renounce the world as he is. Friedrich, who is apparently without any
demanding family or personal ties, agrees to join him, and they set
sail the next day.

On their way toward the Suez Canal, Kingscourt suggests that
Friedrich might want to make a brief detour and have a look at his
"fatherland." Friedrich does not at first know what he means, and
when Kingscourt tells him he is referring to Palestine, his immediate
response is to say that only anti-Semites could call Palestine the
Jewish "fatherland"; Friedrich has not yet left the liberal mentality
completely behind him. They visit the Palestine that Herzl had seen
in 1898, a land largely arid and treeless, made up of towns full of
ancient and dirty streets. There are some signs that the land is being
improved by a Jewish colonization movement, but not enough to
make Friedrich anything but eager to leave there as soon as possible.
They set sail again for their South Pacific island, and the first section
of the novel closes.

The next section begins twenty years later. Kingscourt, now in his
seventies but still vigorous, and Friedrich, in his early forties but also
far more youthful than his years, are returning to Europe, mainly at
Kingscourt's instigation, to see what has become of the world in their
absence. Sailing through the Suez Canal, they discover the traffic
there to be far less than what it had been twenty years before, and,
upon inquiring as to the reason for this, they learn that the chief
corridor of European trade with the East is now the Jewish state in
Palestine. Stunned at the news, they decide to make another visit to
Palestine to see with their own eyes the miracle that apparently has
happened there. They do so, and they discover a technological
utopia, with electric streetcars riding on rails suspended above the
street, motorcars speeding along streamlined highways, telephone
newscasts, and theater and opera in a dozen languages. The prevailing language of the country is apparently German, which shades off
into the "Judaeo-German" of the proletariat, who are mostly of

Eastern European origin. The country is a republic (its degree of
sovereignty is not discussed, since this was still a moot question with
Turkey at the time the book was written), and the economic system
is described as "mutualistic."

The social milieu in which the two men find themselves in Palestine reads like an exercise in wish fulfillment. Just before leaving
Vienna some twenty years earlier, Friedrich had befriended a poor
Jewish family from Galicia, whom he had come to know through
their ten-year-old son, a ragged little boy who used to beg for coins at
the doorway of Friedrich's favorite café. When Kingscourt offered
Friedrich a large sum of money with which to clear up his affairs
before leaving, the young man had taken the money and given it to
this Galician family. Now, upon their arrival at Haifa port, Friedrich
and Kingscourt are suddenly confronted in the street by a well-bred
young man who turns out to be David Littwak, the beggar boy whom
Friedrich had befriended in Vienna. David is now one of the leaders
of the "New Society" in Palestine, and is subsequently, at the end of
the book, to be elected its president. He is married, has an infant son,
and lives in a home that would be the delight of any upper-middle-
class person anywhere. In his household lives his sister Miriam, who
was only an infant at the time Friedrich had known the Littwaks in
Vienna. It is clear from the outset that Friedrich and Miriam are
attracted to one another. Miriam—who, it has been suggested, was
based upon Herzl's bereaved sister, Pauline[10]—is the very antithesis
of the type of spoiled girl that had so upset Friedrich in Vienna.
Simple and straightforward in character despite her social eminence,
she is a schoolteacher, dedicated to the ideal of reshaping the spirit of
her country's youth to a better way of life than their grandparents
had known.

To stress the contrast with Miriam, Friedrich subsequently encounters Ernestine, the love of his youth, here in Palestine—along
with that entire Viennese-Jewish social circle from twenty years
before! Their life is utterly unchanged—Herzl had always advocated
an arrangement whereby the wealthy Jews of Europe could transfer
themselves to Palestine with their fortunes unimpaired. But in the
New Society their wealth alone does not bring them the honor it
once had, and their idle way of life only brings contempt upon them.
They are the vestiges of a kind of Jewish life that is being consigned

[10] Bein, *op. cit.*, p. 400.

to the past. There is a nicely ironic scene in which Friedrich first discovers Ernestine here in Palestine, sitting at the opera. From a distance, he sees at first the beloved of his youth, like an apparition, unchanged, still beautiful. Then he realizes that he is staring at Ernestine's daughter! His former beloved is rather the portly, over-dressed matron sitting at the girl's side. The revenge contained in this vision becomes complete when, at the end of the book, Friedrich becomes engaged to the young Miriam.

The clarity of many aspects of the book as a realization of some of Herzl's dreams helps also to illuminate the elements that are, at first sight, puzzling. Why does he have his hero go off to some distant never-never land that is not even described, instead of going to Palestine immediately? To be sure, Herzl wanted to give Friedrich objective reasons for a complete conversion from liberal assimilation-ism. But Friedrich's experience is also a projection of some of the inner qualities of Herzl's Zionist vision. For, despite Herzl's life-consuming absorption in his project, there still lay at the imaginative base of his hopes the dream that, with the wave of a magic wand, he could somehow *conjure* the Jewish state into being. And this is pre-cisely what he does for Friedrich in the novel. The twenty-year interval in which Palestine is transformed has no reality whatsoever in the context of the novel; when we encounter Friedrich and Kings-court returning from their island only a page after they have departed for it, we experience no sense of time having passed. The device of a twenty-year interval is simply that wave of a magic wand.

Kingscourt, who is one of the few genuinely interesting and three-dimensional characters in the book, is also the most difficult to comprehend. A perplexing conflict, centered upon him, arises through the course of the novel, and is in the end solved only by an unconvincing *deus ex machina*. Friedrich had vowed, when he and Kingscourt made their pact at the beginning of the book, that he would remain the older man's companion until death put an end to the partnership. In the New Society of Palestine, which draws Fried-rich both for its own and for Miriam's sake, it becomes a question whether the non-Jew Kingscourt will want to stay. The American entrepreneur in him is, of course, greatly impressed by the technical wonders and progressive spirit of the New Society, but this alone might not be sufficient to make him want to settle down in Palestine. Friedrich, a man of honor, and hence ever loyal to his vow, is dismayed at the thought that he will probably have to leave Palestine with the old man. But in the end it emerges that old Kingscourt, who never had children of his own, has developed such a deep, grand-fatherly passion for David Littwak's infant son that he cannot bring himself to leave. Friedrich is thereby enabled to remain and marry Miriam.

This elaborately conceived father-son relationship suggests certain passions and conflicts in Herzl's spirit. It is doubtful whether Kings-court, in his totality at any rate, was based upon a specific living person, as so many of the novel's characters were. But he does seem to embody a world, that resolutely liberal world of Bacher and Benedikt, in which any assertion that there is really any difference between Jew and Gentile can only be looked upon as the rantings of a rebellious and troublesome child. Most of the time he is ostensibly that liberal who has rebelled against his Prussian aristocratic origins and gone to make his own fortune in middle-class America. He is capable of occasional anti-Semitic quirks, however, in spite of him-self; it was he who first spoke of Palestine as Friedrich's "fatherland," and not because he was a Zionist! In fact, his inner views on the Jewish Question are, until near the end, clearly ambivalent, even if his external behavior is virtually irreproachable. Herzl means to show through Kingscourt's attitudes the hypocrisy of liberal Europe. It is only Kingscourt's gradual awakening to what Jews are capable of doing once they are given their own homeland that rids him of all ambivalence toward them. Here, Herzl is settling scores again. But, like Friedrich in the novel, Herzl cannot rid himself completely of this relationship, in which he continues to be the son. Kingscourt, as his very name suggests, is that whole European world of dignitaries with which Herzl always deeply yearned to identify himself, in whose corridors he was even permitted to walk, but never as more than an adopted or illegitimate child. In the novel, at least, he can win the father over to his vision. The real world continued to be a more difficult matter.

Just as the European liberal father of Herzl's spirit is represented in the novel, so also is the Eastern European Jewish son. David Littwak (based largely upon the figure of David Wolfssohn, who became Herzl's successor as president of the World Zionist Organiza-tion) is presented as a model of what Zionist regeneration can do for the Yiddish-speaking masses of Eastern Europe. Herzl derived from

the fact of these masses a fulfillment of those impulses that came close
to making a Socialist of him. He sensed that, in their poverty and
simplicity, and in their deep and sincere Jewishness, it was they who
gave dignity to the Jewish people as a whole; they were the salvation
of the spoiled Jewish bourgeoisie of Western Europe. But his attitude toward them, which was basically paternalistic in character, was
never wholly free of a certain condescension. This appears in the
novel in his depiction of a lovable but somewhat boorish Yiddish-
speaking peasantry; they are a bit like unruly children. Their best
hope for cultural self-improvement seems to lie in the fact that their
dialect can be weaned into the Hochdeutsch that David Littwak has
learned to speak. This ambivalence in Herzl's relationship with the
Eastern European Jews was never quite resolved, either in the novel
or in his life. Rather, it produced the undercurrent of tension that
gave tragic force to the last major episode of his career: the Uganda
controversy.

By the spring of 1903 Herzl, who was to have only one more year
to live, was at the end of his strength. For more than six years his life
had been a constant and exhausting pursuit of a revolutionary hope,
largely spent in the compartments of speeding railroad trains. He had
made four frustrating journeys to Constantinople in pursuit of a
charter, and had treated for a time with Kaiser Wilhelm II, who had
dangled before his eyes the prospect of a Jewish Palestine under a
German protectorate, only to pull it suddenly away. By 1902 the hope
of German patronage had begun to fade, and England was showing
the first signs of becoming the center of gravity for Zionist diplomacy.
In that year Herzl held conversations with the Colonial Secretary,
Joseph Chamberlain, and the Foreign Secretary, Lord Lansdowne, in
which the idea was first broached of a possible Jewish settlement in
El Arish, along the Mediterranean coast of the Sinai Penninsula.
Unlike Palestine, this was within the British sphere of influence, and
it had the additional virtue of being contiguous with Palestine. In
response to this proposal, a Zionist commission was sent to El Arish
to investigate its suitability for settlement. The commission discovered a serious scarcity of water there. When it was suggested that
the Jewish settlement might draw its water from the Nile, Lord
Cromer, the British High Commissioner in Egypt, vetoed the whole
plan.

The demise of the El Arish scheme occurred shortly before the outbreak of the Kishinev pogrom during Passover of 1903. The rioting of the peasantry of Kishinev in the Ukraine brought death to some forty-five Jews, injury to more than a thousand, and great loss of property. The immediate effect of this event upon Eastern European Jewry was to stimulate a resurgence of emigration on their part, mainly to America, but also to Palestine. For the young pioneers of the "Second Aliyah" to Palestine, which began the following year, the pogroms had reaffirmed their desire to live and work in the ancient land of their forefathers, irrespective of its current political situation. But for Herzl and other Western European Zionists the pogroms revived their old passion for finding a place in which suffering Jews could take immediate refuge, no matter where it was. This meant seeking a charter at all costs, and if Palestine was not available, then somewhere else would have to do.

It was on April 23, 1903, almost immediately after the Kishinev pogrom, that Joseph Chamberlain suggested to Herzl the possibility of establishing a Jewish area of settlement in Uganda, in British East Africa. Herzl was now fully amenable to the idea of a Jewish "territory" somewhere outside of Palestine. He had not, after all, originally been committed to any particular location for the Jewish state when he had first conceived the idea back in 1895. He had subsequently been converted to "Love of Zion," as he was often fond of saying, by its Eastern European adherents. But constant frustration, the sense of the imminent exhaustion of his energies, and the shock of the Kishinev pogrom had all conspired to bring his heart back to its youthful hope of a sudden and dramatic political breakthrough. He resolved to himself that, if no other prospect arose before the convening of the Sixth Zionist Congress at the end of August, he would present the Uganda offer.

By the time the Congress met, Herzl had already done something to offend the sensibilities of the Russian-Jewish delegates. Earlier that same month he had made a trip to St. Petersburg, where he had held fruitless discussions about the Jewish Question in Russia with the ministers Witte and von Plehve, two of the men most representative of tsarist anti-Semitism in the eyes of Russian Jews. The dim view that the Russian-Jewish delegates to the Zionist Congress took of this visit predisposed them to a suspicion that grew darker still when, upon entering the meeting hall, they perceived that the map of

Palestine which traditionally hung behind the speaker's platform at
every Congress had now been replaced by a map of British East
Africa. In a carefully worded address, Herzl informed the Congress of
the British offer of a territory in East Africa. At first there was widespread gratification: the first concrete gesture of recognition by a
Great Power! But among the Russian-Jewish delegates the initial
mood of joy was quickly replaced by hostility and even despair. What
would become of their hopes for Palestine, the sole raison d'être of
their enterprise, if the Zionist movement were to begin devoting its
energies to some remote African territory? In defense of the Uganda
scheme, its proponents stressed that this would only be a temporary
measure; a Jewish Palestine was still the ultimate aim of the movement, but in the meantime suffering Jews needed what Max Nordau
described as a Nachtasyl (shelter in the night)—a term that only
irritated the opponents of the idea. A resolution was framed on the
Uganda offer. In order to cushion its effects it was formulated simply
as a proposal that the Congress appoint a commission to investigate
the prospects of Uganda. But most of the Russian-Jewish delegates
saw this formulation as mere camouflage of a scheme that they were
coming to look upon as a form of treason: at the end of the first
session a young woman dashed up to the platform and tore the map
of Uganda from the wall.[11]

At the second session the vote was held on the proposed investigating commission. It won a majority: 295 were in favor, 177 opposed;
the negative votes were almost entirely cast by delegates from Russia.
When the results of the vote were announced the great majority of
the Russian-Jewish delegates strode out of the hall en masse. Some of
them were weeping openly. When Herzl, after closing the session,
went over to the small meeting hall in which the Russian-Jewish
delegates held their caucuses, he found many of them sitting on the
floor in the posture of mourning that is assumed at Tisha b'Av, the
anniversary of the destruction of the Temple at Jerusalem. He delivered a speech which "was not humble, but rather that of an
admonishing father."[12] He reassured his listeners of his devotion to
Palestine, but reiterated the need of an immediate place of refuge.
His words were received silently, without applause. When he left the
room he knew he had lost the battle. The majority his proposal had

11 Chaim Weizmann, Trial and Error (New York, 1949), p. 85.
12 Bein, op. cit., p. 461.

received was as nothing compared to the irreparable split in the movement that would have been caused by acting upon it. Weary and dejected, Herzl told a group of his friends later that night that if he did not have Palestine by the time of the Seventh Congress, two years hence, he would offer his resignation—provided he lived that long.

The Uganda proposal was, in fact, revoked at the Seventh Congress, a year after Herzl's death; the diehard "Territorialists," under the leadership of Israel Zangwill, then broke off from the Zionist movement and resolved to seek future Ugandas wherever they might turn up. It was a final victory for "Love of Zion" within the movement. For Herzl himself, however, in the last year of his life that followed the Sixth Congress, there was no longer the strength left to take solace in such patient hopes. He continued to go through the motions of his traditional method of high diplomacy: he had audiences with both the King of Italy and the Pope. But the vigor of his actions had always been founded upon the deep-lying expectation of a sudden and revolutionary achievement; this hope, which had once kindled his life, had reduced itself at last to the merest spark in the Uganda scheme, which then was stamped out. He had founded a historic movement which would in the end be successful, but his private vision was consumed. At that very moment young men and women, guided by the inspiration that the name of Theodor Herzl had imparted to them, were in fact laying the foundation of the Jewish state of his dreams. But Herzl himself, in less than ten years of self-immolating fury, had burned up every vestige of his youth by the age of forty-four. On July 3, 1904, his heart gave out; thus ended for him what he had called "my tragic enterprise."

CHAPTER 2

The Roots of Practical Zionism:

Eastern Europe

I.

THE eventual creation of a state of Israel was the outcome of a successful fusion of the "political" and the "practical" Zionist tendencies. While the political Zionist tradition that had been embodied by Herzl continued, after his death, to develop a worldwide Zionist movement with diplomatic leverage, the practical Zionists set about creating an organic national community on the soil of Palestine, the kernel of the future state. This latter group, almost entirely Eastern European in origin, had been reared in a strongly traditionalist Jewish atmosphere—unlike Herzl and other Western European Zionist leaders—and, for all its modernism of outlook, formed a direct and conscious link with the Jewish past. If Zionism arose in the West mainly in response to secular ideological currents, it arose in Eastern Europe mainly as an organic outgrowth of Jewish traditions. It was an authentically Jewish revolutionary movement, a rebellion against the exile that had been imposed upon the Jewish people nearly two thousand years earlier. But Zionism was not generated suddenly; rather, it was the outcome of a current of revolutionary upheaval in Jewry which had begun with a wave of mysticism in Medieval Spain and had reached a climax in a seventeenth-century messianic movement which left a permanent legacy of

spiritual unrest among the Jewish communities of the world, particularly that of Eastern Europe.

When, in 1666, the news spread throughout the Jewish communities of Europe, North Africa and the Middle East that a certain
Sabbatai Zevi of Izmir (Smyrna) in Turkey claimed to be the
Messiah, a restlessness was created to an extent unknown to Jewry for
more than fifteen hundred years. The last major "Messiah" in Jewish
history had been Bar Kochba (Son of the Star), who led a second
disastrous revolt against the Romans in 135 c.e., but though there had
been a number of outstanding individuals who had claimed messiahship since that time, none of them had shaken Jewry to the core.
Until the appearance of Sabbatai Zevi, the "Next year in Jerusalem"
regularly proclaimed at the annual Passover ritual represented a
prospect no more imminent than the Apocalypse of Christianity. The
Return to Zion was, for the most part, a frozen aspiration, preserved
intact but lacking animation. But the barriers behind which Judaism
had shored itself up through centuries of dispersion were in this era
beginning to crumble. The Jewish spirit was, in places, suddenly out
in the open and exposed to unprecedented influences. In fact, 1666
had originally been anticipated as a messianic year by Christian and
not by Jewish calculators.

The growing mood of crisis in Jewish history was largely provoked
by the expulsion of the Jews from Spain in 1492. For some five
hundred years the Jews of Spain had constituted the greatest Jewish
community in the world, and had been a rival in brilliance and
creativity to the Palestine community of the postbiblical epoch. During much of that time Spanish Jewry need not have been overly discontented with its lot, yet some of its greatest men, such as the poet
Judah Halevi and the philosopher Moses Maimonides, gave vent in
their lives and work to an irreconcilable longing for Zion. But widespread discontent did not arise among the Jews of Spain until the
latter part of the fourteenth century, when the Spanish Inquisition
began forcing conversion upon them under penalty of death. This
policy of crusading Spanish Catholicism, an outcome of the exhilara-
tion of reconquering the Iberian Peninsula from the Muslims, with
whom the Jews were identified, produced one of the strangest
episodes in Jewish history. Large numbers of Spanish Jews accepted
conversion under duress, but inwardly maintained their allegiance to
Judaism and continued to practice its rituals in the secrecy of their

homes. They came to be called the "marranos," a name which may
have had Hebrew or Arabic origins but which in its final form was
simply an old Spanish word meaning "swine." The word specifically
referred to the fact that these converts had to demonstrate their
sincerity by eating pork in front of their examiners, but its abusive
connotations were not minimized. Marranos continued to marry
endogamously and thereby maintained their identity for generations,
many of them converting back to Judaism once they had resettled
outside of Spain. The spiritual tension of marranism contributed
greatly to the growing apocalyptic mood of the sixteenth and seventeenth centuries; the spirit of the marrano seemed to bear the anguish
of Jewish exile with special intensity. Amsterdam, which became a
principal retreat for marranos and Spanish Jews in general after the
expulsion, was a major center of the movement aroused by the proclaimed messiahship of Sabbatai Zevi.

But other upheavals taking place within Jewry at this time were to
give added fury to the Sabbatian movement. In Spain as far back as
the thirteenth century a reaction to the philosophical doctrines of
Moses Maimonides had given rise to a spiritual movement which,
though it claimed its roots in his work, was really antithetical to his
Aristotelian rationalism, and which proved a powerful source of
creative Jewish thought in the centuries that were to follow. The
Kabbalah (a Hebrew word which means, paradoxically, "tradition")
was a mystical movement which, though it usually managed to
remain more or less within the framework of rabbinical Judaism, gave
rise to strong antinomian tendencies among its adherents. Though
Kabbalism was widely varied in its manifestations, the character of
which cannot be summed up in any single body of doctrine, its
general tendency was to counter the Talmudic approach to religious
questions, which had become largely scholastic, with ways of seeking
a more spontaneous and emotionally stirring religious experience.
The school of the thirteenth-century Spanish Kabbalist Abraham
Abulafia, for example, achieved ecstasies and mystical visions through
the contemplation of combinations of Hebrew letters taken from the
biblical text; the supreme form of this experience came through the
contemplation of the letters of the Divine Name, YHVH[1]—a degree

[1] These four Hebrew consonants (Yod, Hey, Vav, Hey) spell the name of
God, which religious Jews will not pronounce. Since the word "Adonai"
("Lord") is traditionally pronounced in its stead, the Tetragrammaton has tra-

of spiritual insight that was reached only through long and rigorous training.

This kind of religious experience was not merely a fetishism, the result of a scholastic passion for the biblical text gone wild. It was also the first latter-day outburst of a truly revolutionary impulse in Judaism, an attempt to return to sources, although it was still mainly under the sway of an established scholasticism. The school of Abulafia represented an authentic revival of the sense of the holy, for if the biblical text had truly been written by the hand of God, then every letter, every punctuation mark, must be charged with spiritual significance. Such a view represents a return to the ancient question of the *logos*, of "the word that was God"—the ancient philosophical problem of the connection between God and the Creation, between Spirit and Nature, between Thought and Act, that had concerned both Jews and Christians in the Hellenistic world, and that was, in another form, to concern the philosophers of revolution in nineteenth-century Europe. This first manifestation of the Kabbalah was another attempt to find the *logos*, to bridge the gap between Thought and Act by transforming contemplation, simply through the intensification of it, directly into experience. But among the followers of Abulafia, the revolutionary implications of this aim were still only dimly present; for the moment, their aspirations were confined exclusively to the area of personal mystical experience. They had not yet become social.

The impact of the Kabbalah grew greater with the appearance of a book written in about the third quarter of the thirteenth century. The Zohar, or "Book of Splendor," which became as central to the Kabbalah as the Talmud was to normative Judaism, is one of the greatest creative religious works to have been written since antiquity. It was apparently the work of a Spanish-Jewish man of letters named Moses de Leon, who wrote a number of books under his own name, but who chose to present the Zohar as an ancient *Midrash* (biblical commentary) composed primarily from the sayings of Rabbi Simeon ben Yohai of the second century C.E. To further the claim that it was the work of an ancient Palestinian, the author wrote the book in Aramaic, a language in which he had only limited technical com-

---

ditionally been vocalized in the Hebrew text of the Bible with the vowels of this latter word. In Western languages the result of this combination has been the word "Jehovah," an artificial construct.

petence. The import of the Zohar is quite different from that of
Abulafia's doctrine, in that it presents, rather than a technique for
achieving mystical experience, a widely ranging theosophic doctrine
that is the product of the insights derived from mystical experience.
The sometimes lengthy discourses on biblical passages that are placed
in the mouths of Rabbi Simeon and his disciples reach for meanings
of a hidden nature; as with Abulafia, the literal prose meaning of the
biblical text does not contain the most profound truth concealed
there. In a way that bears affinities with Freudianism and its out-
growths—a kind of latter-day Kabbalah—the Zohar is prone to search
out the latent meanings contained in metaphors. In the process, the
large metaphors that the book constructs to describe the nature of
the universe are made to stand as the fundamental realities of the
nature of things.

The ruling metaphor in the doctrine of the Zohar is that of the
Sefiroth, or "spheres," of God's manifestations. The universe is
composed of ten Sefiroth, all particularized manifestations of the
activity of the one Divine Spirit. These manifestations, roughly
characterized as (1) the "supreme crown" of God, (2) "wisdom,"
(3) "intelligence," (4) "love," (5) "power," (6) "compassion,"
(sometimes "beauty"), (7) "lasting endurance," (8) "majesty," (9)
"foundation," and (10) "kingdom,"[2] are all real aspects of God's
presence, and not merely abstract ideals. The structural manner in
which they are distributed through the universe is conceived alternately in accordance with two metaphors: one is that of a tree,
whereby the arrangement of the Sefiroth is in accordance with that of
the trunk, roots and branches; the other is the image of a human
being. This latter image leads to the comprehension of the various
Sefiroth in terms of the functions of the various parts of the human
body. The Sefirah of "foundation," for example, which corresponds
to the sexual organs, is imbued with all the powers and ramifications
of fertility that the mystical imagination can bestow.

Such a conception of the world lends a glow to the entire Creation
that is not easily rivaled by traditional theism. Indeed, the greatest
spiritual difficulty encountered by the author of the Zohar was the
tendency toward pantheism in his thinking, an outcome which must

---

[2] Gershom G. Scholem, *Major Trends in Jewish Mysticism* (New York,
1954), p. 213. Most of the discussion of Kabbalah above is derived from Professor Scholem's scholarly masterpiece.

be avoided by anyone who maintains any sort of traditional religious loyalty, since it tends to obliterate all distinctions between the universe and its Creator. For de Leon, the problem worked itself out in a dialectical conception of things that placed great significance in the distinction between two manifestations of God: the *Ein Sof*, or the "Infinite," and the *Shekhinah*, or the Divine Presence. The Ein Sof is the aloof and incalculable Divine Power that resides beyond the universe. The Shekhinah is the presence of God's spirit in the imperfect realm of nature, roughly corresponding to the Holy Ghost of Christian tradition. In the Kabbalah, the Shekhinah is usually conceived of as feminine, and the relationship between God and the Divine Presence is understood in broadly sexual terms: for example, in accordance with the traditional Jewish idea that a man and a woman are each an incomplete being until their union in marriage, so also is God, the Ein Sof, seen as having completed Himself in union with the Shekhinah. In another formulation, God as Ein Sof, the imponderable Divine Power, is understood only objectively and remotely, as "He," whereas God in the unfolding of His manifestations in the universe, the God that can be perceived by the heart, is understood as "You"; but even this is not the end of the process. For the supreme manifestation of God comes when He realizes Himself as "I," when His own self-consciousness becomes completely identified with the universe; it is this Divine Self, this "I," that is the Shekhinah—a conception which goes beyond the one of the Shekhinah, as a separate, feminine presence, and turns to an almost pure pantheism. The clear resemblance here to ideas later developed by Spinoza and by Hegel was to make the confluence between the Jewish tradition and the works of these philosophers a significant one.

The principal limitation of the doctrine of the Shekhinah is that it still leaves unresolved the question of the link between Spirit and Nature, the point at which the Divine Will becomes concrete. To pursue the Kabbalist metaphor of the marriage between God and the Shekhinah, the union calls for issue, just as the Son completes the relationship between the Father and the Holy Ghost in the Christian Trinity. There are the Sefiroth, to be sure; these are the forms under which the Shekhinah manifests itself. But they do not themselves constitute the catalysts, the very points at which Spirit becomes Nature, or Thought becomes Act. The problem of this connection is the perennial one that is contained archetypically in the problem of the Creation. It is to this problem and its ramifications that Isaac Luria, the major Kabbalistic thinker in the epoch that followed the Zohar, addressed himself. Luria represents a more apocalyptic mood than that of his Kabbalistic predecessors; his thoughts bear intimations of universal, and not merely personal, revolution. Living as he did in the sixteenth century, he spoke for an era more concerned than men had been for centuries about the connection between divine ideals and earthly acts.

For Luria, the very Creation of the universe was the act which first gave rise to exile, to *galut* or alienation. The original act of Creation was a *Tsimtsum* (literally a "contracting," but one can also read into it the connotation of "retreat"), wherein God suddenly contracted or retreated into a point, leaving behind some portion or precipitate of Himself, which was the universe. The universe is thus an alienation of God; it is in exile from Him, and man is left with the task of reclaiming this relationship, to whatever extent he can. Now, this task of reclamation is made possible by the fact that the exile is not complete; the world is still suffused with sparks of God's radiance, with fragments of the Divine Presence, or the Shekhinah. The situation in which the Shekhinah finds itself in the universe is depicted in the Lurianic doctrine of the Breaking of the Vessels. When God's radiance poured forth into the world in the instant of Creation, the Vessels which received it—these were the Vessels of the Sefiroth— were incapable of retaining such glory and they smashed to pieces under the strain. As a result, the radiance spilled and scattered itself among the material fragments of the universe, among the *Kelipoth*, or "husks," as the Kabbalah calls the substance of Nature. The sparks of the Divine Presence, of the radiance which spilled and scattered itself among the husks, are therefore to be found everywhere, and it is the perennial task of true men of God to turn them up, to recover them. Every holy act, great or small, that turns up a divine spark is a step toward the reclamation of the world from its exile, toward *Tikkun* ("repair"), or ultimate redemption.

This conception of the relationship between God and the universe in general is also a way of accounting for the history of the people of Israel. Why has Israel been exiled and scattered among the nations? Because it is her task to reclaim the holy sparks from the four corners of the earth. Israel herself can even be conceived of as the sparks, as the Shekhinah, waiting to be gathered up and reclaimed in the time of redemption. But, if the final and universal act of Tikkun can be performed only by the Messiah, at least every son of Israel can further the process until that time by individual acts of reclamation. This conception makes the individual Jew himself into the *logos*, as it were; his own existence is the meeting point between Thought and Act. For, if through piety—if through nothing more concrete than fervent prayer—he can reclaim a divine spark and thus bring mankind one step closer to redemption, then his very thoughts are a form of action. This possibility is at the center of the Kabbalistic principle of *Kavanah*, which was later to be of prime importance to the Hasidic tradition. Kavanah means "intention," but etymologically it implies the more concrete notion of "direction." The very conception of the word suggests a thought that is also an act (indeed, this fusion of properties is a general trait of the Hebrew language). Every human act—praying, reading, eating, and so on—is capable, if accompanied by a fervent and pious Kavanah, of recovering a divine spark. This is a doctrine, in other words, which attributes enormous powers to the pious will. It also is a doctrine which gives a divine force to the routines of everyday life.

In a later era the power in certain elements of the Kabbalah to give new vitality to everyday life was to assume central importance in the traditionalist Jewish communities, but in an age caught up by an apocalyptic mood, such as the sixteenth and seventeenth centuries were, the sanctification of homely everyday acts was not enough. In all eras there was of course the expectation that a time would come when men would see the final reclamation of the sparks in their own lifetimes. Tradition tells of a certain rabbi who kept his boots and walking stick by his bed, ready to pick them up immediately any time he was aroused and beckoned to follow the Messiah back to the Promised Land. But this was the kind of gesture of expectation that had become frozen into unyielding tradition. Only in certain epochs did the routines of conventionalized hopes become quickened with real anticipation. The Jews of the seventeenth century were ripe for such a quickening, and the appearance of Sabbatai Zevi caused it to occur.

Sabbatai Zevi was born in Izmir in July, 1626—on Tisha b'Av, according to the Jewish calendar, the day on which, tradition has

established, the destruction of both the First and Second Temples of
Jerusalem took place, and which is commemorated with a solemn
fast. Sabbatai was, in his childhood, of a solemn and introspective
nature, given to extreme religious piety. While he was still a child, his
father, Mordechai Zevi, a poor poulterer of Spanish-Jewish or Sephardic extraction, suddenly grew wealthy through commerce. This
dramatic transformation of status during his boyhood seems to have
had a strong effect upon Sabbatai's growing sense of personal destiny.
In the customary way, he was married before he was twenty to a girl
who had been chosen for him; but the marriage was not consummated, and his wife sought and was granted a divorce. A second wife
was chosen for Sabbatai and, again, this marriage was not consummated and ended in divorce. To his friends he explained that the
Ruach ha'Kodesh—the Holy Spirit—had told him that these were
not the brides destined for him by Divine Will.

Some of Sabbatai's friends paid the utmost attention to every word
he said, for his extreme piety, his intensity of manner and speech,
and his considerable personal magnetism had convinced them that he
was destined to perform a great mission. They were not disappointed.
In 1648 the twenty-two-year-old Sabbatai Zevi sought to present
himself as the Messiah. The moment was well chosen: for a long
time Jewish messianic speculators had been singling out the year 1648
with remarkable persistence. Furthermore, the news had already
spread to Izmir of the terrible massacres of the Jews of Poland which
took place earlier that year at the hands of the Cossack revolt led by
Bogdan Khmielnitzki. It was understood that the Messiah was to
make his appearance only after a great disaster; this knowledge
needed only the actual experience of fearful suffering to predispose
the spirit to such an eventuality.

One Sabbath morning in that year Sabbatai Zevi strode to the
front of the congregation in the synagogue of Izmir and audibly
pronounced the Holy Name, YHVH. At the moment of final
redemption, according to tradition, the apocalyptic change is to occur
in blasphemy. Sabbatai chose this symbolic act, rather than any
explicit announcement, to signal his advent as the Messiah. If the
time indeed had come, the world would recognize him even through
this indirect identification. But apparently the time had not come; a
few days later the rabbinical court of Izmir placed a ban upon
Sabbatai. The ban was a weapon that was being used with unprece-

dented frequency in Jewry at this time; the Amsterdam rabbinate pronounced a similar ban against Spinoza just eight years later. Roughly equivalent to excommunication, the ban deprived one of the protection of the organized Jewish community. Since the individual Jew had no legal status outside the Jewish community, a ban against him meant that he was henceforth entirely without the protection of law. His only recourse was to convert to Christianity or move on to another Jewish community, in which he was not known.

Sabbatai went to Salonika, but here, too, he ran into trouble because he was unable to contain his messianic aspirations. One Sabbath he walked before the congregation, seized the Torah scrolls, held them to his body, and called upon those present to celebrate his marriage to the Torah: another messianic blasphemy. Again he was banned, and again he moved on. In fact, he continued to wander throughout the Jewish communities of the Near East for more than a decade, performing acts of similar import all the while. By 1662, when he settled in Jerusalem, he had begun to acquire a following which included some young men of considerable talent and dedication. Chief among these was one Nathan of Gaza, a very young man (born in 1644) who was still only a rabbinical student in Jerusalem when Sabbatai first encountered him while passing through there. Nathan, who was a much deeper man than Sabbatai, was an authentic Lurianic Kabbalist. Once he had become convinced that Sabbatai was indeed the Messiah, he proceeded to weave a doctrine around him. It was Sabbatai who was to usher in the era of Tikkun, to reclaim all the divine sparks still scattered among the husks of the universe. Nathan turned up documents written by earlier generations of mystics, predicting the coming of the Messiah, and he demonstrated through close analysis that these writings referred to none other than Sabbatai Zevi. Nathan also calculated that the messianic year was to be 1666, a year that had hitherto been claimed only by Christians as one of apocalyptic import. Meanwhile, the incipient Messiah further prepared himself for the coming dawn by taking a bride, one who was more appropriate to take part in a divine mission than her predecessors had been.

Sarah was a Polish Jewess of obscure origins who had lost both her parents in the Khmielnitzki massacres when she was about six years old. She was subsequently raised in a convent. Upon reaching young womanhood she was visited, according to her account, by her father in a vision, who told her that she must return to her people. She escaped from the convent, and was found by a group of Jews in a cemetery. To the women who gave her shelter she showed the fingernail marks on her body caused by her father's imploring grip. Eventually she settled somewhere in Western Europe, probably in Amsterdam, in the home of a man who was apparently her brother. Around this time she seems to have become convinced that the Messiah was about to come and that she was to be his bride. Seeking her destiny, she wandered through Holland, Germany, Switzerland and Italy, leading a promiscuous life. For Sarah, as for Sabbatai and numerous others throughout history, the grip of messianic expectation led to the conviction that she was exempted from the restrictions of conventional morality. In fact, it was often held that redemption could come only out of the depths of sin: every spark must be reclaimed, no matter how deeply buried in the husks of nature. It was in the midst of this pursuit of the sublime, in Leghorn, that Sarah encountered one of Sabbatai's followers, who wrote to Sabbatai in Jerusalem of her and her claims. Sabbatai promptly wrote back declaring Sarah to be his predestined bride. A splendid delegation, financed by a rich Cairo merchant who had become one of Sabbatai's followers, was sent to Italy to fetch her. The wedding took place in Cairo. Once again, the marriage apparently was never consummated. Sarah, for her part, continued in her old promiscuous habits. Sabbatai compared his marriage to that of the prophet Hosea, who had also taken a harlot for his wife.

Events then proceeded rapidly to the anticipated dramatic moment. In the course of the following year, Sabbatianism grew from an obscure Near Eastern sect into a movement that shook world Jewry, largely through the work of Nathan of Gaza and other skilled publicists among its adherents. In the summer of 1665 Nathan sent out a letter to all the Jewish communities of the Diaspora, proclaiming a vision which heralded the appearance of Sabbatai Zevi as the Messiah. Meanwhile, in Jerusalem, Sabbatai began to manifest his calling in a more open way. He regularly distributed large sums of money (the donations of rich supporters) among his followers and called upon them to defy the prescripts of Jewish Law, as he had already begun to do. Tisha b'Av was defiantly proclaimed a day of rejoicing, because it was the Messiah's birthday. There was an electrified response throughout the Diaspora. Jewish merchants let their affairs lapse, since the time of redemption was at hand. Men made careful preparations for their imminent journey to the Promised Land. Ecstasies and other mystical experiences became rife, and were publicized and contemplated with unusually careful attention. In London wealthy Jews made bets that Sabbatai would be proclaimed the King of Jerusalem within two years.

This latter task of proclamation was presumably to be performed by the Sultan, who was, in fact, at that moment looking with increasing dismay upon the apotheosis of one of his subjects. Whatever was to happen, as Sabbatai well knew, a confrontation had first to take place between himself and the man who was still very much his temporal suzerain. Sabbatai decided to seize upon his destiny, and on December 30, 1665, he set sail for Constantinople. When he landed he was met at the port by a delegation sent to arrest him. The Pasha in charge of the group greeted his prisoner by slapping him in the face; Sabbatai promptly turned his face and presented the other cheek.

Sabbatai was taken to the fortress of Abydos, at Gallipoli, which gradually became a place of pilgrimage during the months he was imprisoned there. His followers, many of whom trekked from distant parts of the world to see him there, called the place *Migdal Oz* (Citadel of Strength). The Turkish officer in charge found he was able to make a handsome income by charging admission. Among the delegations which came to see Sabbatai was one from Poland, which told him of a Polish Jew named Nehemia Cohen who was prophesying the imminent advent of the Messiah. Sabbatai expressed his desire to see Cohen, and when the latter received word of this he promptly undertook the journey to Gallipoli, although he was no longer a young man. Upon his arrival, a disputation began between this mystic and the self-proclaimed Messiah that is said to have lasted three days. At the end of this time Cohen rose and declared Sabbatai to be a false Messiah. Then a strange thing happened. He rushed out of the castle and, before the eyes of the onlookers, pulled his fur cap—the symbol of his Jewish orthodoxy—off his head and flung it to the ground. He then strode up to one of the Turkish guards, seized the turban off the latter's head and placed it on his own. Nehemia Cohen had converted to Islam. From then on he served the Turks by denouncing the false Messiah, Sabbatai Zevi.

In September, 1666, Sabbatai's messianic moment came. He was

transferred to Adrianople, where the Sultan was residing, and he
prepared himself for the confrontation. The Sultan, fully aware of
the dangers of making Sabbatai into a martyr, decided he would offer
the latter the opportunity to convert to Islam as an alternative to
death. The day arrived. Sabbatai was ushered into the Sultan's
quarters, and seeing the turban that was placed before him, did not
even wait to be urged; he threw off his cap and placed the turban
upon his head. He, too, was now a Muslim. He took the name
Mehmed Effendi, and was made chamberlain of the Sultan's seraglio.
Sarah, too, was converted; she took the name Fatima Radini, and
continued to be Sabbatai's wife, although she now had to share the
honor with a Muslim bride provided him by the Turks.

The news of Sabbatai's conversion shocked his followers throughout the world. For some it was an awakening from the dream with
which they had been living for the better part of a year; but for
others, this new development also took on a messianic import. The
Messiah must be *born* a son of Israel, to be sure, but what difference
does it make what religion he pretends to take on in the End of
Days, when all religions, when all men, will be the same? The
messianic era is not to be judged by the standards of normal times.
To suffer, to degrade himself, to plunge with abandon into the husks
of the universe—these are precisely the things that the Messiah must
do in order to bring about universal redemption. Isn't this new
degradation, then, simply part of the process?

Some of Sabbatai's followers waited for further developments,
their expectation unflagging. Others began converting in masses to
Islam. Nehemia Cohen, the Muslim-Jewish prophet from Poland,
now became an ardent Sabbatian. Sabbatai himself continued to
preach from time to time; he was allowed to do so by the Turkish
authorities, since what he preached was conversion to Islam. But in
time the Turks decided that his preaching was perhaps dangerous
after all, and he was placed in custody. He died a prisoner in 1675.
Even at the dreary moment of his death, Sabbatians the world over
awaited his resurrection. Nathan of Gaza, who had written at the
time of Sabbatai's conversion that men were simply being confronted
once again with the incomprehensible, never lost his Sabbatian faith.
He did not convert to Islam, and as a Jew he was constantly imposed
upon by rabbinical authorities to sign recantations of his beliefs. He
signed them, but also paid no attention to these promises. Recanta-

tions, too, were a small matter when one was awaiting the apocalypse. But the apocalypse had already come and gone. After years of wandering, Nathan died in Sophia in 1680, at the age of thirty-four. The Dönmäh, the Turkish Islamic sect made up of the descendants of Sabbatian converts, are in existence to this day.

II

It was among the Jews of Poland that Sabbatianism left its most powerful legacy of messianic expectation and mystical fervor. The ancestors of this community had arrived in Poland in the wake of the persecutions that had accompanied the Crusades and then the Black Plague in Central and Western Europe, and had been welcomed by the early Polish kings, who sought thus to introduce commerce into their realm. In its early days, then, Polish Jewry enjoyed an era of prosperity and cultural ascendancy. With the dispersion of Spanish Jewry and the benighting of the German Jewish communities during the period of religious warfare in the sixteenth and early seventeenth centuries Polish Jewry became the spiritual center of the Diaspora. Polish rabbinism set the standard of Jewish learning and piety throughout the world, and Polish-Jewish teachers were eagerly sought for Talmudical academies in other parts of Europe.

But all this came to an end in the middle of the seventeenth century. The terrible atrocities committed in 1648 by the hordes of Bogdan Khmielnitzki, the Cossack leader who made the Jews bear the brunt of his revolt against the Polish lords, since these latter had used Jews to perform the hateful task of rent collecting, left the once proud Jewry of Poland in utter disarray. This event marked the beginning point in the growth of a widening gulf between Eastern European and Western European Jewry, which was in force for more than two hundred years and had only begun to diminish at the time when the bulk of Eastern European Jewry has wiped out by the nazi exterminations. In the century that followed the Khmielnitzki pogroms, Eastern European Jewry—most of which came to fall within the political domain of the Russian tsars in this period, as the Polish state disappeared from the map—gradually regained stature as a center of piety and traditionalist education, but it was no longer at the forefront of Jewish thought and cultural advancement. This latter role was taken on by the Western European Jewish communities, whose susceptibility to Western culture, however, became so great as to threaten their Jewish identity. In this sense, at least, the persisting medieval atmosphere among the Jewish communities of Eastern Europe became a source of strength. When the fervor of Westernization finally reached them, they were able to synthesize it with a more stable core of traditional Jewish values.

It was in the East that the Jewish mystical and messianic traditions continued to have strength. Amsterdam had been a main center of Sabbatianism, but in the end it was the spirit of that city's own native heretic, Spinoza, that won the day there—at least the Spinoza of Western rationalism, filtered through the eyes of Moses Mendelssohn. In Eastern Europe, Spinoza's pantheistic vision came to be endowed with the animism of the Kabbalah, and the philosopher of Amsterdam was turned into one of the greatest sages of Jewish mysticism. It was the combined impact of the Khmielnitzki massacres and the appearance of Sabbatai Zevi that had produced this mystic ardor among Eastern European Jewry, particularly in its southern reaches, in the forests of Galicia and Podolia, far from the relatively prosperous centers in the north where the more conventional rabbinical learning held sway. The impoverished and poorly educated Jews of the south had no patience with the Talmudic subtleties of the Vilna academies and were much more inclined to favor manifestations of simple pietistic fervor. As with the uneducated Christian peasantries, this mood often lent itself to superstition and to the pursuit of Jewish equivalents of the Black Mass. The outstanding manifestation of this sort was the Frankist movement of the eighteenth century.

Jacob Frank, or Leibowitz, was born in a small town in Podolia (today part of Roumania) in about 1726. His father had strong mystical tendencies and was apparently a Sabbatian, at least for a time. The family settled in Wallachia, where Jacob grew up and worked for his father, who was a merchant. Jacob's commercial travels brought him frequently to Turkey, which is where he received the nickname "Frank," the standard term for Europeans in the Levant. It was also in Turkey that he made contact with the main surviving rump of the Sabbatian movement and became a liaison between them and the small Sabbatian groups that still existed in Podolia. In time he had gathered around himself a small following which considered him to be the Messiah and, in fact, a reincarnation of Sabbatai Zevi. The chiliastic mood of this growing new movement led the members to new conceptions of moral freedom, and their rituals came to include manifestations of untrammeled sexual license. They developed a concept of a Holy Trinity, consisting of God, the Messiah and the Shekhinah. The Messiah was Sabbatai Zevi, now reincarnated as Jacob Frank. This quasi-Christian theology, combined with their increasing friction with the rabbinate, led the Frankists to submit to conversion to Catholicism at the hands of the Polish authorities in 1759. They henceforth dedicated themselves to giving support to the myth that the Talmud enjoined Jews to make use of Christian blood for their rituals. But the Polish government never felt quite at ease with Frank's messianic pretensions, and he was imprisoned. His thirteen years at the fortress of Czestochowa, which his followers dubbed "The Gates of Rome," was a prolonged version of the memory of Sabbatai Zevi at Abydos. When he was released by the Russian authorities, who took over that part of Poland in the First Partition, he settled in Austria. There he served for a time as a Christian missionary among the Jews, and then moved on to the Rhineland, where he lived a somewhat regal life, surrounded by an adoring entourage, until his death in 1791. The Frankish sect continued to exist for a time, but it was eventually absorbed completely into the Polish Catholic population.

Even after this final demise of latter-day messianism, mystical and antinomian tendencies continued to prevail among the southern reaches of Russo-Polish Jewry. The energies of apocalypse now had died, but the spontaneous mystical fervor that was the legacy of the Kabbalah and Sabbatianism had not. In the same century that produced the perverse seizure of Frankism, and indeed in the same geographical locale, there arose the richest and most consequential religious revival in the history of Judaism after the age of the Talmud: Hasidism. This movement not only transformed Jewish religious life but eventually served as the principal folk source underlying the two great secularist religions of the Russian-Jewish intelligentsia in the late nineteenth century: Socialism and Zionism. Hasidism was in some ways the Jewish counterpart of the pietistic revival movements that arose throughout Europe in the eighteenth century. Like Methodism, it was a reclamation of the prevailing religious culture by the less privileged masses, and hence a step toward a fuller democratization of that culture. But its specifically

Jewish role was as a break through the spiritual wall that Judaism had erected and maintained around itself for centuries in order to guard its identity, a wall that had first been cracked by the eruption of Sabbatianism. The Kabbalah, which had reached out for a spontaneous apprehension of an inner vision of Nature, but never with nature itself, provided a doctrinal framework within which Hasidism could retain its hold upon Jewish traditions even as it reached outside of them. For the Hasid, the merest sniff of a flower yielded intimations of the soul of Israel.

The mood of direct and fresh apprehension of nature was imparted to Hasidism above all by its founder, Israel ben Eliezer, called the *Baal Shem Tov* (Master of the Good Name—also called "Besht," from the Hebrew initials of this title). Israel ben Eliezer was born in about 1700 to poor parents living in the region where Podolia meets Wallachia, a point that today roughly corresponds to the border between Russia and Roumania. He lost his parents in childhood, but the charitable aid of the community enabled him to begin a traditional Jewish education, for which he soon proved to be utterly unfit. Unable to keep his eyes on his books, he would wander from the study hall out into the woods, where he would become lost in the contemplation of nature. Here, according to Hasidic tradition, Israel was finding truths that could not be found in books; but he was not behaving in the accepted manner of Jewish boys who were to attain any stature in the world. Nature was buried in the sacred texts, but the degree of direct apprehension of it exercised by Eastern European Jews at this time is indicated by the fact that the Yiddish language was almost totally lacking in—and is today still largely lacking in—any but the most broadly generic words for individual objects in nature. A flower can be distinguished from a tree, but not so readily a lilac from a forsythia—not in words. But words, after all, deaden the mystery that objects can otherwise contain; it must have been precisely this crust of verbal insufficiency that gave an aura of wonder to Israel ben Eliezer's perceptions. His discovery of nature for himself was, within the realm of such a morally fervid imagination, like performing anew the original act of Creation. Besht was one of the greatest of autodidacts in a tradition that is as much characterized by great self-taught men as it is by the persistence of a scholasticism of spirit in its approaches to all forms of learning. It is out of the tension of these opposing tendencies that the great spiritual discoveries of Judaism always spring.

By the time he was twelve Israel ben Eliezer had been expelled from school, and, after working for a short time as a helper to the teacher there, he finally obtained the post of beadle to the local synagogue. By the age of twenty he had settled in the town of Brody, in Galicia, and there married the sister of a prominent local rabbi. His chagrined brother-in-law tried to interest him in devoting himself to the study of Talmud, in keeping with the dignity of the family he had just married into. But Israel did not awaken to such interests, and his brother-in-law finally persuaded him to leave town. Israel and his wife moved to a tiny village where he eked out his living by digging clay in the mountains. His persistence in choosing the most humble occupations seems to have come not by default but out of some kind of a sense of calling. He seems to have been determined, although perhaps not consciously, to make the sparks of his soul rise up from the humblest human experiences. On his clay-digging expeditions he would pray and fast and lose himself in solitary contemplation. During these years he studied Kabbalah.

In time, Israel's spiritual fervor brought him into a new calling. In those days faith healers used to wander about through Polish Jewry, particularly in the south; these men were able to cure or at least bring solace to the ill through their intuitive powers and, above all, through the spiritual force of their presence, which seemed to radiate an aura of holiness. Their incantations usually involved the utterance of the Divine Name in certain contexts, and hence such a healer was called a *Baal Shem*, or Master of the Name. According to tradition, Israel received his calling to become a Baal Shem in a vision that came to him from heaven when he was thirty-six years old—a number which, in the Jewish tradition, suggests righteousness and humility. Starting simply as another Baal Shem among many, Israel soon became unique among them, the first and only one to be designated Baal Shem *Tov*, Master of the Good Name. In time he stopped healing and became simply a religious teacher, one of the greatest in the history of Judaism. Men came from great distances to hear his sayings, to watch even the smallest of his everyday acts, all of which were seen to be charged with an ineffable holiness.

For the Baal Shem Tov, and for the great generations of Hasidim who came after him, the Kabbalah provided an important doctrinal base for their ideas, but they generally tried to eschew extended intellectual constructs. They were at their best in the wisdom of spontaneous instances, in letting the sparks of the soul arise from immediate contact with life. Many of the first great Tsaddikim, or "saints"—the men who formed the religious leadership of Hasidism in the generations following the Baal Shem Tov—did not even write their wisdom down, and the sole repository of their sayings was in the oral tradition that gathered around the figures of these men and was maintained by their disciples. This oral tradition was anecdotal in character, telling stories of particular life situations in which the Tsaddikim found themselves, each one ending, as a rule, with a wise saying made by the Tsaddik appropriate to the moment described. With considerable consistency, the ideal that resides at the center of most of these stories is the doctrine of Kavanah, of "intention." For if even the simplest act is accompanied by a genuinely pious Kavanah, then its ramifications will be felt by God. In this way even the humblest and least educated man, if he is truly pious, can hasten the coming of redemption.

In the whole history of the Diaspora, those who were able to spend some part of their lives walking on the soil of Palestine were always considered to be especially blessed; it was therefore natural that a movement which stressed the holiness of spontaneous experience, especially in direct contact with nature, should give special attention to Eretz Yisroel. Some Tsaddikim made voyages to Palestine, but it was Rabbi Menahem Mendel of Vitebsk who actually transferred a part of the Hasidic movement to Palestine, by going there in 1777 with three hundred of his disciples. He first settled near Safed, the Galilean mountaintop city which had been the home of Isaac Luria and continued to be a center of Kabbalism. Then he settled in Tiberias, a city which, like Safed, was one of the four holy Jewish cities of the Middle Ages (along with Jerusalem and Hebron), but which, unlike the latter, was directly descended from the Jewish commonwealth of antiquity. Thus Menahem Mendel linked the revived Jewish life of the Diaspora with the ancient national past. He saw his mission as being not only one of regenerating himself through contact with the Land but as regenerating the Land by infusing it with the spirituality of his movement. Such a conception parallels that of the Zionist pioneers a little over a century later.

In time Tsaddikism declined. The first generation of Tsaddikim were men who had gathered around the Baal Shem Tov as young disciples, and who themselves went on, after his death in 1760, to become the leaders of Hasidic entourages in various towns of Eastern Europe. The greatest young men among these entourages formed another generation of Tsaddikim, and so on. In these early generations the crown of Tsaddik was inherited not by a man who had some blood claim but by one who demonstrated that his transcendent spiritual qualities entitled him to this designation, no matter what his origin. After a while, however, the title of Tsaddik did become one that was inherited by birth, and the Hasidic sects of today are ruled by enclosed princely dynasties. But this direct line of Tsaddikim has lost the force that once made it great. The progression—or diminution—of Tsaddikism through the generations is described in a classic Hasidic story. It is said that the Baal Shem Tov, when he had some task of great difficulty to perform, would go to a certain spot in the woods, light a fire and say a prayer; the task would then be performed. In the next generation, Rabbi Dov Baer, the great *Maggid* (Teacher) of Mezritch could no longer light the fire as the Besht had done, but he could perform a task by going to the same spot in the woods and reciting the same prayer. In the next generation the prayer, too, was forgotten, but Rabbi Moshe Leib of Sassov at least knew the spot in the woods, and that was sufficient to enable him to perform his task. But for Rabbi Israel of Rishin, in the next generation, not even the spot in the woods was any longer known. All he could do was tell the story of how it was done—yet that, too, was sufficient to perform his task.

This story is at once a demonstration of and an accounting for one of the major legacies of Hasidism to future generations: its treasury of great tales—not to mention a certain unique spirit of storytelling, which reappeared with great vigor in the Yiddish literary revival of the late nineteenth century. The mainstream of the Hasidic *spirit*, in other words, continued on into the latter part of the nineteenth century in a defrocked form, manifesting itself in the heresies of socialism, Zionism, and the writing of literary works which, though secular, were nevertheless utterly Jewish. Tsaddikism, too, had been a heresy in its day, condemned by the scholastic rabbis of the north. It is ironic that the Hasidic sects of today, the descendants in name and external characteristics of those pious revivalists, have become the chief bulwarks of Jewish clerical conservatism, condemning heresy with the same fury that the rabbinical establishment had used against their ancestors two hundred years before. We must now begin to look elsewhere for the sparks that those earliest generations had given rise to.

In the years following the upheaval caused throughout the entire European continent by the French Revolution and the Napoleonic Wars, there came into being the first scattered elements of a secular-minded Russian-Jewish intelligentsia. This newly developing class, the first growing opposition to the long reign of religious obscurantism over Russian Jewry, was partly the creation of the tsarist regime. Under the reign of Nicholas I (1825–1855), the Russian government had evolved a long-range policy of assimilating the Jews of the empire culturally and religiously into the surrounding Christian population. Various methods were tried, from persecution to cajolery, but by 1847 this policy had translated itself into an attempt on the part of the Russian government to gain control of the entire Jewish educational system, down to the smallest village cheder. This never came near to complete success, but the government did in time succeed in creating a small Jewish secular university intelligentsia. But very few of these latter were the good, docile Russians the government had hoped for; most of them succeeded in reconstituting their own heritage either into some kind of secularized formulation of Jewish cultural identity or into the burgeoning revolutionary ideology of the day.

The first current of a secularized Jewish culture in Eastern Europe was an offspring of the German-Jewish Enlightenment that had been inspired by Moses Mendelssohn. As with Mendelssohn, the aim of the Eastern European practitioners of Enlightenment was to teach secular learning to the Jewish masses, and to do so in a language that these teachers could consider more worthy of elevated discourse than the "Judaeo-German" that was spoken in various forms and dialects by traditional Jewish communities from the Rhine to the Dnieper. This desire to find an elevated language was partly the legacy of the eighteenth-century cultural classicism that had produced the Enlightenment, and partly the reflection of a certain intellectual Brahminism which comes from the rabbinical tradition and frequently pervades Jewish learned discourse. For Mendelssohn, this ideal had naturally brought him to German, the language to which the Jewish dialect was most closely related, and which, in Mendelssohn's day, was busy proving its claim to stand alongside French at the pinnacle of European culture. Indeed, the sense of loftiness in their discourses harbored by the German intelligentsia of the nineteenth century and infused into their prose could hardly be rivaled by the French or anyone else. Mendelssohn had also, incidentally, chosen the language of the country in which he lived, but it is doubtful that he considered the claims of German as a language for Jewish cultural expression to be limited by mere political boundaries. This was the era in which the conception of Central Europe—*Mitteleuropa*—as a distinct cultural entity was coming into being, and many Jews were beginning to feel a natural cultural identification with it.

On the other hand, the masses of Jews who lived deep within the "Pale of Settlement" of the Russian Empire, a contiguous geographical and cultural entity that constituted a virtual Jewish national community, were more robust in their cultural self-identification than were those Jews who lived within the Central European sphere of influence. Here, the Judaeo-German dialect was Yiddish, a genuine language, albeit raw and undeveloped. Yiddish was to find its own high literary expression in the latter half of the nineteenth century, but this discovery was to come out of a reaction against Brahminism and classicism more characteristic of that later era (one must allow for a cultural gap in Eastern European Jewry: romanticism, *mutatis mutandis*, did not arrive there for about two generations after its appearance in Western Europe). But in the more eighteenth-century mood of "Enlightenment," when it first struck the Jews of Eastern Europe, the natural product of their combined desire to find a language as elevated as Mendelssohn's German, and yet more Jewish at the same time, was to turn to Hebrew.

There was nothing new about using Hebrew as a language of learned writing; like Latin in the Western Christian tradition, it had served this purpose in unbroken continuity since ancient times. But its use had been almost exclusively religious. The task of the Hebrew Enlightenment, or *Haskalah*, was to adapt this ancient language to largely and even exclusively secular purposes. This was a task of linguistic regeneration that corresponded in many ways to the spiritual one that had been going on for some two hundred years. It is perhaps significant that one of the first practitioners of a modern

Hebrew belles-lettres, Moses Chaim Luzatto (1707–1747) of Padua, was a Kabbalist who thought of himself as the Messiah. Along with his philosophical treatises and religious lyrics, he wrote dramas, but he certainly did not see these latter as a separate realm of activity. All his writings served the same mystical vision on his part. His successors in the gradual secularization of Hebrew, the first Haskalah writers at the beginning of the nineteenth century, were far from being mystics properly so called, but there is often a strong element of mysticism to be found within the ardent rationalist, especially in the Jewish tradition. The first glimmers of Haskalah came not from the Lithuanian strongholds of systematic intelligence (which were still also bastions of rabbinical conservatism) but from the murky recesses of Hasidic Galicia. Its tradition of spiritual upheaval was not the only trait that made Galicia a particularly appropriate breeding ground for Haskalah. Since the Polish partitions of the late eighteenth century, Galicia had been part of the Austrian Empire, and was now turning into the principal crossroads between Germanism and the Jewish culture of Eastern Europe. In later generations it was Galician Jews who both gave a more pronounced cultural vitality to the Jewish life of Vienna and imparted a somewhat German cast to the intellectual life of Eastern European Jewry. The passion for loftiness that is characteristic of the Galician Jewish intellectual made his region into the main stronghold of Hebraism throughout the nineteenth century. The Hebrew prose of a writer of Galician origin usually has a certain German syntactical flavor, even to this day.

When Haskalah moved on from Galicia to the heartlands of Russian Jewry itself in the 1840's and 1850's, it took on a popularizing bent to which the Galician *maskilim* (practitioners of Enlightenment) would not have yielded. Novels and popular scientific treatises began to appear. Eventually, the outcome of this popularizing impulse was even a reaction against the use of Hebrew to serve its purposes. The fact was that the great majority of Russian Jews knew scarcely more than enough Hebrew to be able to read their prayers, if that much (women usually knew no Hebrew at all), and even then the prayers were not necessarily understood. Yiddish, rather, was the language that they knew how to read, just as it was the *spoken* language of all Russian Jews, including the most learned maskil. If, then, a genuine popular literature was coming into being, what other language could it choose but Yiddish? But Yiddishism was not merely the product of a desire to reach a large audience. As the spirit

of romanticism and literary realism made its way into Eastern
European Jewish intellectual circles, and writers sought to describe
not the distant exotic settings of the early Haskalah novelists but the
ordinary life around them, it no longer made sense to translate the
terms of that life into Hebrew. For the writer with an ear genuinely
attuned to the lyricism of human speech, a folk poetry was being
spoken all around him—in Yiddish.

Yiddishism came into its own in the 1860's, a decade which began
with the Hebrew Enlightenment reaching a new height, and then
leveling off onto a plateau. The very beginning of the Russian
Haskalah had been marked by an ardent assimilationism—a first,
favorable response to the tsarist policy in creating this kind of
intelligentsia in the first place—which was soon superseded by a more
vigorous search for national self-identification on the part of those
who continued to adhere to Haskalah at all. At the beginning of the
1860's a new spate of Haskalah periodicals, in Russian as well as in
Hebrew, were founded in response to this new mood. One of the
most prominent of these new journals was the Hebrew daily *Ha'Melitz*
(*The Interpreter*), founded in Odessa in 1860 by Alexander Zederbaum, a prominent Hebraist, and an older relative of Julius Zederbaum, who was to achieve prominence among the leaders of the
Russian Revolution under the name Martov. Recognizing the practical and perhaps the cultural value of Yiddish writing, Zederbaum in
1862 decided to include in his paper a Yiddish-language supplement,
which he called *Kol M'vasser* (*Voice of the Herald*)—a resolutely
Hebrew title. This step soon justified itself brilliantly. It was around
this time that the Russian-Jewish writer Shalom Jacob Abramovich
(1836-1917) made a decision which proved to be momentous not
only in his own life but in the history of modern Jewish literature.
Having written for several years in Hebrew, he decided that this
language alone neither served his literary purposes nor reached the
audience he desired; and so he began writing in Yiddish, under the
pen name Mendele Moicher S'forim ("Mendele the Bookseller").
The very choice of name, homely and unheroically Yiddish as it was,
was an indication of what he was trying to do. Mendele began his
career writing stories in *Kol M'vasser* about the simple and the poor
that were never, however, wholly free of an ambivalence of attitude
toward his subject matter that gives them additional stature. He
subsequently wrote Hebrew versions of all his major works.

This constant and conflicting interplay of Yiddishism and He-

braism was the two-sided legacy of the Hasidic spirit in its encounter
with the world of secular European culture. On the one hand, those
who were influenced by this spirit sought regeneration, the recovery
of a noble lineage that went back to Hebrew-speaking antiquity. On
the other hand, what they sought was a spontaneous communion
with the simplicity and purity of spirit represented by the Yiddish-
speaking masses. At first Hebraism was almost entirely elitist in
character, partly influenced from the outside by the attitudes of a
classical and aristocratic age. For as long as this elitist strain remained
predominant in Hebraism, it naturally yielded in vigor and influence
to the Yiddishism that came with the onset of a romantic and
democratic spirit. Yiddish for a time became the cultural focus of the
Russian-Jewish Socialist and revolutionary tradition. Hebrew recovered its own revolutionary vitality only in the cultural reverberations of Yiddishism at the end of the nineteenth century.

The specific alignment between Yiddish and the Russian-Jewish
revolutionary tradition came about as a result of an event that proved
to mark a turning point in the history of Eastern European Jewry in
general. On March 1, 1881, Tsar Alexander II was assassinated by
members of the revolutionary terrorist organization Narodnaya Volya
(People's Will). The conspirators hoped that this event would
provoke a mass uprising of the Russian peasantry and the advent of a
revolutionary era. But the only response among the peasantry was a
series of pogroms against several of the Jewish communities in the
Ukraine the following month. It was these pogroms that gave rise to
a sudden spurt of Russian-Jewish emigration westward and mainly to
America the following year which eventually turned into the greatest
mass exodus in modern Jewish history. There are reasons to suspect
that the tsarist police were instrumental in directing the energies of
the Ukrainian peasants against the Jews. A mood of crisis among the
peasantry that might, after all, have turned out to be revolutionary
was in this way given outlet in a direction that was harmless to the
regime. The pogroms also perhaps satisfied a certain impulse for
revenge in the part of the new Tsar Alexander III, who saw the Jews
as a bulwark of the revolutionary movement.

Although there was, in fact, only one Jew, a woman, among the
group of terrorists who were hanged for complicity in the assassination, there was truth to the view that Jewish intellectuals were
prominent in the revolutionary movement. Until this time, however,

the Russian-Jewish revolutionaries, like their Liberal and Socialist counterparts in Western Europe, were inclined to disregard the fact of their Jewish origins. They saw themselves as part of a general Russian revolutionary movement, which only incidentally sought to liberate Jews along with all the other oppressed classes. But these men and women had come from a far more intensely Jewish environment than their Western European equivalents, and their cosmopolitanism was rarely more than a veneer. The events of 1881 gave rise to a major crisis of their conscience. Whatever the culpability of the tsarist police in the matter, the actual perpetrators of the pogrom had been Russian peasants, members of that class which was above all dear to the revolutionary movement at that time (Marxism, with its relative indifference and even scorn where peasantries are concerned, had not yet come to Russia). The revolutionary Jewish intelligentsia therefore began to perceive that there was reason for paying more attention to the problems specifically suffered by Jews, even while continuing to take part in a general political movement.

The ultimate outcome of this way of thinking was the formation of the Jewish Workers' Federation, or *Bund*, in 1897. By that time Marxism had fully taken root in Russia, and Jewish radicals took to it as readily there as they had done in Western Europe. Now that the more or less urban class of the proletariat had replaced the peasantry as the focus of revolutionary idealism, it was much more possible to place the Jews significantly into the picture. The Jewish masses were mainly proletarian or semiproletarian, and the confluence of economic and cultural identity that they represented enabled the Bundist to place Yiddish language and culture into a Marxian revolutionary scheme. The cultivation of Yiddish, a language which was at that moment beginning to lose the social foundations of its very existence, burst forth with a sudden revolutionary vitality. Yiddish literature, under the pen not only of Mendele Moicher S'forim, but of Isaac Loeb Peretz and Sholom Aleichem as well, now achieved unprecedented stature. For the ardent Bundist, Hebrew was the language to be scorned; it was the tongue of clerical oppression and, more recently, of Zionism, which was considered by Bundists to be a bourgeois movement.

Bundism served as an important channel between the Jewish working masses and the reform movements of Eastern Europe and America, but its ultimate outcome was not entirely a successful

realization of its early hopes. In America the very success of the
Jewish labor movement in penetrating the economic mainstream of
American life led to the widespread repudiation of Yiddish culture
among a younger generation. In Eastern Europe the Bundists
maintained their identity and vigor more successfully, but they did
not succeed in becoming part of the mainstream of reform. Although
they were largely responsible for the foundation of the Russian Social
Democratic party at Minsk in 1898, their attempt to become an
autonomous organization within that party was repudiated at the
Second Congress in 1903. They later became affiliated with the
Mensheviks, but this party fell by the wayside after the Russian
revolution. From then on until the Second World War Poland was
the center of Bundism.

Hebraism first found its revolutionary vitality with a recovery of a
sense of its roots in Zion. This sense, a natural corollary of Hebrew
nationalism and a natural source of strength for it, did not come to
the fore until the 1880's. Prior to that decade it had at best expressed
itself as a sentimental idealization of the Palestine of the biblical era,
as in the widely read novel *Ahavat Zion* (*Love of Zion*), published in
1853 by the Haskalah writer Abraham Mapu. But the pogroms of
1881 provoked a turning point in the development of Hebrew
nationalism just as they did in the Yiddishist and socialist currents. It
was even shortly before 1881 that the Hebrew writer Peretz Smolenskin had begun to think in terms of founding modern Jewish
settlements in Palestine. Settlement in Palestine had hitherto been
the exclusive province of the very religious, at least among Russian
Jews—of Kabbalists and Hasidim seeking closer communion with
their spiritual brothers in communities there or simply of pious old
men wanting to spend their last days living and praying on the soil of
Eretz Yisroel and to be buried there. These people represented the
very opposite of a secular national renaissance. Smolenskin, born in
Russia in 1842, represented a new and vigorous type of maskil who
could not settle for a cultural renaissance that was in the end merely
sentimental in nature and without real substance, as Haskalah had
been thus far. Having settled in Vienna, where he founded a Hebrew
monthly, *Ha'Shahar* (*The Dawn*), he was in a better position to
receive ideas from the West than most Russian Jews were. In 1878 a
British writer named Laurence Oliphant had begun, out of his own
spiritual compound of religious mysticism and British imperialist

visions, to advocate the establishment in Palestine of a Jewish colony under British auspices. When Smolenskin heard of this idea, he became one of Oliphant's supporters, and he used *Ha'Shahar* as a medium for advocating secular Jewish settlement in Palestine. After the pogroms of 1881 he was joined in this campaign by another prominent Haskalah writer, Moshe Leib Lilienblum, and settlement in Zion began to be a central theme among Hebraists. A group of Jewish students at Kharkov University formed an organization which they called *Bilu* (from the initials of the invocation, *Beit Yaakov, lechu ve'nelcha*, "O house of Jacob, come ye, and let us walk," Isaiah 2:5), twenty of whom settled in Palestine in early 1882.

In the next few years *Hibbat Zion* (Love of Zion) societies began being formed all over Eastern and Central Europe. Smolenskin himself presided over the founding of the Viennese Hibbat Zion organization, *Kadimah* (which means both "forward" and "eastward"), in 1882. Although Smolenskin died in 1885 at the age of only forty-three, Kadimah continued to be a prominent branch of the movement. Nathan Birnbaum, who became its chairman after Smolenskin's death, is credited with having coined the term "Zionism"; after Herzl made his appearance, Kadimah became one of his chief sources of support. But the foremost center of the movement in these years was Odessa, whose Hovevei Zion chapter was considered to be the main one. Its position as the main southern port of Russia, leading to the Middle East and Palestine, made Odessa a natural headquarters for a Zionist colonization movement, but this was not the only reason it became so. Odessa's rapid growth and rise to prosperity had taken place mainly within the nineteenth century, so that it was a city with an unusually liberal and cosmopolitan atmosphere for tsarist Russia. Its southern location had made it a gathering place for many of the non-Russian national groups of the area. Jews had found a way of life there, outside of the Pale of Settlement, which in many ways resembled that of the Jewish communities of Western Europe, except that it harbored a more vigorous Jewish identity. The Jewish community of Odessa formed about a third of the population of the city by the end of the nineteenth century, and enjoyed considerable freedom and prosperity. The young Odessa Jew of this period, unlike most Russian Jews, was likely to speak Russian as his mother tongue (indeed, he often did not know Yiddish at all); he was characteristically worldly and perhaps even inclined to a certain air of aestheticism and decadence, although this latter quality usually concealed an abounding vitality. Odessa became a natural Jewish literary and artistic capital, an outpost of "advanced" ideas, which attracted Yiddishists as well as Hebraists, Socialists as well as Zionists, to its warm climate and Bohemian atmosphere.

It was an Odessa Jew named Leo Pinsker, a son of a maskil, and himself a maskil as well as a practicing physician, who provided the first major work in the literature of Russian Zionism. Provoked by the pogroms of 1881, Pinsker's *Auto-Emancipation* nevertheless aspired to reach beyond the framework of the Jewish situation in Russia. He sought to appeal to Jews everywhere, to make them seek an answer to the universal Jewish Question. He therefore wrote his pamphlet in German and published it in Berlin, in 1882. *Auto-Emancipation* bears some resemblance to its more celebrated successor, Herzl's *Judenstaat*, published fourteen years later. Like the Herzl of 1896, Pinsker does not concern himself, in this pamphlet, with a particular location for the Jewish state that he advocates. If Palestine is available, that is fine; but if not, then some other place of Jewish refuge must be sought. The spirit of Pinsker's pamphlet is entirely that of "political" Zionism. His thesis is that the Jews everywhere are lacking in the sole criterion that the world recognizes for a nation: a sovereign territory. A people living in this disembodied condition, he says, is naturally subject to contempt and abuse. As with Herzl, this is the voice of a disenchanted liberalism speaking. The very title of Pinsker's pamphlet, which had been a favorite phrase of the workers of the First International only a few years before, is a repudiation of liberalism; it is a suggestion that the Jews must now recognize, as the socialist workers have done, that the liberal vision of society as a mere aggregate of individuals equal before the state is an illusion and that the underprivileged groups in any society must develop a sense of solidarity and organize in their own interest.

Yet the earmarks of the Liberal are also present in Pinsker's work, primarily in the view that a nationality is not really such until it resides in a state of its own. This is not at all the Hibbat Zion view (and certainly not the view of Bundist nationalism), which considered a rich Jewish national tradition to be already in existence, unbroken through almost two thousand years without a state, and which merely sought to have the Jewish settlements in Palestine serve as a focus and an anchor for the national existence of Jews everywhere. In the undertones of vestigial liberalism and overtones of political Zionism that are contained in *Auto-Emancipation*, Pinsker manifests himself as a common type of Odessa Jewish intellectual, cosmopolitan and culturally a bit detached from Jewish traditions. But there was clearly also another side to his nature, the side expressed by the interest in Hebrew letters that he had inherited from his father. Shortly after the publication of his pamphlet, he was approached by the Hovevei Zion of Odessa; he joined that organization and eventually became its president. His search through the world for a place of Jewish refuge promptly found its focus in Zion after all. Furthermore, the political Zionism of his pamphlet was soon replaced by an apparently complete concurrence in the Hibbat Zion idea of gradual colonization without any short-range political ends in view.

The actual process of colonization in Palestine that the Hovevei Zion sponsored proceeded with some energy through the decade of the eighties. The Bilu group sought to make themselves into farmers, and, upon their arrival in 1882, settled in Petah Tikva (Gate of Hope), a Jewish agricultural village just northeast of Jaffa which had been founded four years before by a group of young religious Jews from Jerusalem, under the auspices of the *Alliance Israélite Universelle* of Paris. Some members of the Bilu group subsequently founded a new colony, just southeast of Jaffa, which they called Rishon le Zion (First in Zion). In the meantime the foundations of a Hebrew national culture in Palestine were being laid largely through the work of one man, a fanatically dedicated young maskil named Eliezer Perlman, who changed his name to Ben-Yehuda, settled in Jerusalem in 1881 and began refusing to address or be addressed by a Jew in any language but Hebrew. All these steps were valuable preliminaries to the ultimate formation of a Jewish national community in Palestine, but they were too scattered and tentative to achieve much success by themselves. In the end it took the concentrated purposiveness of Labor Zionism, which arose among a new generation at the turn of the century in response to the challenge of Bundism, to make the leap from desultory settlement to organizing the revival of a Palestinian Jewish nation. The Labor Zionists learned from socialism the techniques of their unique nationalist enterprise. Knowing full well that the Jewish community of the Diaspora was suffering from a lack of the occupational distribution proper to an ordinary nation, the

Labor Zionists sought to regenerate themselves economically, in particular to turn themselves into laborers and farmers, through collective enterprise. The collective was the way in which these young socialist pioneers absorbed the shock of one another's mistakes and learned from them.

But the Bilu and other pioneers of the earlier period had not yet learned the methods to keep up with their ambitions. They became private farmers, and soon resorted to hiring Arab laborers, who were cheaper and more used to backbreaking work than Jewish laborers were, to be their field hands. This practice was later deplored by the younger generation of Labor Zionists, who said that a true nation must be prepared to do its own "dirty work"—another manifestation of the confluence of socialist and nationalist ideals among that generation. Furthermore, the private farms that were established in the early Hibbat Zion period, which ambitiously sought to raise crops for which the land was not well suited, soon fell into economic difficulties. It looked as if they were heading for complete financial disaster until, through the good offices of the Alliance Israélite Universelle, an appeal was made to Baron Edmond de Rothschild in Paris. The Baron immediately began subsidizing the Jewish-owned farms of Petah Tikva and Rishon le Zion. The first Zionist colonization effort was thus turning into simply another form of Jewish philanthropic enterprise.

This situation was subjected to a scathing criticism in a Hebrew-language essay published in Odessa in the spring of 1889, and which came to serve as a major step in opening the way to a new and decisive frame of mind in Russian Zionism. The essay, published in Zederbaum's Ha'Melitz, was forthrightly entitled "This Is Not the Way" and was signed with a pen name then unknown but soon to enjoy great eminence in Hebrew letters, "Ahad Ha-Am," which simply means "one of the people." Ahad Ha-Am argued that it was a hasty and thoughtless pursuit of merely practical achievements that had brought Hibbat Zion to its present state, as an enterprise sponsoring a few struggling Palestine outposts dependent upon the good will of Baron de Rothschild in Paris. The proper aim of such a movement was not, after all, a few scattered colonies but a national renaissance. This latter aim, however, did not mean a "political" Zionist policy to Ahad Ha-Am, as it had meant to the Pinsker of Auto-Emancipation and was to mean to Herzl a few years later. He did not share their view that nationality depended upon statehood. The Jews had been a nation without a territory for almost two thousand years, although, to be sure, the conditions of exile and suffering had imposed a period of moral decline upon them. But a time of spiritual revival was now at hand, and this was not a mere matter of physical enterprises. This is not to say that Ahad Ha-Am scorned worldly activity in favor of some separate realm of the spirit; on the contrary, he insisted (as Moses Hess had done) that the Jewish tradition was not the Essene and medieval Christian one of a dichotomy between spirit and flesh, but the Pharisaic one of a balanced combination of the two—that, indeed, for Judaism there was not really even a clear line of distinction between spirit and flesh. He therefore did not oppose colonization in Palestine; in later works, in fact, he was to elaborate his conception of the role of a Palestine Jewish community as the "spiritual center" for the national renaissance of which he spoke. He merely considered it wrong to put the practical task of colonizing before the moral and cultural task of national regeneration.

Ahad Ha-Am, whose real name was Asher Ginzberg, was born in the Ukraine in 1856 to a wealthy Hasidic family. Shortly after Asher's birth, his father leased the estate of a Russian nobleman, and this is where the boy grew up. His childhood was thus an unusual combination for a young Jew of worldly ease and unworldly religious engagement. This combination subsequently marked his whole life, for the Hasidic inclination to scorn engagement in the practical problems of life in favor of intellectual pursuits was reinforced in him by his having enjoyed a childhood free of practical cares. His whole life was marked by a certain passivity in worldly matters. In accordance with Orthodox Jewish traditions, he was married at the age of seventeen to a girl whom he saw for the first time when they met under the bridal canopy; he accepted the pleasant woman who became his wife loyally and without much joy, had children by her, came home to her all his life, and kept his deepest feelings to himself. In his twenties he decided that he wanted to go to a university, and even went by himself to Germany for a while with the intention of pursuing his studies there, but he could not bring himself to take the step, and he returned to his father's estate in despair. His essay, "This Is Not the Way," which began his literary career, was written only after Zederbaum had spent considerable effort in convincing him to do so. After

1885, when his family's fortune collapsed, he was forced to earn his own living, but was reluctant to do so through his writing and intellectual activities—again, an old Hasidic ideal, but one that was reinforced by the diffidence of Ahad Ha-Am's personality. Most of his life he indifferently retained a post with the Wissotzky Tea Company. In 1906 he was offered the possibility of becoming the director of the new Dropsie College of Jewish studies in Philadelphia, and he was interested in the offer, but he hesitated, and the opportunity passed.

This quality of diffidence in his personal life bears affinities with a philosophy that refused to lay stress upon practical activity. For he believed that practical activity, given the proper frame of mind at least, would simply take care of itself. His view was, in effect, the quintessence of Hasidism. To Ahad Ha-Am, Spirit was a force that could somehow become Act, not by some sudden and concrete implementation of a plan but by the sheer emanation of its power. Although this motion of the continuity of Thought and Act bears affinities with that of Moses Hess—both he and Ahad Ha-Am saw this continuity as being of the essence of the Jewish tradition—it is here being viewed from the other side; whereas Hess saw activity as a way in which the Spirit defined itself, for Ahad Ha-Am activity is only the emanation of Spirit, which has already defined itself within. Ahad Ha-Am's view is a supreme affirmation of the ideal of Kavanah, of the notion that the internal direction of the Spirit is sufficient to change the world. This, then, was the reason that he laid stress upon the moral regeneration of the Jewish people. For him, the Jews were the spiritual nation par excellence in history, the people who had once given mankind a great moral vision, and who would now do so again. For this task a "spiritual center" was important, a place where Jews would speak Hebrew and generate a purely Jewish cultural life. Such a center, furthermore, could be nowhere but in Palestine. But in this scheme of things the practical tasks of establishing such a Palestine community were only a secondary matter, not the be-all and end-all of a national revival.

But, for all its apparent disdain of practical matters, Ahad Ha-Am's "cultural" Zionism was not unrelated to the essence of the Hibbat Zion ideal, particularly as manifested by the younger generation of Labor Zionist pioneers who began to arrive in Palestine after 1903. These latter, too, were after all seeking a national cultural renaissance. The difference between them and Ahad Ha-Am turned out to be mainly one of emphasis, and began in time to disappear altogether. Instead, Ahad Ha-Am found the main focus of his disdain not in them but in the political Zionism of Herzl. He attended the first Zionist Congress at Basel in 1897, as a visitor rather than a delegate, and was immediately repelled by this attempt to project whatever he had disliked about the old Hibbat Zion policies onto an epic scale. The diplomatic approach to what in the end had to be a spiritual renaissance seemed to him vulgar, futile and un-Jewish. For him, the Jews were a people of prophets, not of diplomats. He remained an opponent of Herzl and of political Zionism all the rest of his life.

It was this conflict that finally had the effect of placing him in the camp of the practical Zionists in spite of himself. He became their teacher. His philosophical essays, calling for a reformulation of Jewish values—above all, of Judaism's great moral and prophetic vision—into modern terms, gave spiritual substance and direction to their activities. His clear and subtle Hebrew prose, which took Hebrew literary style completely out of the Middle Ages for the first time, gave them a linguistic ideal to which to aspire. He was the major spiritual catalyst between the Jewish tradition and a new phase of Jewish history.

But that new phase of history was also the outcome of a political movement, of the Herzlian Zionism that Ahad Ha-Am had scorned. In the end it was this movement that validated his work, in spite of his own opposition to it. And this is an appropriate outcome, for all its ironies. Ahad Ha-Am belonged to the tradition of the great Hasidic teachers, and at heart he shared their revolutionary impulse, for all his diffidence in worldly matters. As a thinker and moralist, he broke through to the realm of general European culture with the ardor of a Baal Shem Tov stepping forth from the darkness of the cheder into the open countryside. Like that great Tsaddik, he was throwing off the accumulated and overbearing superstructure of the past, but not in order to repudiate the past completely, as Western European Enlightenment ultimately tended to do. Rather, the step away was taken only so as to be better able to draw out the essence of the past and to refresh it through contact with something new. For Ahad Ha-Am the refreshing new contact was the revolutionary turmoil of nineteenth-century civilization, which he savored in the

manner of a Hasid slowly inhaling the scent of a wild flower. It was
enough for him that this aroma caused a turmoil within his spirit; he
then made it his life work to contemplate the meaning of that inner
confrontation. But whatever its meaning was, its ultimate manifestation was bound to be activity. This outcome was not, however, for
Ahad Ha-Am himself to realize, but for a younger and hardier
generation that rushed forth inspired by his teachings. It is Ahad Ha-
Am's place in history to have passed on the spark of an ancient
revolutionary vision to a generation that was to translate it into
political reality at last.

PART TWO:

The Mandate Era

CHAPTER 3

Establishment and Decline
of the British Mandate

I

THE growing concern with Zion throughout the nineteenth century, in both the Jewish and the non-Jewish European mind, was in part an outgrowth of the ideal of national revival fostered by the French Revolution, but was above all tied up with the increasing interest on the part of Europeans in that phenomenon which came to be known as the "Eastern Question." Briefly stated, the Eastern Question was the whole set of problems that emerged—particularly for the European foreign ministries—out of the steady dissolution of the Ottoman Empire, a process which took place with growing speed in the nineteenth century. The diminution of Turkish power had at first been a question of the utmost concern only to the expanding Russian state in the eighteenth century, when the tsars sought first to establish themselves on the shores of the Turkish-dominated Black Sea—an aim in which they were successful—and then to achieve control of the Black Sea straits leading out into the open waters of the Mediterranean. They were frustrated in this latter aim because, by the nineteenth century, both France and England had become committed to preventing any Great Power from achieving such decisive control of the Near East. France and England became the protectors of the crumbling Ottoman state, as well as rivals for influence over it, and the Crimean War of 1854–1856 was their crusade to help the "Sick Man of Europe" throw off his Russian persecutor.

But since this compassion for the Turk was never based on any larger sentiment than political self-interest, both France and England, as well as Russia, also sought ways throughout the nineteenth century to establish a foothold in whatever political vacuum might remain should the Ottoman Empire ever be completely dismembered. When Bonaparte essayed to become the conqueror of Egypt and Syria in 1798–1799, France—even the new revolutionary France —was still smarting from the defeat she had suffered at British hands in India some forty years earlier. The French by no means considered the matter of domination in the East to be settled. But it was the French Revolution, with Bonaparte as its missionary, that produced the novel idea of achieving power in some areas not by right of conquest alone but also by fostering the renaissance of suppressed nationalities. This idea had worked admirably for Bonaparte in Italy, and it was later to work again in Poland. Pursuing the idea into Egypt, Bonaparte brought with him a portable academy of scientists, philologists and poets, and the modern science of Egyptology was founded during his stay there. The weight of this massive catalyst of French civilization must have been far too much, however, for any Egyptian national revival it hoped to foster. As for Syria (a term which then included Palestine), the idea seems to have occurred to Bonaparte, at least briefly, that he could lead a crusade of Jews to reconquer the Holy Land. But this dream vanished when the French were expelled from Syria by the British in the spring of 1799.

In the century following the Napoleonic Wars and the Congress of Vienna the major center of attention in the Near East was the Balkan countries. The Serbian national revival was under way even before the final defeat of Napoleon. But it was the Greek revolt against Ottoman domination from 1821 to 1831 that won the abiding attention of the Powers and captured the imagination of the Western European peoples. For men like Byron, Hugo and Delacroix the renaissance of the nation that had founded Western civilization was of far greater historic import than the small size of the country would ordinarily imply. Later on, the national uprisings in Roumania and Bulgaria were to be, among the men who wielded political power in Europe, of greater concern than Greece had been, but the romantic intelligentsia of Western Europe were scarcely excited by them. The only equal to the Greek uprising for the romantic imagination got under way at the end of the nineteenth century, when the people who had given Jesus and the Bible to the world also began seeking a national renaissance. To a certain extent the Greek and Zionist revivals coincided with appropriate phases in the evolution of the cultural mood of Western Europe. The early nineteenth century still felt the impact of the era of classicism that had preceded it, so that Byron, for example, achieved a fusion of the Augustan and romantic states of mind. The Greek War of Independence was an ideal focus for such a combination of feelings. But modern Greece was not solely the repository of a Hellenic ideal, purely outlined and white as a marble frieze; it also shared in the baroque outlines and flamboyant colors of the Near East. The heightened interest in the Near East on the part of the Byronic generation soon found its focus in the exotic, in objects that reflected the growing antirational and anticlassical mood. For Delacroix, the freedom of color and form that he found in the Muslim world of North Africa was an extension of the ideal that he had sought in themes from the Greek revolution. In time Syria became a major focus of interest for both Anglo-Saxons and Frenchmen, and their missionary activities in Beirut in the middle of the nineteenth century did a great deal to foster an Arab cultural revival. Ultimately this attention extended, especially among the British, to the deserts of Arabia itself.

This growing fascination with the Arab and Muslim Middle East was bound up with religious attitudes, which gained new energy with the progress of romanticism. The romantic may proclaim his immunity to religious ideas as loudly as the rationalist does, but he is really quite susceptible to them. In a sense, modern romanticism is a revival of the religious impulses of Western man. Among the European intelligentsia of the nineteenth century these impulses characteristically expressed themselves in a more or less secularized form, but this was not true in every case. In this respect England and France differed somewhat in their general tendencies. In France, as in the Latin Catholic countries in general at this time, the dominant outlook of the liberal intelligentsia was anticlerical and hence, at least on the surface, against religion in the traditional sense. In England the Protestant tradition had allowed for a reconciliation between liberal aspirations and traditional religious loyalties, so that the outlook of the British liberal intelligentsia was always more deeply imbued with more or less orthodox religious attitudes than was that of their French counterparts. This difference in the French and British outlooks—or at least the British conception of this difference —was expressed in David Lloyd George's remark, made early in the First World War, that it would be an outrage if the Holy Places in Palestine were to fall into the hands of "agnostic, atheistic France."[1]

This is one reason why Zionism, with its simultaneous appeal to both the revolutionary and the religious outlook, found a greater response in England as compared to France. But one must not conclude that the less enthusiastic response to Zionism in France was due to a relative lack of religious piety there. A small but fervent anticlerical group has almost always been pre-eminent there since early in the nineteenth century, but the French people on the whole are as deeply Catholic as the British are Protestant. In fact, the cultural influence of Catholicism in France does not really stop at the borderline between clericals and anticlericals. Catholic universalism is a powerful force in France among religious and nonreligious alike; its secularized form is the French cultural universalism that dominated the eighteenth century and the revolutionary epoch. The kind of cultural pluralism that characterizes the Anglo-Saxon countries is scarcely to be found among the French. In the areas in which French language and civilization are predominant, cultural variation is usually tolerated only on the folk level, among a peasantry bound up with the traditions of a particular locale. All higher forms of cultural expression must, as a rule, take up their place in the spiritual mainstream that emanates from Paris.

At its best, this spirit manifests itself in an outlook that is singularly free, for a European people, of anything like racist attitudes. This, in general, is the finest manifestation of Catholic universalism, but it is often antithetical to the better possibilities of the development of subcultures within a nation. This has proved to be the case in France not only in distinct linguistic-geographic entities such as Provence or Brittany but also in relation to the Jews. A people which chooses to maintain its particularist traditions without having any geographical center of its own is not readily comprehended anywhere, but especially not in nineteenth-century France. To a certain extent there was a Jewish geographical center in and

[1] Leonard Stein, *The Balfour Declaration* (New York, 1961), p. 111.

around Strasbourg (although it was in no way a center for the large
Sephardic Jewish population of France), but this region derived its
identity from the German cultural sphere within which it was
located. In fact, French anti-Semitism in the nineteenth century
tended to look upon the Jew as some kind of German. During the
Dreyfus Affair, the fact that an alleged spy for Germany was also an
Alsatian Jew corroborated a popular myth. Jewish particularism was
also considered to be somehow Protestant in character, pietistic in a
somewhat crude way, like Germans, and like that Old Testament
which Protestants always tended to favor and which French Catholics often looked upon as barbarous. And yet the most virulent kind
of anti-Semitism in France, that which came to the fore in the last
two decades of the nineteenth century, was really a German import,
itself appealing to a kind of warped pietism and provincialism that is
not characteristic of the mainstream of French civilization. Although
racist attitudes have had some vogue in France, the racist variety of
anti-Semitism has never had much strength there. Rather, the
French, when they have taken a critical view of Jewish particularism,
have more often done so on cultural grounds. It is hard for the
cosmopolitan type of Frenchman, whether he is Catholic or anticlerical, to understand why the Jews want to maintain a separate identity.
For the cosmopolitan Catholic, the religion of the *Évangiles* is the
logical culmination of the universalist vision of the Hebrew prophets;
therefore the Jew, if he were true to the spirit of his own religious
heritage, would convert to Christianity. For the cosmopolitan anticlerical in France, the Jew might want, for reasons of his own, to
cling to a clerical tradition that seems no less obscurantist than the
Catholic variety; but if he should not want to, there is no clear reason
why he should be anything distinct within the universalist family of
republican France, a brotherhood which carries its own prophetic
traditions.

British Protestantism is far more prone to acknowledge the existence of cultural and religious minorities, and to allow them the
energy to flourish, even when it is not necessarily tolerant of them.
During the course of the long struggle on the part of the various
religious minorities to gain their rights in Britain from the sixteenth
century onward, the Anglo-Saxon spirit developed a talent for cultural and especially religious proliferation that was not easily rivaled
among nations. The very badgering of one group by another there

has often caused them to thrive, since it is above all persecution that causes the Calvinist soul to rise to heights of self-assertion. Furthermore, the fundamentalist mood that prevailed among these groups often led to a particularly strong sense of kinship with the people of the Bible (although not necessarily always with its descendants). Their imagination was captured not only by the Old Testament vision of a God of wrath but also by the idea of a chosen people, singled out by God from the idolaters amidst whom it lived, and driven to pursue its hopes through a wilderness.

In Britain this sense of belonging to a holy brotherhood was strengthened when it also implied membership in one of the national minorities. Indeed, this often completed the inner sense of being a religious nationality that rose up in many Britons when they were confronted by the Zionists, whom they saw as a reflection of their own spiritual identity. This range of feelings is present in the remarks made by the Welshman (and pro-Zionist) Lloyd George before a gathering of the Jewish Historical Society of England in 1925:

> I was brought up in a school where I was taught far more about the history of the Jews than about the history of my own land. I could tell you all the kings of Israel. But I doubt whether I could have named half a dozen of the kings of England, and not more of the kings of Wales. . . .
>
> We were thoroughly imbued with the history of your race in the days of its greatest glory, when it founded that great literature which will echo to the very last days of this old world, influencing, molding, fashioning the human character, inspiring and sustaining the human motive, for not only Jews, but Gentiles as well. We absorbed it and made it part of the best in the Gentile character. So that, therefore, when the question was put to us, we were not like Napoleon,[2] who had never been in a Sunday School and had probably read very little of that literature. . . .
>
> You call yourselves a small nation. I belong to a small nation and I am proud of the fact. It is an ancient race, not as old as yours, and although I am very proud of it, I am not going to compare it with yours. One day it may become great; it will perhaps be chosen for great things. But all I know is that up to the present it is the small races that have been chosen for great things. . . .

This is not to say that Lloyd George, or for that matter most of the prominent British Gentile pro-Zionists, were free of anti-Semitic

[2] Napoleon was the subject of the lecture by Philip Guedalla that had just preceded Lloyd George's address (Philip Guedalla, *Napoleon and Palestine*).

sentiments. On the contrary, their special passion about Jews contained a vexing ambivalence of attitude toward them. The admiration these men felt for Old Testament Hebrews often only heightened their predisposition to feel a certain contempt for Stock Exchange Jews or for East End peddlers. Zionism appealed to them because it proposed to make Jews into Hebrews once again.

The British spirit, then, became fired with the Zionist idea in a way that the French never could. The notion of an exiled people seeking their land had resided in the British soul for centuries and had made them the greatest colonizing people in history. Indeed, the condition of exile, the wandering itself, has always been more exciting to the British Puritan imagination than its outcome, the condition of rootedness and ease on the soil. Ease in Zion is a state of the soul that is alien to the ideals of British Puritanism, which is inclined to look upon it as a phenomenon of moral decline. It is the French who are the landed people, the peasant society par excellence. French Catholics, to whom Zionism meant little in its pioneer days, are probably more excited today than any other Western group about the fact of a Jewish peasantry living on the soil of the Holy Land. Here, once again, are the Hebrews of the New Testament, that ancient, settled agrarian civilization which produced Jesus. But the British Puritan is less interested in the peasant than he is in the nomad, the Hebrew of the Old Testament. The British were, in fact, far better at sympathizing with a Zionist movement, a phenomenon of the Diaspora, than they were at yielding to the demands of a Jewish community settled in Palestine. In fact, this British passion for the nomad often led to a greater feeling for Arabs than for Jews—especially for the ideal type of Arab represented by the desert wanderers of Arabia, members of the Shi'ite sect, the Puritans of Islam. T. E. Lawrence more than once referred to nomadism as "that most deeply biting of all social disciplines." For the most part, the British were more attracted by the Arab nomads of Arabia than by the peasants of Syria, whereas it was upon the latter that the French focused their attention almost exclusively. Lawrence seemed to be fulfilling an ideal deeply embedded in the British Puritan soul when he led a nomadic crusade from Arabia northward to conquer Syria. But at least one British Puritan was able to formulate this ideal in his own mind so as to make him lead a Jewish crusade in the Land of Israel. Captain (later Brigadier General) Orde C. Wingate, who organized and led Jewish

self-defense units in Palestine in 1938, was one of the few British
Gentiles to become converted to Zionism on the soil of the Holy
Land itself. Only a short time before arriving in Palestine for his tour
of duty there, he had spent two months exploring the Libyan desert.
Perhaps his arrival in the Holy Land after a time in the wilderness
caused him to feel an innate kinship with the Hebrews who had
arrived in Canaan under Joshua, and were now once again returning
from exile.

A slow but steady acceleration of the pace of Jewish colonization in
Palestine, and the gradual transformation of this exodus from a
religious into a secular national one, began to attract the Western
Powers of the nineteenth century to the notion that the Jews of
Palestine might become a European enclave in the Levant. Since
Jews were primarily Europeans, it was more reassuring to have the
Holy Places entrusted to them than to Muslims. More zealous about
its culture than its religion, nineteenth-century Europe was ready to
reward Europeanized Jews with a trust that its medieval counterpart
never would have given them. But gradually, as the dissolution of the
Ottoman Empire became imminent, the notion of a general European enclave was replaced by the idea that a Jewish Palestine could
be a cultural and political advance guard in the Middle East for one
or another of the Powers. The first glimmers of the Zionist vision, on
the part of both Jew and Gentile, had a way of appearing throughout
the earlier part of the nineteenth century in one or another country
according to the flowering of that country's aspirations in the Middle
East.
The first major initiative toward establishing Jewish settlements in
Palestine under the auspices of a Western Power was that of Sir
Moses Montefiore of England, which started in the 1830's. Montefiore was the son of an old Sephardic Jewish family that had been
settled in England for two generations at the time of his birth in
1784. By the age of forty he had made a fortune on the London Stock
Exchange, and he then retired to spend the rest of his life in
philanthropic work. He made, in all, seven trips to Palestine, the last
of which he undertook at the age of ninety-five (he lived to be one
hundred one years old!), in a period when the Middle East was still a
test of the hardiness of even the youngest European traveler. He

hoped to get a grant of land for Jewish settlement in Palestine, but he did not succeed. But he did do a great deal to improve the lot of the Jewish communities, mainly ultrareligious and not economically robust, that were already established there. He built synagogues, hospitals and residential quarters—it was his initiative that built, in 1860, the first Jewish quarter of Jerusalem to stand outside the dank walls of the Old City, in the sunlight of the surrounding hills.

But Montefiore's work, although it took place in a period when British interest in Syria was beginning to grow, did not capture the abiding attention of the British government. In the middle years of the nineteenth century it was the French who showed the greater interest in the Middle East. This interest reached its height in the 1860's, when French initiative built the Suez Canal, and undertook missionary work in Syria which laid the foundation of the powerful French cultural influence still felt in that region today. It was in 1860 that a group of young Jewish business and professional men of Paris founded the Alliance Israélite Universelle, which went on to reign for a time as the foremost Jewish philanthropic organization in the world. Founded in response to a sudden recrudescence of anti-Semitism in Europe and the Middle East that took place in the 1840's and 1850's, the Alliance was concerned with Jewish welfare anywhere in the world, but in time its activities in Palestine took on some pre-eminence. In 1870 the Alliance founded *Mikveh Israel* (Hope of Israel), an agricultural school, in Palestine just outside of Jaffa. Its primary purpose was to teach useful agricultural occupations to the offspring of the ultrareligious Jews living in Palestine, who usually relied upon Jewish charitable donations from abroad for their sustenance. Mikveh Israel gradually made its influence felt, and in 1878 a group of religious Palestinian Jews founded Petah Tikva, the first Jewish agricultural settlement in Palestine. But these settlers were not able to dispense entirely with the principle of *halukah* (Jewish charitable donation from abroad); it was Baron Edmond de Rothschild who came to the rescue of their still unprofitable enterprises in the 1880's. By the time the Zionist movement came into being, Jewish settlement in Palestine was something of a French philanthropy. Both Baron de Rothschild and the Alliance Israélite Universelle were opponents of Zionism in its early days.

Despite this confluence of French-Jewish initiative in Palestine and

French initiative in the Middle East in general, the idea of using Jewish settlement to gain a foothold in Palestine never took hold of French policy makers. Not that the idea was not discussed in France. In 1860 there appeared a pamphlet, *La Nouvelle Question d'Orient*, by Ernest Laharanne, which advocated the revival of an Egyptian and an Arab empire, and a Jewish state in Palestine, all under French influence. Laharanne was aware of his project as above all being a political move against growing British power in the Middle East— indeed, it somewhat resembles the projects that the British later evolved, during the course of the First World War, to push back French influence in the area. But Laharanne had his romantic as well as his practical side, and the idea of a revived Judaea seems to have captured his imagination in a way unusual for Frenchmen at that time. But his book did not gain much response in France.

In the next decade the idea of a restored Jewish Palestine was taken up more robustly by a British Christian. Laurence Oliphant was a Puritan fundamentalist if there ever was one. Born in Cape-town in 1829, the son of a British barrister and civil servant, he seems to have spent most of the first four decades of his life as something of a *bon vivant*, who wandered through many parts of the world writing accounts of his travels. But in 1865, shortly after he had successfully contested a seat in Parliament, he underwent a religious conversion, and joined the Brotherhood of the New Life, a society of Sweden-borgian mystics centered in the United States. Two years later he settled in the Brotherhood's community at Amenia, New York, where he devoted himself to manual labor. His mother, now a widow, came to Amenia shortly after him—sixty years old, a British woman of the upper middle class, she settled down to working in the Brotherhood kitchen. After three years at Amenia, Oliphant returned to England, apparently on an agreement that he would be of more use to the Brotherhood in the outside world. In 1872 Oliphant met a young Englishwoman who agreed to adopt his religion; they were married, and, in accordance with the highest ideals of the Brother-hood, lived together as brother and sister rather than as husband and wife.

In the meantime Oliphant had been continuing to develop the worldly side of his nature, so that he would be able to perform practical tasks for higher spiritual purposes. He had resigned his seat in Parliament shortly after settling in Amenia, but he was a talented journalist and was always able to command good fees for his assignments. His publicity work had now come to receive attention. It was in 1878 that he began publicizing a project he had conceived for obtaining a grant of land in Palestine from the Turks and developing it through Jewish settlement, all under British auspices. He spent some time seeking a subscription for the purchase of such a concession, and he visited Palestine in 1879. By 1882 his activities on behalf of Jews were well enough known that he was employed by a charity established in Britain to aid the emigration of victims of the Russian pogroms, and he traveled to Eastern Europe on this mission. He later wrote of the Jews he saw in Galicia on this trip that "at every station they were assembled in crowds with petitions to be transported to Palestine, the conviction having apparently taken possession of them that the time appointed for their return to the land of their ancestors had arrived, and that I was to be their Moses on the occasion."[3] It was at this time that Oliphant came into contact with the nascent Hibbat Zion societies, his work having become known to Peretz Smolenskin a few years earlier. By the end of 1882 Oliphant had settled in Haifa, which remained his home for the rest of his life. His wife Alice died in 1886, but in England two years later he met and married Rosamund Dale Owen, the granddaughter of Robert Owen. Oliphant brought his new bride to Haifa and died a few months later. His widow remained in Haifa the rest of her life, where she devoted herself to what she considered to be the two great world problems of her time: the Jews and sexual purity.

It was Oliphant's generation that saw the publication of what must be considered the foremost Zionist novel ever to be written by a Gentile. George Eliot's *Daniel Deronda* was published in 1876, just two years before Oliphant began publicizing his scheme for Jewish settlement in Palestine. The novel's hero, Daniel Deronda himself, is an Oxford-educated gentleman, the adopted son of a British aristocrat, who discovers after a long inquiry into the secret of his origins that he is a Jew. But this fact emerges only at a point in his life when, through love of a Jewess and through a heightening moral and intellectual passion, he has begun to study Judaism and the Hebrew language. Deronda's history has the ring of a fulfilled wish on the

[3] *Episodes in a Life of Adventure* (London, 1887), p. 353.

part of British fundamentalism; it has particular affinities with the
myth of the British Israel movement, which claims that the Anglo-
Saxons stem from the Ten Lost Tribes of Israel. For Deronda, the
discovery of his Jewish identity is part of a process of moral regeneration, which lifts him above the spiritual emptiness of his milieu. He
marries the poor and beautiful Jewish girl whom he loves, and at the
end of the novel is making plans for a lifetime of journeying, in
which he will seek to organize the Jews of the East and resettle them
in Palestine. Although Eliot makes some attempt at presenting
Eastern European Jews in the novel, the Jewish image in the book is
basically Sephardic—aristocratic, more aesthetic than intellectual,
Mediterranean in look and temperament. The spirit of Disraeli
hovers over it all. There is a certain feeling present that a man like
Deronda, Jewish in blood but English to the core, makes the best
kind of Jew—or Hebrew—after all.

This feeling that there is some fortunate chemistry in the meeting
of Jewish and British traditions was to take on great strength a
generation later, both for British Gentiles and for Jews, even Jews
who were not of British birth. No man could have been more deeply
imbued with this ideal than was Chaim Weizmann. Indeed, his
strength as a diplomat and Zionist leader lay primarily in the firm
combination within him of an aristocratic temperament that inclined
him to British aristocratic traditions as if he had been born into
them, even though he did not settle in England until he was thirty
years old, and a proud and manifest Jewishness that was utterly
Eastern European in character. He was the very fulfillment of what
many an Englishman of the type of George Eliot wanted a Jew to be:
a gentleman, and yet not the sort of craven assimilationist that so
many members of the oldest Anglo-Jewish families were; a man
whose pride in his origins even included an unabashed Yiddishness,
and yet who bore no trace of the worst qualities of East End
peddlers. England was perhaps the only country in the world in
which this combination of qualities could have been so fully realized.
It was also perhaps the only country in the world, as Weizmann and
many other Zionist leaders came to feel, whose cultural traditions and
political power combined in such a way as to enable it to foster the
birth of a Jewish state in Palestine. At the time that the unknown
young Zionist activist and chemist, Chaim Weizmann, born near
Pinsk, and educated in Darmstadt, Berlin and Geneva, decided to try

to make his life in England in 1904, this was hardly more than a random choice on his part. In the sequel, it was a move that proved to be historic.

II

To a certain extent Chaim Weizmann's career from 1904, the year of his emigration to England and of Herzl's death, until the Balfour Declaration in 1917 stands as representative of the entire history of the Zionist movement in that period. His move to England and his emergence there as the leader of the world Zionist movement are the story of the shift of the center of gravity of that movement from Continental Europe to England. Furthermore, the rise to eminence as a political leader and diplomat of this Eastern European Jew, who had been schooled in Hibbat Zion traditions and always remained cognizant of the spiritual debt he owed to Ahad Ha-Am, was a manifestation of the fact that the clear line of distinction between Herzlian, "political," Zionism and practical Zionism—between the Western European and Eastern European approaches to the problem—was coming to lose its meaning. In his own person and career Chaim Weizmann, who had been among those delegates who walked out of the meeting hall when Herzl offered his Uganda proposal to the Congress in 1903, was a reconciliation and a fusion of these two tendencies. His "political" approach was free of any of the old hopes for a sudden diplomatic coup followed by the swift and mass colonization of the Jewish commonwealth, but his "practical" approach, his policy of fostering steady, gradual colonization, was firmly directed toward political ends, however far off they might be. And there were never to be any Ugandas, any "shelters in the night" for Weizmann; his "love of Zion" was absolute and uncompromising.

When Weizmann moved to England and set up a small chemistry laboratory for himself at the University of Manchester in 1904, the Zionist movement was entering upon a period of doldrums. The great dramas of Uganda and of Herzl's career had ended in a storm of controversy, and a time was at hand for the recovery of energies, for retrenchment, and for working out the lines that the movement was now to follow. The first major development in the decade that followed until the outbreak of the First World War was the gradual shift of the base of the movement from Germany to England. Herzl,

despite all setbacks and the focusing of his aspirations toward England that began taking place at the end of his life, had mainly
centered the hopes of his Zionist program around Germany. In 1897
Germany was at the height of her vision of *Drang nach Osten*, an
aspiration contrary to everything Bismarck had stood for, but a favorite
one for the young Emperor who had dismissed him in 1890. In 1898
Herzl had audiences with Wilhelm II both in Constantinople and in
Palestine during the course of a voyage in which the Emperor sought
to clinch Germany's growing influence in the Ottoman Empire. The
Emperor had at first shown some interest in Herzl's idea. He seemed
convinced that Zionism would bring about the emigration of many
Jews from Germany, and he shared in the view that a Jewish
commonwealth was bound to be an outpost of German civilization.
But by the time he granted a last, brief audience to Herzl in a chilly
tent in Jerusalem he had apparently had a chance to see what a dim
view the Sultan took of the Zionist idea, and he dismissed the matter
brusquely.

The Zionist movement, however, could not readily bring itself to
shrug off the hope of a German protectorate in Palestine, especially
after the Uganda controversy. Right down to 1917 the German
protectorate seemed to many Zionist leaders the most natural aim of
their policy. Under Wilhelm II, Germany became the most influential European Power at the Sultan's court, and Turkey was Germany's ally in the war. But the Zionist stress on Germany was not
based upon a political appraisal alone; it also came out of the
traditional Jewish attraction to German culture. This was not only a
feeling on the part of Central European Jews; as Weizmann himself
often put it, in the eyes of most Eastern European Jews in those days
Europe extended westward to the Rhine and no farther. Many of the
Russian-Jewish intellectuals of his generation sought their university
education in Germany, as he did. This cultural flirtation between
European Jewry and Germany did not completely come to an end
until Hitler's time, in the ruins of the Holocaust. But the Zionist
movement achieved its cultural separation from Germany somewhat
earlier, between 1904 and 1914, as it gradually transferred its affinities
to England. It is noteworthy that Weizmann, who was rather
contemptuous of the aspirations of the German Jews to become like
the middle classes of their country, was in no way reluctant to
identify with the British upper-class milieu of which he became a

part. But for a man like Weizmann, Jewishness was, precisely, an aristocratic and not a bourgeois identification.

The transfer of the focus of the movement from Berlin to London did not take place quickly and easily. Technically, Berlin remained the headquarters of the Zionist movement through the First World War, since this was the city in which the Zionist Executive sat. Even at the moment when he reached the height of his diplomatic career by being foremost in bringing about the Balfour Declaration, Weizmann was not a member of the Zionist Executive. The ultimate adhesion of Zionism to the Allied side and to the British government in particular, as a result of the initiative of Weizmann and others, was a somewhat "wildcat" move on their part. They were able to do so by taking advantage of the anarchy in the organization of the Zionist movement that the war had produced. Although it seems most natural in retrospect that Zionism should have aligned itself with the Western Powers, the course to take was not at all so clear at the time. Jews throughout the world were thoroughly anti-Russian at this time, because of tsarist anti-Semitism. The fact, then, that Russia was on the side of the Allies, along with the traditional Jewish admiration for German culture, caused considerable pro-German feeling among Jews at the beginning of the war, especially among the Russian-Jewish immigrants in America. It was the Russian Revolution, followed by America's entry into the war on the Allied side, that made American-Jewish sentiments overwhelmingly favorable to the struggle against the Central Powers. One of the British motives for the Balfour Declaration later that same year was the hope that it would place Jewish opinion, particularly in America, completely on the Allied side; but to a large extent this had already been accomplished by the course of events.

The British makers of the Balfour Declaration also hoped that their pro-Zionist pronouncement would bring about a wholesale cooperation with the British war effort on the part of the Jewish community in Palestine. At the beginning of the war the situation was a highly ambivalent one for the Jews living in Palestine. Their hearts were in no way inclined toward Constantinople, but since its government was still the only one in charge of Palestine, the most active Zionist leaders there reluctantly cooperated with it. As a demonstration of their readiness to be good tenants, many of them had accepted Turkish citizenship even before the war. Service in the

Turkish army was quite a large order, however, and many young Palestinian Jewish men—particularly the offspring of the non-Zionist Jewish settlers—emigrated to other countries at Turkey's entry into the war. But to the committed Zionist leaders in Palestine there seemed little alternative to military service for the Power that governed their country, and so some of them joined the Turkish army.

But these men soon came to feel the new currents toward London and the Allied side that were working in the movement. The military problems of the Zionists were being provided with a solution by 1915 through the efforts of two of the most dazzling personalities in the movement: the Russian Jews Joseph Trumpeldor and Vladimir Jabotinsky. Trumpeldor had served as an officer with the Russian army in the Russo-Japanese War, in which he lost an arm in combat. Jabotinsky was a slightly younger man who had been born in Odessa in 1880 and had spent a romantic period in his youth as a journalist and writer in Italy. Both men were rather highly assimilated Jews, and they were drawn to Zionism above all by a romantic conception of revived Jewish valor, by memories of Joshua and Samson. Together they conceived of the formation of a Jewish Legion under British auspices, which would aid in the liberation of Palestine from the Turk. They were soon able to win some interest in Whitehall for their proposal. The British government was at this time looking with growing concern upon the East End of London, where thousands of young Jews of military age were remaining exempt from service because they were still technically Russian subjects. The fact that these young men were claiming exemption because of citizenship of a country that was, after all, an ally, led to such resentment among the public at large that the government was even considering allowing the Russian army to conscript those among them who were eligible to serve. When the idea of a Jewish Legion was broached, it was considered that large numbers of East End Jews might enlist in such an enterprise.

Despite such hopes, bureaucratic conservatism resisted the immediate formation of such a legion, and the idea had its first manifestation instead in a small Jewish detachment called the Zion Mule Corps. Trumpeldor led this corps, which served at Gallipoli with distinction, but Jabotinsky's more baroque spirit was repelled by such an idea and such a name, and he refused to take part in it (later he admitted he was wrong to have refused). Instead, Jabotinsky enlisted, at the age of thirty-five, as a private in the British army. The charm of his unusual personality was such that he became a favorite among fellow soldiers who could not even pronounce his name (they called him "Private Jug o'Whiskey"), and the force of his will so great that, by insinuating himself into offices in which a private normally had no right to appear on his own initiative, he obtained the Jewish Legion that he sought, and himself led one of its battalions in the Galilee in 1918 as Lieutenant Jabotinsky. The effort to form a Jewish Legion was taken up by the Palestinian Zionist leaders, and by 1915 David Ben-Gurion, who had been expelled from Palestine by the Turks, was in the United States to solicit enlistments for the Legion. The lonely rump of a Zionist Executive in Berlin continued to have dreams of another sort, but the wager made on an Allied victory by the Zionist movement was now complete.

By 1916 the Entente Powers were firmly committed to the dismemberment of the Turkish Empire as a war aim; the only question that remained was how the prize was to be divided among the victors. It was generally understood that Russia was to have Constantinople and the Black Sea straits, to which she had so long aspired—an understanding that was wiped out by the Russian Revolution. But the division of Syria and Mesopotamia between England and France had yet to be worked out. A fairly detailed arrangement between these latter two Powers was essayed in the spring of 1916, in the Sykes-Picot agreement. Broadly speaking, this agreement was based upon the same principle that prevailed after the war, whereby the northwestern sector of the Syria-Mesopotamia region was acknowledged to be a French sphere of influence and the southeast a British sphere. Beyond this basic principle, however, substantial modifications of this arrangement were made necessary by subsequent developments of the war. The disappearance of Russia from the scene affected the power distribution in the Middle East, and in particular allowed for the retrenchment of the Anatolian Turkish State at the end of the war. This reduced the large French claims in Anatolia that were incorporated into the Sykes-Picot agreement. In general, French claims in the area had to be reduced by the end of the war because of the substantial shift of the balance of power there in England's favor. This latter development was of particular importance in the eyes of the effective Zionist leadership in London.

From the point of view of the Zionist leaders, the Sykes-Picot agreement was untenable because of the way in which it handled Palestine. In the first place, it dismembered the country. In the second place, it placed too much of Palestine in French hands. The French sphere of influence over "Syria"—a somewhat nebulous concept at that time—extended well into the Galilee. Much of the remaining part of Palestine was to be placed under an international administration, with the exception of Haifa, which was to remain a British port. But the Zionist wanted neither a French nor an Anglo-French administration. They had often discussed among themselves the relative merits of British and French colonial administration, and they agreed that their cultural aspirations for a genuinely Jewish national community would do better under the British. The usual policy on the part of the French of imposing l'esprit français in their colonies was, in the Zionists' view, too overbearing.

One of the most remarkable developments to take place in favor of Zionist aspirations at this time was the awakening of sympathy in their favor on the part of Sir Mark Sykes himself, during the very period when his agreement with Picot was being considered for acceptance by the British government. By this time Zionist leaders had begun to make their influence felt in government circles. Herbert Samuel, later the first High Commissioner in Palestine, was sympathetic to Zionism, even though he was of the type of established Anglo-Jewish family that tended to resist and even oppose it in this period. A member of the Cabinet from the beginning of the war, Samuel was the man responsible for calling Mark Sykes' attention to the subject of Zionism. An established expert in Middle Eastern affairs who was at this time working with the Foreign Office in a semiofficial capacity, Sykes was struck by what seemed to him a confluence of historic import between Zionist and British aspirations. Although he was a Catholic, his imagination was caught up with the notion of Jewish regeneration to which the British Puritan spirit has always been so susceptible. Furthermore, on a practical level, he saw a Jewish Palestine under British sponsorship as a way of pushing back French influence in the Middle East; he was in no way committed to maintaining permanently the compromises he had himself made with M. Picot. In view of the way in which Zionist opinion was becoming pro-British, Sykes saw that the establishment of a moral commitment to a Jewish national home in Palestine on the part of the Entente would also be, in effect, an establishment of British hegemony there.

When this vision came to guide his policy, the fact that Sykes was a Catholic also stood him in good stead, since French Catholics could not easily claim that he did not have the best interest of the Holy Places at heart.

The year 1917 brought a remarkable confluence of events in the history of Zionism. By this time Sykes and Samuel were openly exercising their influence in the government in favor of Zionist aspirations in Palestine. The pro-Zionist influence of the *Manchester Guardian* also was important; this was a reflection of the favor Chaim Weizmann and his political aspirations had won in his home city during the years that he taught chemistry at the university there. A change of government at the end of 1916 had brought Lloyd George into the Prime Minister's chair, and placed the Foreign Office in the hands of Arthur James Balfour. Both of these men, quite unlike outgoing Prime Minister Herbert Asquith, were inclined to strong pro-Zionist sentiments. The Russian Revolution and America's entry into the war changed the balance of forces in the Allied war effort; these complementary events, each in its own way, gave a new significance to the Jewish communities of those countries, the two largest in the world. On the one hand, the British government wanted to reinforce American Jewish opinion in favor of the Allied cause; on the other hand, the British sought to persuade Jewish opinion in Russia to favor their country's remaining in the war. (The inflated and somewhat mystical notion of Jewish power in the world that is manifested here is another revelation of the anti-Semitic under- tones that often underlay the British Gentile's favorable approach to Zionism.) A pro-Zionist statement was widely thought to be the best way to realize these aims. In the Middle East itself, British forces seized the initiative in Palestine in 1917, and they had captured that entire region by the end of the year. Even by the fall, British troops in Palestine had already in effect annulled the Sykes-Picot agreement. But the British government sought to give a moral basis to the claim to Palestine.

Chaim Weizmann, in the course of more than twenty years of life in England, had done a great deal to impress the men who were now holding power with his personality and beliefs. He had first met Balfour as far back as 1905, less than a year after his arrival in the country. Balfour, who was then Prime Minister, and who had held a seat for Manchester since 1885, was always interested in maintaining good relations with the large Jewish community in that city. His first conversation with Weizmann, who was already a young man of some importance in Zionist affairs, took place briefly at the end of a political meeting. But in December of 1905, after Balfour had resigned from the Prime Ministry and was contesting his seat in a new election, they held a longer conversation. Balfour was interested in sounding out Zionist opinion, since Jewish matters loomed large in that year's election: earlier that same year Balfour had signed the Aliens Act, which severely curtailed Jewish immigration into Britain. In the course of an hour's conversation Weizmann succeeded in convincing Balfour that the Zionists had been right in not accepting the Uganda offer (Balfour himself had been Prime Minister when the offer was made). The young man made an impression upon Balfour that the latter never forgot.

Years later, during the course of the war, Weizmann came to the attention of Lloyd George while the latter was still Minister of Munitions. A new and cheap way of producing acetone, a necessary and rare component for explosives, was being sought by the British government at that time. It became known that the chemist Chaim Weizmann had been able to produce it in small quantities in his laboratory through his work on fermentation processes. Weizmann was called to work in Lloyd George's ministry in September, 1915, and in time he became the scientific director of a large acetone-producing program. This important work naturally brought his Zionist activities to the atttention of the government, and particularly of Lloyd George. In later years Lloyd George was fond of saying dramatically that "acetone converted me to Zionism." This has led to the widespread myth that the Balfour Declaration was simply the British government's reward for Weizmann's work in producing acetone. Such was clearly not the case, but there can be no doubt, on the other hand, that the acetone project was an important factor in inducing government sympathy for Zionist aims.

By the end of August, 1917, the British government was prepared to make a statement of policy concerning Zionist aspirations in Palestine. Between that time and November 2, the actual date of the Declaration, the delay in its promulgation was caused primarily by the opposition of certain prominent British Jews who feared that the recognition of a Jewish nationality in Palestine would constitute a threat to their own status as British subjects. Furthermore, the government itself came to feel a certain flagging of intentions at this time, since certain of the purposes envisioned for such a Declaration were now no longer valid: American Jews were now as firmly in favor of the Allied war effort as their country was, and Russian Jews no longer seemed a significant factor in deciding the outcome of revolutionary Russia's vacillating position on participation in the war. Some pause was also given by the emerging apparent contradiction with Zionist aims represented by the nascent Arab nationalism, which had also been fostered by the British. But the moral commitment had been made, and on November 2 a statement of British government policy on Palestine was delivered in the form of a letter from Balfour to Lord Rothschild. The decision to address the letter to Lord Rothschild instead of to one of the official Zionist leaders was the outcome of a slight difficulty in protocol. Chaim Weizmann was president of the English Zionist Federation, but he was not a member of the Zionist Executive, which was still the official governing body of the movement and was still in Berlin. The one member of the Executive who was in England was Nahum Sokolow, but he was not yet a British subject. Therefore, it was decided to send the letter to the most prominent of British Zionists holding no position in the movement. Unlike his French kinsman, Baron Edmond, the British Lord Rothschild had been a Zionist most of his life.

The Declaration as finally presented on November 2 was a somewhat modified version of earlier drafts. Without the introductory and closing amenities to Lord Rothschild, the complete final text ran as follows:

> His Majesty's Government view with favor the establishment in Palestine of a national home for the Jewish people, and will use their best endeavors to facilitate the achievement of this object, it being clearly understood that nothing shall be done which may prejudice the civil and religious rights of existing non-Jewish communities in Palestine, or the rights and political status enjoyed by the Jews in any other country.

The significant differences between this final text and the original draft that had been submitted by the Zionists in July were: (1) Palestine, in the original Zionist draft, was to be "reconstituted as the national home of the Jewish people," instead of its merely being the place *in* which there was to be a Jewish national home; (2) the government was, in the original draft, to use its best efforts to "secure" rather than to "facilitate" this object; and (3) there was no mention in the Zionist draft of the rights of non-Jewish communities in Palestine or of the rights of Jews in other countries. The changes were of course partly the work of a government naturally more cautious in its Zionist aims than the Zionists were, but this does not seem to be the whole story. Actually, the draft first written by Balfour himself in August, on the basis of the Zionist draft, was scarcely different from the latter at all. It was not until Lord Milner's draft, later that same month, that "Palestine . . . as the national home of the Jewish people" became "a home for the Jewish people in Palestine." But even in this latter, less favorable draft there is still no mention of the rights of Jews abroad and of non-Jews in Palestine. This introduction of the question of rights was clearly the work of the influence exerted by some prominent non-Zionist British Jews, such as Edwin Montagu, the newly appointed Secretary of State for India. The Zionists objected to the introduction of this passage into the text because such an explicit precaution carried with it the implication that Zionism somehow represented a danger to the rights of these other groups mentioned. It is therefore possible, though not proved, that, as Weizmann and other Zionist leaders later contended, Montagu and the British anti-Zionist Jews were also primarily responsible for the change in the text from "Palestine . . . as a national home" to "a national home" in Palestine, since this latter formulation assured Englishmen of the Jewish faith that their own national identity was not to be construed as somehow Palestinian. However it came about, this change was to provide the most significant loophole for the modification of Mandate policy in later years, as the assurance on the part of the British government about the aims represented by the Balfour Declaration rapidly declined. The change of wording from "secure" to "facilitate" was a foreshadowing of that decline of assurance.

Among the Zionist leaders there were some misgivings about these changes, but none of them could seriously entertain thoughts of further delaying the appearance of a document that represented a turning point in Jewish history. After the official conveyance of the letter to Lord Rothschild on Friday, November 2, the Declaration was made public, but not until the following Friday, November 9, so that the announcement could make its first appearance in that week's issue of the London *Jewish Chronicle*. Unfortunately, by that date the news of the Bolshevik Revolution was usurping the headlines of the day. The new Cyrus proclamation appeared in Jewish history almost unnoticed.

III

The Balfour Declaration made a commitment that was unprecedented for a Great Power. Conceived in an era when European colonization of outlying parts of the world had already been the rule for centuries, this commitment could of course pass at first for simply another imperial project; indeed, it has passed for this in the eyes of its enemies down to the present day. Unquestionably, it was formulated under the aegis of the colonial frame of mind; but it was also unlike any colonial project that had ever existed. Had the Jews of Palestine simply been British *colons*, they would have been far more zealously protected than they were by the British government under the Mandate. Unlike other *colons*, the Jews were a stateless people, who were settling in Palestine, not out of an aggregate of personal ambitions but in order to reconstitute their nationhood. This was hardly an aim that could readily be understood by the normal type of colonial administrator. The British statesmen who made the Balfour Declaration, although they were certainly able to find the practical grounds for justifying this project even in their own minds, were not mere practical men but visionaries, whose imaginations were captured by a religious or quasi-religious ideal. When the implementation of the policy proclaimed in the Declaration was eventually taken over by purely practical men, this document came to seem in their eyes nothing but a great mistake.

The foremost practical difficulty to come from the morally inspired Balfour Declaration was due to the fact that its intentions ran immediately into conflicting moral claims. At the very moment of this spectacular near-fulfillment of Jewish national aspirations, the Arab nationalist movement came to the fore to oppose it. Zionism may be said to be the last of the European nationalisms, and Israel (despite its Asian location) the last of the European nation-states to achieve independence. But since the Jews had lacked a single territory of continuous national settlement, such as all other European nationalities had, and since their own national traditions were embedded in a land that was located in Asia, Zionism had to make its appearance before non-Europeans as the last of the colonization movements. Arab nationalism, like all the other non-European nationalisms that have come into being in the past century, has made no distinctions between one form of European colonization and another, finding them all equally intolerable. To a Europe that had colonized undeveloped areas for centuries—creating a United States, for example, in the process—and that had despoiled Jews for a much longer period of time, there was considerable reason on grounds of conscience for granting an area of settlement to Jews, especially since Jewish settlers had already been in that area for some years before the European Powers arrived to claim influence over it. But the Arabs have always disclaimed any responsibility for European problems. They maintained from the start that, since they did not create European anti-Semitism, their conscience did not require them to allow a Jewish Palestine to be carved out of land they considered to be theirs.

The atmosphere for the Arab-Jewish conflict over Palestine was established during the First World War, when the British, seeking all available means of support for their efforts in the Middle East, threw out a net of policies so wide as to begin gathering in contradictions. With a notable lack of coordination, British policy makers cultivated both Zionism and a nascent Arab nationalism that was not necessarily prepared to grant Jewish hegemony in Palestine. It was as early as in the fall of 1915, two years before the Balfour Declaration, that the first major concession to Arab nationalism, and at the same time perhaps the most damaging blow to Zionist aspirations in that epoch—although the two things did not necessarily have to go together—was delivered by Sir Henry MacMahon, the British High Commissioner in Egypt, in a letter to the Sharif Hussein. At this time the groundwork was being established for the Arab revolt of the following year, which was to make such a great impact upon the imagination of the world through the exploits of Colonel T. E. Lawrence. It was the Sharif Hussein of Mecca and his sons, Abdullah, Feisal, Ali and Za'id, who were to provide the Arab leadership of the revolt and thereby further their claims to being the political leaders of the Arab nationalist movement. Hussein, who was taking a great risk in offering to help the British fight the Sultan, whose subject he nominally was, had made contact with the High Commissioner in the summer of 1915 in order to obtain preliminary assurances of British intentions concerning the Arabs.

In his first letter to MacMahon, Hussein requested a guarantee of "the independence of the Arab countries" from the Mediterranean to the Persian Gulf. MacMahon sent a politic reply, assuring Hussein that the British government sought such an outcome, but suggesting that the question of the boundaries of the Arab territories be discussed at some later date. This reply was not satisfactory to Hussein, who wanted an explicit statement as to boundaries. It was understood and accepted on both sides that the British government would maintain its foothold in Aden. The question was, what other exceptions did Great Britain propose to make? The question applied in particular to Syria, over which Britain was already engaged in a struggle for influence with France. Hussein waited more than a month for MacMahon's reply.

The British High Commissioner finally wrote back a generous acceptance of the frontiers sought by Hussein (who had excluded Aden to begin with), making only the following modification:

The districts of Mersin and Alexandretta, and portions of Syria lying to the west of the districts of Damascus, Homs, Hama and Aleppo, cannot be said to be purely Arab, and must on that account be excepted from the proposed delimitation.

Now, the expression "cannot be said to be purely Arab" would have been a most appropriate way of accounting for the exclusion of Palestine—a focus of European Christian as well as of Jewish aspiration and settlement—if Palestine had been intended as part of the area excluded by MacMahon's proviso. But if Palestine was meant to be excluded, as the British government always later claimed, then the geographical comprehension that went into the formulation of the proviso was rather fuzzy, to say the least. Palestine is indeed to the west of Damascus, Homs, Hama and Aleppo, but it is also considerably to the south of any of them. If MacMahon had really intended to exclude Palestine, why couldn't he also have mentioned Amman, or some place still farther south, as districts "to the west" of which lay the excepted portions of Syria? The British government was later to argue that the answer to this question was in the intention behind the use of the word "district." In the context this word was meant, according to the British, to have the force of the Turkish word "vilayet," which is the term for an administrative district. By this construction, "the district of Damascus" could be taken to mean the

vilayet of which that city was the administrative center, and which
extended all the way down to Aqaba. The proviso could thus be
understood as taking in all of Palestine, including the Negev. But if
this was indeed the intention, then the choice of words was most
inept, since the "district" of which Damascus was the capital was
properly called "the Vilayet of Syria." One might as well refer to
Massachusetts as "the district of Boston." It was a strange vagueness
of usage for a man who was an acknowledged expert in Middle
Eastern affairs.

The explanation for this lapse probably does not lie in the area of
specific intentions. On the contrary, the British government no doubt
still hoped to keep its intentions vague, as indicated by MacMahon's
earlier statements to Hussein. Many questions, after all, still remained open in 1915. First of all, how much of Syria would be
available to England by the end of the war, as against French claims
upon it, to dispose of between herself and the Arabs as she would see
fit? It is noteworthy that the area unambiguously designated in
MacMahon's proviso was entirely within a French sphere of influence
that was virtually uncontested from the European point of view, and
that did in fact become part of the French mandated territory at the
end of the war. This indicates that MacMahon sought at least to
exclude specifically what it was not in the power of the British to
guarantee in the first place. Outside of this necessary precaution, it
was really in the interest of British policy to be as vague as possible in
making guarantees to Hussein. How serious a phenomenon, after all,
was the proposed Arab revolt? This was not to be known until the
following year. Moreover, how seriously could one take Hussein's
claim to speak for the whole Arab people—if it was indeed one
people at all? Hussein had his rivals. Even in 1915 his vision of a
unified Arab Empire under his family's rule was clearly preposterous.
Why, then, should the British government have regarded promises
held out in the heat of wartime to this one man, whose political
authority was uncertain, as binding upon it in all its future dealings
with the Arabs? But in the sequel, even after all of Hussein's family
except Abdullah, who was scarcely more than a British puppet, had
disappeared from view, England was never allowed to forget the
MacMahon letter.

In this matter the British had done nothing worse than follow the
established practices of nineteenth-century European diplomacy.

These practices reached their height during the First World War, the history of which is rife with unfulfilled promises between nations. But the First World War was also a revolutionary era, in which the world of the nineteenth century began coming to an end. Each in its own way, Wilsonian idealism and the Russian Revolution brought an unprecedented atmosphere of moral considerations into international affairs. This atmosphere came to apply with harrowing force upon the British as they took up their prize in the Middle East. Throughout four years of one of the bloodiest wars in history, they had sat at conference tables with their wily French allies, staking claims and counterclaims in the Middle East, jockeying for position, making promises that could always be withdrawn as soon as the realities of power made them obsolete—in short, exercising the diplomatic prerogatives that were understood to pertain to all European nations, friend and foe alike. And in the moment of British victory, the legacy of it all was a cry of moral outrage from two nations which had not been at the bargaining table at all, and which, in fact, had not even existed as political entities during the time of negotiations.

But, aside from having a common recourse to moral arguments, the claims made by these two nations were quite different in character and in the emotional responses they evoked. The Arabs presented the face of a simple and chivalrous people who had been defiled by European subtleties. This had particular appeal to a certain type of mind that combined the British sense of fair play with a stolid lack of imagination. In this outlook, the Jews were seen not as a nationality seeking its sole piece of sovereign territory in a small corner of the vast region that the Arabs were otherwise quite free to claim as their own but as the hard bargainers of the market place, always ready to take advantage of the less sophisticated. Even the Balfour Declaration could be seen in this light. What had the wily Jews done now to win the support of a tiny handful of men in the highest circles of power? In any case, the Jewish claim was the one that was far more difficult to understand or to sympathize with, because it was revisionist. The Arabs were the people who had long been settled there, and the Jews were now being pushed upon them: this was the simplest view of the matter.

In this connection it was perhaps not entirely to the advantage of the Jews that they were far better versed than the Arabs in the methods of traditional European diplomacy. Throughout the entire

Mandate period, the Arabs adopted a stance of unrelenting moral outrage over the Palestine question. Moral absolutism in political matters is hardly possible for liberal democracies, but for this reason it often gives rise to an outburst of guilty admiration on the part of the citizens of a liberal democracy when they are confronted with it. One's conscience can far more easily deal with a diplomat. In the end, the Jews, too, were to have recourse to moral outrage, once they had suffered one of the greatest disasters in human history. But until then, precisely because their claim was more problematical than that of the Arabs, there was no course for them to follow other than to practice diplomacy.

For this task the Zionists had a master. Chaim Weizmann, who was to be the predominant figure in the Zionist movement for as long as diplomacy was the necessary course to follow, and who was to be swept aside when this course began to lose its exclusive validity, has been described by the British historian Sir Charles Webster as one of the greatest diplomatists of his time. Weizmann's scientific background stood him in good stead for this work. As a chemist, he knew that political configurations, like the configurations of nature, are in a constant state of flux. For him diplomatic agreements were at best like hypotheses, perhaps unvarying in their broad outlines but always subject to modification with changes of the external conditions within which they were formulated. This understanding was the source of his success in bringing about the Balfour Declaration in the first place. Some of the more ardent proponents of a traditional "political" Zionism had sought from the British government an explicit guarantee of a Jewish state. But the ambiguity of the term "national home" in the Balfour Declaration was intended precisely for the purpose of deferring the more difficult question of statehood until some later date. For Weizmann, this was a satisfactory arrangement for the time being. The question of statehood would arise organically in time, once the "practical" Zionist task of building and rooting an authentic Jewish national community in Palestine had been performed. A patient man, Weizmann was even prepared to consider this development as not likely to take place within his own lifetime.

Weizmann also understood that, now that the framework for the Jewish national home had been established, it was one of the most important tasks of Zionism to find a way of living peacefully and cooperatively with the Arabs. There can be no doubt that many of the Zionists, both Jewish and Gentile, pictured Palestine in the halcyon era prior to 1917 as scarcely more than a desert, waiting to be populated. It was not until the war itself that the presence of a rooted population there began to make an impression upon the European mind. For many Englishmen of the type that served in the British administrations in Palestine after the war, the fact that there was such a population there immediately disqualified the claims of the colonizers (since the colonizers were not British). It was soon forgotten that the greater part of Palestine had, in fact, been wasteland before the Zionist settlers came. During the years of the Mandate it was a frequent complaint on the part of the Arabs to the Administration that the Jews were taking over the most fertile parts of Palestine; but the truth was that many of these fertile places had been created out of swamp and arid land by the Jewish settlers. For many of the early Zionist pioneers it was a very important fact for their conscience that only *parts* of Palestine were occupied by the indigenous Arab populations. Their vision was the creation of an entire Jewish community in the spatial interstices of the country. From the purely economic standpoint, the Palestine Arabs were bound to benefit from such a development. The problem was not the economic one, however, but the spiritual one of reconciling Arab nationalism to Zionist aspirations in Palestine.

In principle, such a reconciliation was never impossible. Chaim Weizmann was able to obtain, in January, 1919, a written agreement in principle to Zionist aims from Hussein's son, the Amir Feisal. Arab nationalism was then and still is a broad ideal, spread through a vast region and a multiplicity of cultures, which has yet to attain the clear political definition that is characteristic of almost any European nationalism, including Zionism. As with most nationalist movements in their early stages, Arab nationalism prior to the Second World War was primarily the ideal of a small elite, and it scarcely reached the great peasant majority. Peasant traditions of attachment to a specific locale are somewhat different from the nationalist ideal of loyalty to an abstract political and cultural entity, and though they are amenable to the latter, they become so only in the period when technological change begins uprooting the peasant spiritually and physically. Palestine did not become a distinct and separate political entity in the Middle East until Zionist aspirations and British administration made it so. Until then, the peasant majority in Palestine had no sources of political identification larger than their own villages, and these were not being threatened by Zionism. The Arab nationalist elite, on the other hand, had a world for the realization of their aspirations which was vast enough even without Palestine. To be sure, their political claims upon Palestine had some validity, but these claims came to seem morally equal to the Zionist ones only when the myth arose that the Palestine Arab population was somehow a distinct and separate political entity in the general Arab world, which needed its own sovereign state. The British Mandatory Administration allowed itself increasingly to be swept up by this myth. Organized Arab opposition to Jewish settlement in Palestine was at first only the work of a few ambitious and powerful leaders and their hirelings. Only subsequently did the mood of opposition begin to spread and take on a more popular character. This latter development might have been prevented by an administration able to maintain control, in the first place, over abuses and provocations committed by Jews as well as Arabs and, in the second place, over the general political development of Palestine. But this could only have been done within the framework of a firmly defined commitment and policy for that country, which is precisely what the British lacked.

From 1917 onward, British policy in Palestine increasingly vacillated between two utterly irreconcilable aims. One aim was the Jewish "national home" in Palestine. Ultimately, this could only mean a politically autonomous or sovereign territory containing a Jewish majority. A permanent Jewish minority in Palestine would have been in basically the same situation as a Jewish minority anywhere else in the world, and in such a case the "national home" idea would have had no meaning. The other aim was to accord fulfillment to separate Arab nationalist aspirations in Palestine; in other words, to foster the development of a hitherto nonexistent Palestinian Arab nation. But such an incipient national community could not possibly have consented to being turned into a minority. Therefore, the Palestinian Arab leaders were irreconcilably opposed to unlimited Jewish immigration, which was, on the other hand, the very lifeblood of Zionist hopes. The vitality and central importance to the Zionist program of Jewish immigration to Palestine were not fully appreciated by the British at the outset. The widespread British assumption, shared by Sir Herbert Samuel, who served as the first High Commissioner in Palestine, was that Jewish settlement there had been the work of an isolated few idealists, whose numbers would not be appreciably added to in the years to come. From this point of view, the Balfour Declaration was simply a guarantee of protection to the Jewish community already existing in Palestine. In the eyes of most of the British administrators, the purpose of the Mandate was to create self-governing institutions as soon as possible in Palestine on the basis of the existing population distribution there. Jewish immigration was a continual challenge to this conception.

The British policy of reconciling the two nationalisms in Palestine, therefore, inevitably had recourse to increasing restrictions upon Jewish immigration (a practice irreconcilable with the Jewish nationalism). The Arab riots of 1920 and 1921 led to a temporary ban on Jewish immigration, but the long-range method of restriction used at this time took the form of a reduction in the size of the territory in which Zionist settlement was permitted in the first place. In the 1922 White Paper, drawn up under the direction of then Colonial Secretary Winston Churchill, Transjordan was definitely excluded from the area designated by the Balfour Declaration. It was separated from the Palestine Administration and established as an Amirate under Hussein's eldest son, Abdullah, who subsequently became king of the independent Jordanian state. Although parts of Biblical Palestine had extended into Transjordan, this excision was not vehemently opposed by many Zionists. Only one small area of Zionist settlement had been established east of the Jordan, around the southern rim of Lake Tiberias, and this was carefully excluded from the Transjordanian territory designated by the White Paper. From the Zionist point of view, the 1922 White Paper was a reasonable compromise with reality. By setting limits to Zionist territorial aspirations, the area of potential conflict between Jew and Arab was reduced to those places where the Jews were already established. It was hoped that such a clear delimitation would placate Arab feelings. Otherwise, the White Paper gave robust support to the Balfour Declaration with its statement that the Jewish people "is in Palestine as of right and not on sufferance." This phrase redounded with the personality of Winston Churchill, who remained favorably disposed toward Zionism all his life.

But the spirit of this statement gradually disappeared from British

policy in the ensuing years. The turning point came after the Arab
riots of 1929. Tension between Jews and Arabs had grown considerably throughout the preceding year, centering upon a controversy
over the Wailing Wall. This most sacred of Jewish shrines, the sole
remaining fragment of the Jewish Temple destroyed by the Romans,
stands on the edge of an area sacred to the Muslims as well, since the
Dome of the Rock, an Islamic holy place, was built upon the ruins of
the Temple. For both physical and symbolic reasons, this area was a
natural source of tension. When, on the Yom Kippur of 1928, Jewish
worshipers at the Wailing Wall set up a screen to serve as the
traditional partition between men and women at prayer, Muslims
protested that this was an unlawful obstruction of the area in front of
the Wall, and the British police removed it. In the following months,
Muslim religious leaders threatened to reroute a thoroughfare onto
the pavement in front of the Wailing Wall. Even nonreligious
Zionists protested at this provocation. Demonstrations were held in
front of the Wall and tension mounted. Then, in August of 1929, a
Jewish boy entered the garden of an Arab's home in Jerusalem to
retrieve a football he had kicked there. A brawl ensued, and the boy
was stabbed to death. There were Zionist demonstrations at the boy's
funeral. A few days later large numbers of Arabs arrived in Jerusalem
carrying arms. The ensuing riots lasted several days and spread from
Jerusalem to other parts of the country. When the trouble had
ended, 133 Jews were dead and 339 wounded, all at the hands of
Arab rioters. A total of 116 Arabs were killed and 232 were wounded
by the British police in their efforts to quell the rioters.[4]

Two investigating commissions were sent to Palestine by the
British government, and both concluded that unrestricted Jewish
immigration was the chief provocation of Arab unrest. In response to
their recommendations, the White Paper of 1930—drawn up under
the aegis of the Colonial Secretary for the Labour government, Lord
Passfield, the former Sidney Webb—suggested, in cautious language,
the restriction of Jewish immigration. But Zionist protest in London
was so strong that Prime Minister MacDonald was prevailed upon to
publish a clarification of the White Paper policy which was, in effect,
a repudiation of it. The issue thus hung fire a few more years.

In April, 1936, a series of isolated incidents culminated in rioting
between Jews and Arabs even more severe than in 1929. This began a

[4] Christopher Sykes, *Crossroads to Israel* (London, 1965), p. 138.

period of constant Arab attacks which lasted until the outbreak of
the Second World War. In response to the 1936 riots, the British
government sent another investigating committee, the Peel Commission, which performed the most intense and enlightened survey of
any of the British commissions of inquiry thus far. Like its predecessors, the Peel Commission suggested in its report that Jewish
immigration might have to be curtailed, at least for the time being,
but the investigators appreciated the moral questionableness of such
a policy at a time when Jewish suffering was mounting in Europe. It
was precisely the threat of Nazi persecution that had caused the
sudden leap in immigration responsible for the new outburst of
tension. As a result of the riots, the immigration quota for 1936 was
cut to 30,000, half of what it had been the previous year. The
situation in Palestine had deteriorated to such a point by this time
that the Peel Commission could foresee only one viable alternative to
a severe curtailment of Jewish immigration: the partition of Palestine.

The Peel Commission's recommendation of partition was the first
of a long series of partition proposals through the ensuing years,
which culminated in the United Nations scheme in 1947. It was also
the first official and explicit recommendation for a Jewish state to be
made by the British. Sovereign in their own territory, the Jews would
at least be able under this scheme to pursue their policies of
immigration and economic self-improvement without any outside
interference. But the territory of the Jewish state proposed by the
Peel Commission was to be quite small, and was to be divided by a
corridor extending from Jerusalem to the sea, an area designated to
remain under a permanent mandate. The prospect of independence
at last drew Chaim Weizmann to the partition idea at first sight, but
he rapidly cooled toward it as he saw its limitations. The Arabs were
even more adamant in their opposition to it. For one thing, the
proposals, if implemented, would have necessitated a transfer of
populations—Arabs from the Jewish state, Jews from the Arab
state—which would unquestionably have affected the Arabs more
severely than the Jews. But, above all, the Arabs simply remained
unwilling to concede even a square inch of Palestine as sovereign
Jewish territory. In other words, by 1937 the Arab-Jewish conflict in
Palestine had reached a point at which it could no longer be resolved
in any other way than by force. The Mandate refused to use force

for any other purpose than that of maintaining the status quo. As a result, no course remained open but an armed contest between the Jews and the Arabs in Palestine. But this outcome was deferred for several years by the outbreak of the Second World War.

By 1939 the partition scheme had died by default, but the need to placate Palestine was felt more urgently than ever by the British government. A war was in the offing and London could not afford to wear out its energies over a quarrel between small competing nationalities in the Middle East. Chamberlain had agreed to the dismemberment of Czechoslovakia out of such considerations; Palestine was just as much a nuisance for him, especially since it stood to become a sensitive strategic area during the war. In formulating the remedy for its Palestine headache, the British government took the line of least resistance. The conditions of the brewing conflict with Hitler, unlike those of the war that broke out in 1914, left the Jews no choice but to be on the Allied side. It was Arab support that had to be bargained for. The British government therefore settled upon a formula that seemed on the surface to be a balanced compromise between Zionist and Arab claims, but which, in effect, was a complete surrender to the Arabs. The White Paper issued on May 17, 1939, proclaimed that the purpose of the Mandate was to create neither a Jewish nor an Arab state, but a binational one, based on the presently existing population balance plus another 75,000 Jews. The additional Jewish immigrants were to be admitted at the rate of 15,000 a year for the next five years, after which immigration would cease entirely. The "binational" state thus provided for would, in effect, have been an Arab state with a Jewish minority. As a long-range policy, it threatened the downfall of Zionist hopes. As a short-range policy, it was more disastrous still, for this severe restriction upon entry into Palestine came at the very moment when Europe was about to be turned into an execution ground for the Jewish people. But the Chamberlain government was right in one respect; as it anticipated, there was nothing for the Jews to do for the moment but join the British in the fight against the common enemy. David Ben-Gurion summed up the double and conflicting task that the Zionists had to face in that tragic moment: "We shall fight the White Paper as if there were no war, and the war as if there were no White Paper."

CHAPTER 4

Catastrophe and Resurrection

I

THE world of nineteenth-century Europe came to a final end in the death factory at Auschwitz. The nineteenth had been the German century to a large extent. A race of sturdy, hard-working burghers, looking out through their shop windows at the cobblestoned streets of decent provincial towns like Bergen-Belsen and Dachau, had created a civilization that commanded the imagination of Europe. It was a civilization that had discovered in full the possibilities of sober and pious immersion in monumental toil as a way of shutting out the sound of howling goblins in the forest. It began with Immanuel Kant proclaiming the world external to man's spirit to be unknowable, and characterizing virtue as the performance of painful acts of duty, or with Faust setting aside his magic potions to build a dam, and it ended with the clank of an industrial-age Walpurgis-nacht, made up of freight cars packed with human cargoes heading for doom, trucks carrying portable gas chambers, great compounds enclosed by electrified barbed wire, the massive steel doors of ovens roasting human flesh, shower rooms spraying poison gas and soap dishes filled with the precipitate of ravaged existences.

The nineteenth century had been founded upon a conception of human decency organized through the state. Although the liberal ideal was always qualified by the fact that some people in any given society held power at the expense of others, the more predatory possibilities of this relationship were held in check by the laws and customs of those Western states which came to see that the fullest possible reconciliation of interests within the society not only served ideals that were the legacy of Christianity but also provided the best climate for the organization of state power. In the course of the nineteenth century the state learned not only to protect its citizens from one another but also even to begin providing some of the minimum needs of a decent existence to those citizens who would not otherwise have been able to obtain them. For the most part, the old *omnium bellum contra omnes* was relegated to the realm of international relations, and man's destructive instincts were reserved for the battlefield. In the Western world prior to the two World Wars, martial honor was a virtue organized into a rather civilized military arrangement. At least once in every generation, strong young men, eager to demonstrate their courage and physical prowess, kissed their wives, fiancées and mothers, left them tearfully standing in doorways, and went off to some distant field of battle. From then on, whatever the men did to one another, it was between themselves. If they survived, they did so with a knowledge that they could keep to themselves, that did not have to intervene upon the sweet peacefulness of the living rooms to which they returned. If they died in battle, the impact of this terrible event was to some extent absorbed by the vast and stirring ritual of honor within which it had become incorporated even before it took place.

But in nazi-occupied Europe, such conceptions of honor and the family were swept away. Here is a conversation which took place between a brother and a sister in one of the nazi death camps during the war:

"You know, Eva, I saw Mother . . ."

"Mother?" Eva began to tremble and was afraid to ask any more.

"A shipment came from Plaszow. Straight to the gas chamber. I was there, loading the chamber. You know how I try not to look at them. Then, suddenly I heard a cry and sobs, 'My little boy!' I raised my eyes and my heart stopped. She hadn't changed. Meanwhile, we were holding things up, the Kapo was screaming at me, and the S.S. men were coming towards us.

" 'Mother, I'm doing my job now,' I told her. 'This is very responsible work, and they're very strict here. Go take a shower now and after work I'll come and get you. You'll stay with Eva. She's here too. You'll be all right with us.'

"She looked at me with love in her eyes, you remember how she used
to be. 'You've grown so tall and strong, my little boy,' she said, and
stroked my hair. And then she went . . ."[1]

In the concentrationary universe, which is placed under the supervision of men who murder upon a whim, and whose murderous
whims have the sanction of the state, the very framework in which
such a conception as "honor" is established no longer exists. Liberalism broke the resistance of communal and institutional traditions and
made men into the grateful servants of the state. When the state
itself became the betrayer, men were left with little or no moral
recourse against it. Honor was turned into a sham by a crushing and
omnipresent malevolence. The question has often been asked why
thousands of victims, watched over by only a few dozen guards, did
not more often leap out and overwhelm their persecutors, but almost
always marched docilely to their death. But what resources of heroism is a man to call upon marching in such a line, his pregnant wife
in front of him, his aged grandmother behind him, naked, all of
them naked? Death is no longer the worst thing that can happen at
this point; the foundations of the will have been destroyed. And yet
there were times when the will to resist was summoned up all the
same.

The Nazis entered Warsaw on September 9, 1939. The disabilities
that they had long been imposing upon the Jews of Germany were
now brought down with still greater force upon the *Ostjuden* of
Poland, considered by the Nazis to be a species even more inferior
than the German kind. All over German-occupied Poland, Jews were
made to wear an identifying armband and were gradually deprived of
their means. Jewish-owned businesses were turned over to "Aryans,"
although sometimes the displaced proprietor was given the "privilege," at least for a while, of being employed in the enterprise he had
founded. Increasing indignities were imposed. A Jew had to step off
the sidewalk when a German walked by, and, eventually, was expected to salute him. The penalty for not saluting might be a
beating, or perhaps even a sudden and humiliating death. The
German soldiers manifested a genius for sadistic experimentation
upon their victims. Frequently Jews were rounded up in the streets

[1] Alexander Donat, *The Holocaust Kingdom* (New York, 1965), pp. 307–308.

and taken away on forced labor details, sometimes never to return. But the mass extermination of the Jews had not yet begun in the first year of the war.

The Ghetto was created in Warsaw in October, 1940. Jews had gradually been uprooted from their homes and pushed into the part of Warsaw in which the greatest concentration of Jews had lived in the first place. The overcrowding in this area became immense, and typhus grew rampant. Walls began going up around the quarter in September, under the pretext of quarantine. Then, on October 16, a decree was published, giving two weeks for all the Christians within the quarantine area to move out, and for all Jews still living outside of it to move in. On November 15 the openings in the Warsaw Ghetto wall were sealed off, with the exception of a few guarded points through which only carriers of permits could pass. From that moment the Warsaw Ghetto became a world by itself. At first it contained roughly 350,00 Jews, but this number swelled to more than 400,000 by the end of 1940, as deportees from other parts of Poland were placed within it; all this within an area that had normally housed about 150,000 persons. Several families would live in a single apartment. Life went on—there were even makeshift schools and theaters in the Ghetto—but death from disease and starvation was rampant. A regular work gang combed the streets daily to pick up bodies and cart them by wheelbarrow to the cemetery. But a few opportunists—smugglers, collaborators, and other forms of self-seekers—managed to make life virtually pleasant for themselves. There were a few cabarets for them, prohibitively expensive to the starving majority, in which they could drink all night; getting up to go home only in the early hours of the morning, they would make their way cautiously over the bodies lying in the streets.

The administration of the Ghetto was placed entirely in Jewish hands. The official Ghetto government was the *Judenrat* (Jewish Council), and there was even a Jewish police force. This became the standard administrative structure in every one of the ghettos created by the Nazis in Eastern Europe. These Jewish Councils and police forces rarely were made up of men of good character, and there were many abuses. But for the most part ordinary Jews were relieved at seeing the brutality of nazi governors replaced by the mere venality of Jewish ones. For the time being, the everyday scenes of wanton sadism in the streets were a thing of the past. Some of this new breed of Jewish administrators—men such as Adam Czerniakow, the president of the Warsaw *Judenrat*—believed sincerely that they were performing a mission to alleviate the sufferings of their people. From the standpoint of the fleeting moment, this was even true: they were more humane than the Gestapo. But such judgments of value were based upon a frame of reference derived from the normal world of laws and stable virtues. The nazi universe, unlike that stable world, was a headlong dialectic of extinction; all men who served it, whatever their motives, ultimately became executioners. When the Nazis began demanding of the *Judenraete* that they fill regular quotas of Jews for deportation (it gradually dawned upon all the victims that this meant the death camps), many of the Jewish administrators still believed they could salvage some good from the mouth of disaster by carefully selecting only those least eligible for survival. The virtuous intentions of mediocre men thus became the intermediaries for an almighty malevolence. When Adam Czerniakow was first called upon to make such a selection in July, 1942, he saw with terrifying clarity where the logic of his own position was bringing him, and he shot himself.

It was in the summer of 1941, shortly after the German invasion of Russia, that Hitler had arrived at the decision to move beyond mere persecution and begin the "Final Solution" to the Jewish Question—the extermination of all European Jewry. This plan was first implemented in Russia, by special squads, called *Einsatzgruppen*, who came immediately behind the advancing German armies. They went from town to town rounding up as many Jews as they could find, brought them to pits dug outside the cities (often these were dug by the victims themselves), and shot them down inside what became huge mass graves. The victims, men, women and children together, were usually first made to strip naked; then they waited in line for their turn to be shot. The executioner at one of these scenes was described thus by the Nuremberg Trials witness, Hermann Friedrich Graebe: "He was an SS man, who sat at the edge of the narrow end of the pit, his feet dangling into the pit. He had a tommy gun on his knees and was smoking a cigarette." Before him in the pit lay some 1,000 bodies piled onto one another, some of them still writhing, covered with blood. The nazi leaders began to fear that such methods were turning their ordinary soldiers into sadists, and so they sought more "humane" methods of extermination.

Gassing had originally been used for another aspect of the black hygiene of nazism: to eliminate congenital idiots and other forms of physically defective types. It was first used upon Jews in mobile gassing vans transported by the *Einsatzgruppen*. The victims were loaded into airtight chambers in the backs of trucks, and the exhaust was turned on. But by the end of 1941 the more systematic techniques of the death camp had begun to evolve, particularly at the Chelmno and Auschwitz camps, both in Poland. Here, a quicker and "cleaner" method of extermination was developed through the use of a gas called Zyklon-B, which had originally been used as an insecticide. The gas chambers in these camps were disguised as shower rooms; the victims were led into them with instructions to wash themselves, but out of the shower heads came gas, not water. Once this assembly-line method of extermination had been developed, the chief technical problem for its administrators became that of disposal of the bodies. At first they were simply piled into huge pits (after such valuable commodities as gold teeth and hair had been removed from them) and cremated. This task was performed by the *Sonderkommando*—special work units selected from among the physically more sturdy of the Jews themselves. But the turnover of victims—at Auschwitz, in mid-1944, it reached as high as several hundred thousand a month—made this method too unwieldy. Ovens were built within the very buildings in which the gas chambers were located. In this way the entire extermination process was organized to take place under a single roof. Huge chimneys gave off their dire smoke, smearing the heavens with the abominable stink of the crematoria.

It was on July 22, 1942, that the mass deportations from the Warsaw Ghetto began. By this time the Nazis had begun operating the death camp of Treblinka, only a short distance northeast of Warsaw, and directly connected with it by rail. The death trains were able to make the round trip in a matter of hours. The selections of those to be deported were made on the street, in the *Umschlagplatz* (a word which simply means "transfer point," but which came to ring with connotations of doom for the Jews of Warsaw), an open square by the railroad siding at the northern end of the Ghetto. Every day for more than two months the Jewish police stormed into buildings and herded every Jew they could find—or wanted to find—out into the streets and toward the *Umschlagplatz*, until they had filled the quota for the day. The line of candidates for the day's selection gathered in the square, where Gestapo men decided in a moment's scrutiny who would be put onto the trains and who was physically fit enough to remain for work details in Warsaw. As they waited their turn, bent, hungry men straightened their backs and forced their faces into grotesque expressions of well-being; women, wearing their best available dresses, pressed down unresponsive hairs and primped themselves with whatever cosmetics they possessed. Parents carrying small children faced certain doom. Some men tried to conceal their infants in their luggage; occasionally a mother pretended not to know the child weeping by her side. More often, healthy young women who otherwise stood a chance of being spared preferred to die with their infants. In this way more than 300,000 persons were deported from the Ghetto. The roughly 40,000 who remained by the end of 1942, for the most part the youngest and the hardiest survivors of a man-made Darwinian jungle, were left for possible forced labor, and for death at some future date. The area of the Ghetto was greatly reduced in size; from the administrative point of view, it was now considered to be a sort of urban concentration camp.

The edge of any Jewish inclinations toward armed resistance had been dulled until this moment by two principal factors. The first was the feeling, which died only slowly, that Jewish resistance was to be construed as part of the general Polish resistance movement. This view had particular strength among the members of the Bund, whose traditional capacity for revolutionary organization made them one of the natural foundation stones of a resistance movement, but whose philosophical predisposition to view Jewish suffering as part of the plight of oppressed men in general led them to construe the Jewish struggle with the Nazis as a not especially distinct part of the general antifascist cause. But the Poles of Aryan Warsaw on the other side of the Ghetto walls had, on the whole, shown indifference to the fate of their fellow citizens within the walls of the Ghetto. Many heroic efforts were made to conceal Jews—and especially Jewish children— who had got to the Aryan side, but little had been done to forestall the doom of the Ghetto itself. As the realization of this fact heightened in the twilight of the *Umschlagplatz*, the last vestiges of Jewish misgivings at forming into a separate Ghetto resistance movement were destroyed. The second factor holding up organized Jewish resistance had been, of course, the continuing existence of anything like family life, with elderly men and women and small children still present to entangle the emotions and the wills of those who were young, strong and inclined to fight. But, after the great mass deportations, this was no longer the case. By October, 1942, the Warsaw Ghetto had been reduced to a bivouac. In that month the Coordinating Committee of the Jewish Resistance Movement was formed.

Even then, there was at first some dispute over the question as to whether Ghetto resistance should be coordinated with resistance activity on the Aryan side. But this question was put to rest on January 18, 1943, when the SS entered the Ghetto in an attempt to hold a new roundup for deportation. The Jewish Fighting Organization met them with armed resistance, and some twenty Germans were killed in the ensuing battle. Stunned by this unprecedented reception, the Germans quickly retreated. There was elation in the Ghetto as the sense of the dignity of being able to fight back spread among its inhabitants. In the following weeks the administrative authority of the *Judenrat* gradually yielded to that of the Jewish Fighting Organization. This organization consisted mainly of very young men and women—its commander in chief, Mordechai Anilewitz, was twenty-four years old—who had been weaned and toughened in the primeval world of the Ghetto streets and alleyways. They had been schooled in improvisation, a talent they needed in order to fight with the few weapons that had been smuggled in and preserved in Ghetto hiding places. Their sense of solidarity and their orientation toward revolutionary activity and the development of physical prowess were furthered by the fact that they were, for the most part, members either of the Bund or of the various Zionist youth organizations. These two opposing trends in the modern revolutionary spirit of Eastern European Jewry had thus found common ground at last, in a situation redolent with the memory of Eleazer ben Yair's band on top of Masada.

For that the lives of the Ghetto resistance fighters were as doomed as those of the Zealots of Masada was virtually certain. On April 18, 1943, SS General Jurgen von Stroop arrived in Warsaw carrying a personal order from Himmler that the Ghetto be destroyed. The next day the Germans entered the Ghetto and began their slow advance, burning every building they reached and leveling it to the ground. They found themselves confronted by the fierce resistance of men and women who were now fighting not for their lives—this was out of the question—but to assert their dignity in the eyes of heaven, or history, or their own proud spirits. "The dream of my life came true," wrote Mordechai Anilewitz on April 23 to one of the Jewish resistance leaders stationed on the Aryan side. "I was fortunate enough to witness Jewish defense in the Ghetto in all its greatness and glory." He died fighting a few days later. By May 16 the entire Ghetto was in flames, and some 2,000 survivors presented themselves to the Germans as prisoners. The few surviving members of the Jewish Fighting Organization managed to escape, mainly through the sewers, and were hidden in the forests. "And I only am escaped alone to tell thee."

The final act of the Holocaust took place in Hungary. Until March, 1944, Hungary had been a nonbelligerent state aligned with the Axis Powers. The Jews of that country, although they suffered disabilities imposed upon them by laws passed by the Hungarian government to satisfy its German suzerains, lived in an island of safety, in which their lives could seem relatively privileged as compared with those of their brethren in Europe all around them. They still owned some property, and their social and economic situation had become rather stable by the beginning of 1944. When the German armies finally occupied Hungary in March of that year, some 750,000 Jews were residing there.

The deportations were begun on May 15. By this time the German machine of human annihilation had reached a peak of efficiency. With the relentlessness of an assembly line, 380,000 Jews were deported from Hungary in a little more than six weeks. Most of these were sent directly to Auschwitz, where 250,000 of them were exterminated, usually sent straight from the trains to the gas chambers. But on June 27, succumbing to pressure from the Allied governments, Admiral Horthy managed to call a provisional halt to the deportations.

At this time one of the strangest episodes in the history of the Holocaust was unfolding. Since January, 1943, a secret Jewish organization in Budapest, the *Va'ad Ezra v'Hatzala* (Aid and Rescue Committee), had been helping Jewish refugees from the surrounding German-occupied countries to escape to safety. It was a Zionist organization, whose principal work consisted in securing entrance certificates to Palestine (on the quota of 15,000 immigrants a year that was still being enforced by the Palestine Administration) for the refugees in its charge. For a time its members hoped also to form a full-fledged resistance organization, and to aid in this project three Palestinian Jews of Hungarian origin, one of them a young woman, were parachuted into Croatia on April 14, 1944. The three managed to cross the border into Hungary, but they were captured by the Germans in Budapest, and two of them, including the woman, Hannah Szenes, were eventually executed. From then on, the Va'ad Ezra v'Hatzala concentrated solely upon its rescue operations. In April, 1944, two of the organization's leaders, Rudolph Kastner and Joel Brand, made contact with the SS officer, Dieter Wisliceny, who was Adolf Eichmann's assistant in the Jewish operation in Hungary. It turned out that Wisliceny could be bought. The bargain made was that, for a payment of about $1.6 million to Wisliceny, the rescue committee would be permitted to select 1,600 Jews who could live. The money was raised, the selection was made, and the 1,600 were eventually shipped westward to Bergen-Belsen instead of to Auschwitz. From there, a number of them finally reached Switzerland in December of 1944.

The success of this deal led the Germans to aim for a larger bargain, which they presented on May 8, one week before the start of the mass deportations. Eichmann himself appeared this time and, in a talk with Joel Brand, offered to spare a million Jewish lives in exchange for 10,000 trucks from the Allies. The trucks were to be stocked with such supplies as coffee and soap. No weapons were asked for, and it was promised that the trucks would be used solely on the Eastern Front. The rescue committee, caught up in this calculus of survival, had reason to believe that the German offer was sincere. Emotionally, they found themselves in no position to question their own right to become arbiters of human destiny. On May 17, Joel Brand, accompanied by a man named Grosz, left for Istanbul, with the intention of making contact with the Jewish Agency there and of using its good offices to persuade the Allies at least to negotiate the German offer. But in Istanbul he was taken prisoner by the British, brought to Cairo, and held in custody there for several months. In October he was released in Jerusalem, where he then spent the remainder of the war at the doors of the Jewish Agency and other organizations, seeking a hearing for his scheme. A deeply sincere man, Joel Brand never ceased to believe that a million Jewish lives might have been spared had he been heeded. Rudolph Kastner, who had remained behind in Budapest until the end of the war, emerged from this strange episode more compromised than Brand in the eyes of many. Years after the war Kastner, who, like Brand, had settled in Israel, brought suit for libel against an Israeli journalist who had accused him of collaboration with the SS. In March, 1957, while the case was under appeal to the Israel Supreme Court, Kastner was murdered in the street. He was subsequently exonerated.

On November 26, 1944, Heinrich Himmler ordered that the "Final Solution" be stopped. As the Russian armies pushed forward into East Central Europe, many survivors were liberated in the camps, but thousands of others, forced by the Germans to evacuate westward, made their way on foot through the snow. Thousands died on this trek. By the end of the war some six million Jews were dead as a result of nazi persecution—a million had been killed at Auschwitz alone—and some 100,000 (the figure soon doubled) stood in the Displaced Persons camps of Europe, waiting to find a home. These were the castoffs of an ancient relationship between the Jews and European civilization, now brought to an end in an apocalyptic thrust into the twentieth century during which the Old Europe extinguished itself forever. The Jewish orphans of that dead Europe now began pouring outward to wherever they could gain admittance and find peace—to Britain and the Commonwealth, to the United States, to South America, or, for those who now believed that settlement anywhere else would only invite a recapitulation of the same old history of suffering, to Palestine.

II

It is one of the glories of the Anglo-Saxon nations that their institutions and public acts are, for the most part, based firmly upon the tradition of law. French democracy is inclined, like the Latin Catholic cultures in general, to seek its ideals every so often in a vision that transcends the laws of the state; but in the Anglo-Saxon tradition morality is determinedly treated as immanent in the social contract itself. For this reason, Great Britain and the United States, even with their faults, have served the world as models for their combination of institutional stability with the ideals of liberal democracy. Because their systems are plastic as well as stable, they are amenable to long-term social and economic changes. But, on the other hand, they do not readily accommodate revolutionary upheavals. The British Administration in Palestine, although it was abused in practice by the excesses of some individuals (as in all colonial administrations), was for the most part unimpeachable in its exercise of the principles of lawful procedure. Seeking to impose and maintain peace in Palestine, and to act in a way that it deemed to be equal fairness to both major communities there (which came increasingly to be considered a task of redressing the balance in favor of that community—the Arabs—which seemed in its own eyes to be suffering the greatest disadvantages, due to its general cultural inferiority and its lack of powerful "connections" in London), it had used its prerogative as the Mandatory power to limit Jewish immigration, and once this policy had become law, it sought to enforce that law with the utmost propriety.

But this unfortunately was the very moment when the reign of lawlessness was beginning in Europe, and when the most extreme sufferers under this regime were being reduced to a condition in which the sole valid law was that of survival. The Jews of Europe were no longer citizens, subject to the protection of legal systems and obliged to honor them in return, but a naked mass, subject only to the demon whim of an absolute power. Herded behind barbed wire and ghetto walls, the Jews gazed across a magical dividing line on the other side of which stood a world of more or less sovereign bodies politic which were able to afford to their Aryan nationals varying degrees of protection or cushioning against the hand of the conqueror. Magical documents—passports, Ausweisen, baptismal certificates—suddenly had greater power as shields than guns or the claims of human decency. It had become a world in which the sole form of legitimacy was nationhood, and the Jews of Europe were nationless, illegitimate.

There was one place outside of Europe, however, in which they were legitimate, in which the magic of nationhood existed for Jews as for all men. For this matter of Jewish legitimacy and nationhood in Palestine was now no longer one of administrative or constitutional legality; it was the primeval conviction of a suffering people. The traditional British stress upon the rule of law had no relevance to the revolutionary situation in which the fleeing Jews of Europe were now living. If unrestricted immigration was illegal in the eyes of the Palestine Administration, then the Jewish refugees would enter there illegally; but they would enter.

Aliyah Bet—as the illegal immigration was called by Palestinian Jews—was first organized in 1937 under the auspices of the Haganah, the illegal or semilegal Palestinian Jewish defense organization. It was conceived in reaction to the severe cut in immigration quotas that had already been made the previous year, even before the restrictions of the 1939 White Paper. It was administered with the aid of a handful of adventurous Greek sea captains and small shipowners, and used the Black Sea and the Dardanelles as the principal route for its traffic. The refugees destined for Palestine were first transported to ports in Bulgaria or Roumania (from 1938 to 1940, this was often even done with the aid of the Nazis, some of whom, like Eichmann himself, at first envisioned the Final Solution as a program for resettling the entire Jewish population of Europe), where they were then picked up by the small and often antiquated and unseaworthy craft that were to take them to the Promised Land. Often a stopover was made in Istanbul, but the passengers would always be kept aboard the crowded ship, suffering the usually intolerable conditions that prevailed there, until it had arrived at a landing point in Palestine.

The growing atmosphere of desperation and imminent disaster that accompanied these ships with the onrush of the war was signaled by the case of the *Tiger Hill*. This ship was overloaded with more than 1,400 refugees, two of whom died from the inadequate food and unsanitary conditions aboard. When, after two weeks at sea, the *Tiger Hill* finally entered Palestinian territorial waters near Ashdod, it was suddenly confronted by a British coastal patrol, which fired upon it and killed two of its passengers. The boat managed to make an escape back into international waters. Its commanders then decided to make a desperate landing by simply running it onto the beach at Tel-Aviv. Haganah members on shore were alerted, and when the boat finally appeared out of the darkness and pushed its prow onto the sand, a crowd of Jews was already there, ready to hustle the new arrivals off into hiding. The British police arrived and there was a melee. Many of the refugees managed to escape into hiding, but those who did not were impounded in a British army camp. This happened on the night of September 2, 1939, the day after the German invasion of Poland.

Soon, the recurring histories of these ships became like the scenes of a mounting tragedy. On Friday, November 11, 1940, another small, battered and overloaded Greek ship, the *Pacific*, entered Haifa harbor with another cargo of refugees. Held on board, the passengers restlessly awaited the decision that was being made for them by the authorities ashore. In the meantime a second group of refugees arrived on the Greek ship *Milos*, which had left its Bulgarian port of debarkation together with the *Pacific*. The results of administrative deliberation soon came forth with devastating clarity. The refugees from both ships were loaded onto a large ship anchored in Haifa harbor at this time, the *Patria*, which was to take them to internment for the duration of the war on the British-held island of Mauritius, near Madagascar. A third refugee ship, the *Atlantic*, arrived on November 24. The new arrivals were also about to be transferred when suddenly the *Patria* rocked with an explosion. A hole had been blown in its side. The ship rolled over, its passengers leaping into the water, and sank beneath the surface in a little more than an hour. On the slopes of Mount Carmel, the population of Haifa watched in horror as men, women and children who had narrowly escaped death at the hands of the Nazis sank into the ocean within sight of their hoped-for place of refuge. Some 240 refugees and a dozen policemen were killed in the disaster.

For a time the widely held belief was that the explosion had been a mass suicide attempt made by a group of people who had reached the limits of desperation. But it later became known that the explosion had, in fact, been a miscalculated attempt to delay the ship's departure by putting its engines out of commission, and that it had been organized from ashore by members of the Haganah. This was a dire responsibility. And yet the knowledge of the real facts of the case never had the effect of transferring the focus of the blame, in the eyes of the Palestinian Jewish community, from the British authorities. From the Jewish point of view it was above all British intransigence that was driving a desperate people to desperate measures in Palestine. This attitude applied itself with equally undiscriminating severity more than a year later, in the case of the *Struma*. This Bulgarian cattle boat, carrying another cargo of Jewish refugees, mysteriously exploded and sank to the bottom of the Black Sea on February 24, 1942. Out of 769 passengers aboard only one survived. There was as much reason to blame the Turks for some share of responsibility in this catastrophe as to blame the British. It was the Turkish authorities who grew impatient after the boat had stood in Istanbul harbor for two months, and who finally had it tugged out to the open sea,

labor federation, which became one of the central institutions of the growing Yishuv. Whereas the predominant outlook of the Yishuv leadership was socialist and the foremost elements among the world Zionist leadership were not, there was nevertheless harmony between these two centers of power in the Zionist movement; only Jabotinsky, who was rapidly becoming an opponent of the main Zionist establishment, was militantly antisocialist. The policy agreed upon by the Yishuv and the world Zionist leadership was to seek to cooperate with the British as much as possible. This policy, which manifested the ascendancy of Chaim Weizmann in the Zionist movement, remained almost unshakably in force until the end of the Second World War. It was a policy which naturally led to ambivalence in certain matters, one of the foremost among these being the situation of the Haganah. Technically, the Haganah remained an illegal and clandestine organization, since the British government would openly tolerate no army on the soil of Palestine but its own. But the British connived at the existence of the Haganah, which, in effect, was given a semilegal status. This state of open clandestinity even reached the point that, for a time in 1938, a British officer was in effect serving as a Haganah commander, although not with official sanction. Captain (later Brigadier General) Orde Wingate was a religious fundamentalist of the classic British nonconformist variety, who could quote at length the biblical passages referring to any section of Palestine in which he found himself. Shortly after being stationed in Palestine in 1937 he became a rabid Zionist. On his own initiative he organized a network of "Special Night Squads" among the Jewish settlements in the Galilee, and led them in counterattacks against Arab bands seeking to pillage Jewish property. He also gave a course in military tactics to the Jewish fighters and began studying Hebrew (he was already an accomplished Arabist). But he was quickly transferred back to England in the fall of 1938. He never gave up his dream of commanding a Jewish army in Palestine, although he went on to make his fame in the Second World War as a commander in Ethiopia and then in Burma, where he lost his life. His brief spell of influence was instrumental in helping to form the cadre of an Israeli military establishment.

But even the Special Night Squads, whose tactics were purely defensive, remained within the framework of the general Haganah policy of *Havlagah*, or "self-restraint," which was in force throughout this epoch. This refusal to use offensive tactics was the Haganah's quid pro quo for its semilegal status. The policy of Havlagah was praised and firmly upheld by the Zionist leadership in London, but it was not always easy to maintain in the Yishuv, especially during the period of continual Arab attacking from 1936 to 1939. There were dissident tendencies among the rank and file, both on the left and on the right of the ideological spectrum. In the 1920's some of the most robust elements in the Haganah came from kibbutzim who wanted to use the organization as the military arm of a social revolution. But this tendency subsided during the Arab attacks of 1936–1939, which imposed a long-range and countrywide discipline upon the Haganah for the first time. The leftist tendencies had been mainly localist in character, founded upon an ideal of kibbutz autonomy, and so they lost their strength when the Haganah became a truly national organization in this period. In the 1930's the greatest trouble came increasingly from the right.

After his release from prison in 1920, Vladimir Jabotinsky grew increasingly insistent that Jewish military organization in Palestine not settle for a clandestinity or quasi clandestinity that he considered to be humiliating, but that it come out defiantly into the open, whether the British liked it or not. In the years that followed, his pronouncements became highly militant and cavalier in style. While traveling through Europe in 1923, Jabotinsky was approached by a Zionist youth organization in Riga which called itself *Histadrut Trumpeldor*, in honor of Jabotinsky's lamented friend and comrade-in-arms, who had fallen in the remote Galilean settlement of Tel Hai during the Arab riots of 1920. He was asked to become their leader, and he accepted. In time, this group expanded into an international Zionist youth organization, paramilitary in character, which was called *Brith Trumpeldor*, or *Betar*. (The word "Betar," formed from the Hebrew initials of Brith Trumpeldor, is also the name of the town at which Bar Kochba made his final stand against the Romans in 135 C.E.) Betar became the training ground for some of the most talented elements in the Haganah, but its militant tendencies created tension in the latter organization. Jabotinsky's opponents began to accuse him of quasi-fascist tendencies. There were aspects of the organization and spirit of Betar which did indeed suggest some degree of influence from Mussolini's Italy. As in the latter, Betar made liberal use of uniformed pomp and display, of a highly charged and heroic phraseology, and of an emphatically antisocialist stance,

which it applied vigorously against the predominant ideological outlook of the Yishuv leadership. Furthermore, as in Italy at that time,
Jabotinsky's followers assumed an irredentist political stance, openly
demanding the inclusion of Transjordan in a Palestinian Jewish
state.

In this connection it is probably not insignificant that Jabotinsky
had spent the formative years of his young manhood in Italy.
Between the ages of eighteen and twenty-one, from 1898 to 1901, he
had lived a carefree Bohemian life in Rome. Showing remarkable
precocity both in intellectual achievement and in self-assurance, he
mastered more than one Italian dialect, and supported himself as a
correspondent and feuilletonist for a newspaper in his native Odessa,
writing under the pseudo-Italian pen name of "Altalena." Jabotinsky
shared in the cosmopolitan and rather broadly Mediterranean character of many Odessa Jews of his generation (he did not learn Yiddish
until his manhood, when he mastered it, as he did many languages),
and his spirit harbored the cavalier romanticism of those other
semifeudal knights of the twentieth century, Trotsky and Isaac Babel,
who also were products of Odessa. Always inclined toward the
Mediterranean spirit, Jabotinsky became a great admirer of Sephardic
Jewry when he eventually discovered them in Turkey and then in
Palestine; it is not insignificant that much of the support obtained in
the Yishuv for his policies came from the Sephardic community.

It was probably a more or less Sephardic conception of Jewish
character that enabled Jabotinsky to affirm his Jewish identity in the
face of the strong pull that the Latin cultures exerted upon him.
Sephardic Jewishness is Latin in character; it is not abstractly ideological like the Bundist or Labor Zionist nationalism of the north,
which Jabotinsky deplored, but is rather visceral, spontaneous and
highly aesthetic. It lacks the continuous tension of self-control that
marks a more bourgeois culture, but rather only rises to scattered
moments of spiritual tension, which are then extreme in their force.
This is characteristic of a culture that has a powerful sense of
rootedness in the soil upon which it finds itself, a culture that is
either peasant or aristocratic, but scarcely middle class. Jabotinsky's
vision was of a Jewish Palestine founded upon such a culture. This is
not to say that Jabotinsky himself was free of the kind of Nordic,
Ashkenazi rigor in his soul that repelled him in so many of his
colleagues. Rather, he was a supreme example of it. This was one of

the paradoxes of his life, this opposition between the two fundamental tendencies of his spirit, and he gave expression to it in his
novel *Samson*, which he wrote in the 1920's. The hero of this novel
has two identities. He is of course Samson the warrior, the dedicated
leader who seeks to organize the scattered tribes of Israel into a
militant and truly national community. But he is also emotionally
drawn to the way of life of his Philistine enemies. In his guise as the
Philistine Tayish, he is a carefree vagabond, a merry drinker, a robust
womanizer, and in general a lover of luxury. But as Samson the judge
he is a puritanical son of the stark hills of the Galilee. After ten years
of this austerity, however, he meets Delilah, and his old passion for
the sensuality of Philistia erupts to destroy him. Except for an
occasional literary indulgence, the attention of the mature Jabotinsky
was never so diverted from his own austere vocation.

By the end of the 1920's Jabotinsky, who had in the meantime
been permanently barred from Palestine by the British authorities,
had become the leader of a quasi-autonomous faction within the
Zionist movement which called itself the Revisionists. In 1931 a
corresponding Revisionist faction, called *Irgun Bet* (Organization
B), was formed within the Haganah. Then, in 1935, Jabotinsky's
Revisionist group broke entirely with the World Zionist Organization
and formed itself into a separate movement. A large portion of the
Irgun Bet followed suit two years later, breaking away from the
Haganah and establishing itself as the independent *Irgun Tzva'i
Leumi* (National Military Organization), usually referred to simply
as the "Irgun" in the English-speaking countries. In the two years
that remained until the outbreak of the Second World War, controversy between the Irgun and the Haganah centered upon the latter's
policy of self-restraint. The Irgun found an opportunity to break with
this policy in the Ben-Yoseph affair of 1938. The nineteen-year-old
Shlomo Ben-Yoseph and two other youths, all members of Betar,
had decided to take it into their own hands to retaliate for an Arab
attack on a busload of Jews, in which fourteen persons were killed
and four women raped. The three young men opened fire on an Arab
bus, which escaped unscathed. They were caught, and although the
courts ruled one of them insane and sentenced another to life
imprisonment, Ben-Yoseph was condemned to hang. He went to the
scaffold singing *Hatikvah*, the Jewish national anthem. In retaliation
for the hanging of Ben-Yoseph, the Irgun kidnaped an Arab in Haifa
and hanged him. Then in February, 1939, the Irgun undertook its

first major reprisal action, exploding bombs in the market places of several Arab towns in retaliation for Arab attacks upon Jews the previous month. Jabotinsky himself opposed these actions; but by this time the Irgun, like all other institutions in the Yishuv, was taking on a life of its own.

With the outbreak of the war in 1939, the Irgun declared a truce and went along with the Haganah policy of cooperation in the war effort. The illegal immigration was, for the time being, the only area in which organized resistance against the British continued. But there continued to be dissident elements who claimed that noncooperation and armed resistance should continue despite the war. They were given ammunition for their claims by the continuing intransigence of those who were responsible for British policies in Palestine. The status of the Haganah continued, strictly speaking, to be illegal. Uneasiness at the outbreak of the war and at the wave of terrorism that had just preceded it caused the Administration momentarily to renounce its unofficial policy of connivance at the Yishuv military organization. In the fall of 1939 forty-three Haganah members, including the young Moshe Dayan, were found engaged in military drill exercises and were arrested. But it could not be proved that these men were doing anything but preparing themselves for military service with the British, and they were released. Later they served in the British army with distinction, most notably in Syria, where Dayan lost an eye in combat. The Haganah background of these men made them valuable soldiers, but they were unable to gain the distinct status as a Jewish military organization that they sought, either inside or outside the British army. Throughout the entire war the Zionist leadership in London pressed for a Jewish Legion. Their pleas grew particularly urgent in 1942 when, until the British victory at El Alamein in the fall of that year, the German advance through North Africa led to the widespread fear that the persecutors of the Jews would reach Palestine itself. But a separate Jewish military detachment was not formed until the last year of the war.

Dissidence against the policy of cooperation with the British began in 1940 with the splintering off from the Irgun of a small extremist faction known as the Stern Gang. Its leader, Abraham Stern, had been born in Poland in 1907 and had come to Palestine in his teens. At the Hebrew University in Jerusalem he was a brilliant student of languages and literature, and gained some reputation as a poet. In 1929 he received a graduate fellowship to study in Italy, where, like

Jabotinsky, he became passionately devoted to Italian culture and perhaps somewhat susceptible to the martial splendors of the Musso-lini regime. His poetry abounds with violent imagery, with a passion for the glitter of the sword combined with an uncanny sense of impending apocalyptic disaster. He signed himself "Yair" (Illumi-nator), the name of the Zealot commander at Masada. By the time of the outbreak of the war Stern was a member of the Irgun. He soon was the leader of a faction within the Irgun which spoke up in the early part of 1940 against the policy of cooperation with the Haganah and the British. At first he attempted to have his way within the organization, and he challenged the leadership of David Raziel, the Irgun commander. But when Jabotinsky, then in the United States on a lecture tour, received word of the quarrel, he cabled an order that Stern submit to Raziel's authority. Jabotinsky died immediately afterward, while visiting a Betar camp in New York State. Stern's group then broke away from the Irgun altogether. The Sternists returned to the practice of violent reprisal actions, until February, 1942, when Stern and other leaders of the group were killed by the British police.

The months that followed the death of Stern were a period in which the mounting tension of the war suppressed all tendencies toward extremism. But the British victory at El Alamein changed the climate of feeling in Palestine. The general war effort now became somewhat more remote than it had been, and the specifically Jewish and Zionist issues came once again to the fore. In this atmosphere dissidence and terrorism reappeared. In the summer of 1943, under the leadership of Nathan Friedman-Yellin, the Stern Gang reconsti-tuted itself as the "Fighters for the Freedom of Israel" (F.F.I. or, from its Hebrew initials, Lehi). The F.F.I. remained a completely independent and clandestine organization, as much opposed by the Zionist authorities as it was by the Palestine Administration. It cultivated a fanatical, self-immolating dedication among its members, who were expected to be prepared to lay down their lives upon order. Not satisfied with mere reprisals, the F.F.I. sought to affect history with some more apocalyptic manifestation. After several unsuccessful attempts upon the life of Sir Harold MacMichael, the British High Commissioner in Palestine, it turned to a higher if more remote symbol of British colonial authority, Lord Moyne, in Cairo. Two very young men, weaned into young manhood by the demon prescripts of this organization, fired point-blank at the Deputy Minister of State and at his chauffeur, who had tried to intervene. At their trial the young men defended themselves in terms of the ideal of a free Jewish nation living in its homeland. Like Ben-Yoseph, they sang *Hatikvah* as they stood upon the gallows. They had committed the assassination in November, 1944, only a matter of days before the ovens of Auschwitz came to a final halt.

Earlier, in January, 1944, the Irgun had also declared its independence from the Haganah policy of cooperation with the British. The Irgun was now, after the death of David Raziel, under the leadership of Menahem Begin. A member of the Polish army at the beginning of the war, Begin had been imprisoned by the Russians but then released when Germany went to war against Russia. He then went to Transjordan with a unit of the free Polish army, from which he was given indefinite leave by a Polish officer sympathetic to Zionism, so as to enable him to take part in the Jewish underground in Palestine. From the beginning of 1944 to the end of the war the Irgun and the F.F.I. now both pursued dissident terrorist policies, although there was, in principle at least, an important difference in their approaches. Whereas the Stern Gang was ready to pursue a policy of assassination whenever it saw fit, the Irgun tried to destroy British installations without taking lives. The latter prided itself on its policy of giving advance warnings to personnel in installations they were about to blow up. But lives were often lost in their raids anyway.

With the war's end the Haganah found itself between two stools. It had not yet been accorded the legitimacy it sought in the eyes of the Administration, and yet it had not chosen to respond to this situation by becoming a full-fledged underground movement. At first the Haganah tried to play it both ways. In October, 1945, it called for a united Jewish front, a "Jewish Resistance Movement" which would include the Irgun and the F.F.I. along with the Haganah. On the diplomatic level, on the other hand, the Zionist leadership both in Palestine and abroad continued to claim to repudiate the underground movement. Responsible to the established political authority of the Jewish Agency, the Haganah continued to be diffident about terrorism, but not to the extent that there was not some degree of high-level cooperation between the Haganah and the Irgun during the ensuing year. On general lines at least, Haganah members were in agreement with the Irgun plan to blow up a wing of the King David Hotel in Jerusalem in 1946. The Haganah men sought assurance that the hotel would be evacuated completely before the explosion, and the Irgun promised to do this. Still, the former were hesitant about the matter, and the Irgun leadership, losing patience, seized the initiative on July 22. Since it housed the military headquarters of the Palestine Administration, the King David Hotel was well guarded; but by creating a temporary armed diversion in front of the hotel on the morning of the 22nd, the Irgun enabled several of its members to enter unnoticed from the rear and place in the kitchen several milk cans filled with high explosives. Other Irgunists then promptly telephoned the hotel and the offices of the *Palestine Post*, announcing that the bombs were to go off in half an hour and that the building should be evacuated. But for reasons that are not clear, no evacuation took place. At 12:37 P.M. an explosion larger than anyone had anticipated destroyed the entire south wing of the hotel, killing 91 persons and wounding 45 others—Englishman, Jew and Arab alike. In the anguish and political confusion that ensued, the Haganah repudiated the united front it had called for the previous fall and once again declared war upon the Irgun and the Stern Gang.

III

During the years of Hitler's ascendancy in Europe the center of gravity of the Zionist movement shifted away from Europe and even to some extent away from embattled London, moving outward in two directions, to Palestine and to America. The vast American Jewish community that had grown up in the course of half a century, now largely Eastern European in character, was a product of the same folk exodus that had created the Jewish national community in Palestine. Of course, the Jews who had gone to America were motivated by purposes very different from those of the Palestine pioneers, and among Yiddish cultural circles in the United States, largely Bundist in inclination, there had even been considerable hostility toward Zionism. But once a nation of Jews, mostly of Russian and Polish origin, had become a reality in Palestine, ideological reservations gave way to a sense of kinship. The problem of Jewish suffering in Europe furthered growing American-Jewish sympathy with Zionist aspirations. By the end of the war the wealth and size of the American Jewish community, combined with a passionate desire on its part to make atonement to its European Jewish brothers for the safety it had enjoyed during the Holocaust, gave the American Zionist leaders central importance in the worldwide movement.

Like the American Jewish community, the Yishuv had grown and come of age in the course of half a century. Prior to the First World War the most important Zionist elements in Palestine had been very young men and women who were mainly preoccupied with the task of remaking themselves into farmers, laborers and other humble but essential elements of a reconstructed national existence. The major political initiatives governing their enterprises naturally came from older and more sophisticated men living and working in the European capitals. But these pioneers were mature men and women by the time of the Second World War, and their political leaders could claim more than twenty years of administrative experience in the very Land which was the focus of all Zionist activity. These men no longer had reason to submit passively to the tutelage of Zionist leaders in London; furthermore, as a result of their own firsthand experience with the Palestine Administration, they were less inclined than were their colleagues in the more polite atmosphere of London to have consistent faith in the workings of British good will.

These two new elements, the American and the Palestinian Zionist leadership, came rather suddenly to the fore in 1942, during the course of a Zionist conference held in May of that year at the Biltmore Hotel in New York. The "Biltmore Program," drawn up at that conference, condemned the 1939 White Paper and called for the establishment of a Jewish commonwealth in Palestine—the first open and official statement on the part of the Zionist movement since the Balfour Declaration that it sought Jewish statehood as an outcome of the "national home" idea. Chaim Weizmann wholeheartedly endorsed this statement, which was, in effect, a repudiation of his own more Fabian approach; he subsequently gave his energies to fight for it, but the initiative in drawing it up had in no way come from him. It came rather from two new major leaders in the Zionist movement: the American Reform rabbi, Dr. Abba Hillel Silver, and David Ben-Gurion, the Chairman of the Jewish Agency Executive in Jerusalem. The final years of the struggle toward statehood were to be dominated by the forces represented by these two men: the financial and political strength of American Jewry and the physical energies and will of a Palestinian Jewish community that had now become a nation.

The initiatives taken by the Yishuv were at this time coming to be increasingly identified with David Ben-Gurion's will. He was a classic representative of the heroic age of pioneering in Palestine. Born in the town of Plonsk, Poland, in 1886, he was taught Zionism at his father's knee, and he joined a local branch of the movement while still a boy. In 1905, at the age of nineteen, he emigrated to Palestine and went to work there as a farm laborer. He was one of the founders of Ha'Shomer, the self-defense organization of the pioneers in remote settlements. It was around this time that he changed his name from Green to the Hebrew one of Ben-Gurion (Son of the Lion), the name of one of the defenders of Jerusalem in the war against the Romans. He was soon drawn from agriculture into the political activities of the growing Yishuv, and by the time of the outbreak of the First World War he (along with Itzhak Ben-Zvi, later the second President of Israel) was in Constantinople studying law, with the hope of eventually sitting as a Jewish representative in the Turkish parliament. When he was expelled by the Turks in 1915 he went to America, where he helped recruit volunteers for the Jewish Legion. Later he fought in Palestine in one of the Legion's battalions. After the war he returned to Palestine and participated in the formation of the Histadrut; he was elected its secretary general.

By the 1920's, Ben-Gurion had become a major advocate of the view that the true Zionists were those who had made their home in Zion and that the major political initiative in the movement should therefore come from them. He was given a new opportunity to realize this political philosophy when the Jewish Agency was created in 1929. One of the purposes of the Jewish Agency was to be the official instrument for the effectuation of Zionist policies within Palestine itself. In Palestine it became, in effect, the official governing institution of the Yishuv, and treated with the Palestine Administration as such. The Jewish Agency Executive became the virtual Yishuv cabinet of ministers under the Mandate, a government within a government. Its parliament was the Va'ad Leumi (National Council), the elected governing body of the Yishuv. With the declaration of the independent state of Israel in May, 1948, the Jewish Agency Executive and the Va'ad Leumi simply became the cabinet of ministers and the parliament of the new state. In 1931 David Ben-Gurion became the Chairman of the Jewish Agency Executive, and it was in this position—which he held until statehood in 1948, whereupon he promptly became Prime Minister—that he established his authority as the main representative spokesman of the new national community.

Ben-Gurion's political pre-eminence came not only from the fact that he was a genuinely charismatic personality, a virtual historical force flung up by events, a man of immense will and energy, whose craggy figure, bald dome and white mane evoked images of Hebrew prophets; but also from his ability to combine a large historical vision with a keen sense of practical politics. After 1945 his task was simultaneously to create and to defend the Jewish state. This double task demanded a policy that was often seemingly contradictory; he had to utilize to the fullest extent possible the nationalist idealism and fighting capacities of the Yishuv, but he had at the same time to establish unity and submission to a single authority among a people who had been without secular political institutions of their own for nearly two thousand years, and who were never prone to be submissive. In the long run his difficulties in achieving unity came from the left as well as from the right (Ben-Gurion was the leader of the moderate Socialist party, *Mapai*, which was middle-of-the-road by Yishuv standards); but in the three-year period between the end of the war and the establishment of the state, the greatest problems by far were created by the terrorist right, the Irgun and the Stern Gang.

At times he put these two groups down ruthlessly; but at other times he did not pursue them as relentlessly as he might have done. On the grounds of morality as well as of the need for unity in the Yishuv, Ben-Gurion could not but oppose the barbarism of the terrorists. But he was also, after all, leading a nation engaged in a fight for its very existence, in an era in which the night of barbarism had descended upon mankind in general and driven men of all walks of life into extremes of cruelty that they themselves would never have condoned in ordinary times. Under these circumstances the central, rational forces of the nascent Israeli nation—forces such as the Haganah, the Jewish Agency and the Va'ad Leumi, all embodied in Ben-Gurion's leadership—could not but temper their own zeal to put terrorism down, and some of these elements occasionally even co-operated with it. This contradictory approach was perceived by the British Labour MP, Richard Crossman, when he was in Palestine in early 1946 as a member of the Anglo-American Committee of Inquiry. It seemed to Crossman, in listening to Ben-Gurion's testimony before the committee, that the latter wanted to have it both ways: "to remain within the letter of the law as chairman of the

Agency, and to tolerate terror as a method of bringing pressure on the Administration."[2] Crossman felt at the time that Ben-Gurion should either have gone all the way to a Sinn Fein, Irish terrorist, position or have more wholeheartedly joined Weizmann's utter disapproval of the use of such tactics. But Ben-Gurion, standing between the more dispassionate approach of a Zionist leadership living outside of Palestine and the whole range of passions of an embattled community fighting to keep from being driven into the sea, took the only position appropriate to the historic role he was assuming. He was the catalyst between a world movement and the nation-state it had created.

There were now two principal forces intervening upon the matured Palestinian Jewish national aspirations that Ben-Gurion represented. One was, of course, the Arabs, with whom the decisive struggle was eventually to take place. But in the period immediately following the end of the Second World War the Yishuv was not inclined to regard the Arabs as its major problem, and its leaders did not necessarily foresee that there would have to be a war with the latter at all. Rather, it was the Palestine Administration that was viewed as the major opposing force. In the bleak months of late 1945 and early 1946 it came increasingly to seem that the new postwar Labour government in London, whose advent had been greeted in Tel-Aviv with dancing in the streets, was not only not going to revoke the policy of the 1939 White Paper but was determined to keep Britain in Palestine indefinitely. In the meantime an estimated 100,000 Jewish refugees were sitting in the Displaced Persons camps of Europe, many of them hoping to get to America, but most of them sharing the feeling that, if America was not open to them, then Palestine was the place to which they wanted to go. To obtain an evaluation of the postwar problem of Palestine in the light of the situation of European Jewry, the British government called for American cooperation in a commission of inquiry. The Anglo-American Committee, consisting of six Englishmen and six Americans, from both political and private life, began its work in the latter part of December, 1945.

The members of the committee first went through the Displaced Persons camps of Europe before going on to Palestine itself to complete their investigation. The major element in their recommen-

[2] Richard Crossman, *Palestine Mission* (New York and London, 1947), p. 129.

dations was that, as President Truman had already requested, 100,000 Palestine entry certificates be issued among the Displaced Persons immediately. They also called for the eventual establishment of a binational state in Palestine. But the generally favorable attitude of the report toward Zionism, particularly in the provision concerning the 100,000 certificates, which was, in effect, a recommended abrogation of the 1939 White Paper, met with widespread disapproval in the British government. In particular, it met with the disapproval of the man who had brought the committee into being and who was steadily assuming final authority over British policy in Palestine, Foreign Minister Ernest Bevin.

Bevin was a large and boisterous man whose overbearing, rough-and-tumble personality had brought him great success as the leader of the labor movement from whose ranks he had risen. His often rather crude style was not the usual manner of foreign ministers, although he showed considerable talent in the post and scored one major success in the British withdrawal from India. It is quite possible that his approach to the Palestine question came from a mistaken application to it of attitudes that were appropriate in the case of India. In the era immediately following the Second World War anticolonialism was rapidly becoming a major element in the creed of the European political left. Many members of the left were prone to regard Zionism as simply the same old European colonialism in a different guise. Men of this outlook tended to see the unsophisticated Arabs as the victims of an unwarranted onslaught at the hands of a shrewd, well-organized and powerful world Jewry. Nazism had demonstrated to those who cared to learn the lesson that Jewish wealth and power, whatever its mythic dimensions, was as nothing compared to the sovereign control of the merest scrap of land, the one thing that the Jewish people lacked. But Bevin, for one, never understood Jewish history in this way. He seems always to have been sure that 100,000 Jewish DPs could—and would be willing to—be reabsorbed into the countries from which they had come, and he at least once indicated that he did not understand why a state should be formed on "religious" grounds. This inability to understand the point of Zionism was combined with an unfortunate penchant for making remarks that, however intended, had an anti-Semitic ring to them, such as his celebrated remark that "if the Jews, with all their sufferings, want to get too much at the head of the queue, you have the danger of another anti-Semitic reaction through it all."

Bevin had made the mistake of announcing to the Anglo-American Committee, upon their departure at the end of 1945, that he would "do everything in his power to put it [their report] into effect," presumably certain that their findings would conform with his own convictions on the subject. When, in the end, he ignored their proposals, Zionist opposition to him grew strong, and he felt the pressure of unfavorable opinion with particular force from American shores. It was in this period that American views on the Palestine question began to be of decisive importance. President Truman was becoming the chief force among the world powers in favor of the establishment of a Jewish state. This was partly out of his own inclinations, partly as a result of the pressure of a politically significant and now largely pro-Zionist American Jewish community, and partly due to a growing pro-Zionist sympathy at this time among American Gentiles as well (given greater force by a traditional American Anglophobia). Truman's inclinations favorable to Zionism frequently found their chief obstacle in the State Department, where lack of sympathy with Zionism was an old tradition, as in most foreign ministries. Men whose approach to international relations is technical are instinctually opposed to any kind of force which would revise the existing political structure in any given area.

By early 1947 Palestine Jewish resistance had become so pronounced that even the Haganah had turned to sabotage, by blowing up two of the boats in Haifa harbor that were used for transferring the passengers of illegal immigrant ships to Cyprus. In February the British government decided to turn the Palestine question over to the United Nations. In April a United Nations Special Committee on Palestine (UNSCOP) was created, made up of representatives of eleven of the smaller or less developed nations. They arrived in Palestine at the beginning of June. It was during the committee's stay there that Bevin committed one of his most egregious blunders. His anger had already been aroused by the events of May 4, when members of the Irgun and the Stern Gang blew a hole in the side of the prison-fortress at Acre, enabling some 200 other prisoners to escape along with the 41 comrades of their own whom they had set out to rescue. Then in the middle of July the *Exodus 1947* arrived in Haifa harbor carrying about 4,500 Jewish refugees. Determined, as he put it, "to teach the Jews a lesson," Bevin ordered that the ship be returned to its port of embarkation in southern France. The French government agreed to the British request that it receive whatever passengers debark, but stipulated that none of them were required to do so. The passengers of the *Exodus*, now transferred to three British boats, remained aboard them in the harbor of Port-de-Bouc for a month, during which period only a few sick persons went ashore. It was during this same month that the Palestine Administration captured five of the leaders of the Acre prison break and sentenced three of them to death; in retaliation, the Irgun murdered two British sergeants and hanged their bodies to a tree, attaching a booby trap to one of them. In the wave of revulsion that struck the British public, Bevin ordered that the *Exodus* passengers be brought to Hamburg, which was in the British occupation zone of Germany. Many of the Jewish survivors of nazi terror would sooner have touched their feet upon the rim of hell than upon German soil. This callous act cost the British government any sympathy that it might have received from UNSCOP.

The UNSCOP proposal was for the partition of Palestine into a Jewish and an Arab state. It allotted less territory to the Jews than had a plan submitted by the Jewish Agency in 1946, but it was more generous to them than any of the previous non-Jewish partition schemes. It included the Negev, with the exception of an area roughly corresponding to, though somewhat larger than, the Gaza Strip of today. The plan also gave the Jewish state Eastern Galilee, and a complete coastal strip from a point north of Haifa (and just south of Acre) to a point well south of Jaffa; the almost entirely Arab city of Jaffa was to be included in the Jewish state. Jerusalem was to remain under a permanent international trusteeship. The chief disadvantage of the plan was its checkerboard arrangement; both Jewish and Arab states were made up of three separate enclaves which met one another only at points. Nevertheless, the Zionist leadership was inclined to favor the proposal, *faute de mieux*; it would be some kind of sovereign Jewish territory at last. The Palestinian Arab leadership opposed it. By the time the plan came up for approval by the General Assembly, the proposed map of Palestine had been revised to the advantage of the Arab territory: portions of the proposed Jewish state were removed in the southwestern and northern parts of the Negev; Beersheba now was allotted to the Arab state. On November 29, 1947, the partition proposal came before the UN General Assembly. Palestine had by this time become a focus of the growing cold war conflict, and the Soviet Union rushed in to rival the United States in currying the favor of Palestine Jewry. With the support of those two Great Powers, the partition proposal managed to obtain the necessary two-thirds majority in the General Assembly. A Jewish state as the final outcome of Zionist endeavors in Palestine had now been officially recognized by the world. On the next day severe Arab rioting broke out in various parts of Palestine. In effect, the Arab-Israeli War had begun.

The first phase of the war, which lasted until the official termination of the Mandate on May 14, 1948, was technically an underground affair. For a long time neither the Jews nor the Arabs were certain that the British would really withdraw from Palestine, despite the UN resolution, and although the British government announced in December that it would terminate the Mandate on May 15, this announcement was not taken seriously at first. But in the meantime the Jews and the Arabs prepared for the all-out war between them that was now virtually inevitable once the British should withdraw. This was done in a series of campaigns fought behind the woodshed as it were, under the noses of the British forces as they withdrew step by step from various parts of the country. In this way the Jews and the Arabs established the positions they would be holding once the British had left completely.

Until the end of February this was a diffuse affair. Arab volunteer armies infiltrated across the borders into Palestine, made scattered raids, and were sometimes chased back across the border by the British. The Haganah scored a major success in repelling an Arab offensive in the Beisan Valley in February; but throughout this early period of the underground war its tactics were purely defensive. In fact, until the end of March the Haganah was seriously unprepared for all-out warfare. Its own arms store, gathered in clandestinity, was inadequate; and its ability to obtain arms was severely restricted by the fact that America, anxious to avoid an arms race in the Middle East, had placed an embargo upon all arms shipments into that area. In the meantime the British government was selling arms to the Arab states. In December, Ehud Avriel, one of the organizers of the illegal immigration, was sent to Paris on a mission to obtain arms for the Haganah and arrange to have them smuggled into Palestine. He eventually succeeded in making a deal with Czechoslovakia, and the first shipment of arms from that country arrived in Palestine at the end of March. These arms, combined with the remarkable home-made mortar that the Haganah had developed, called the "Davidka" (Little David) in honor of its inventor, David Leibovitch, enabled the Jews to embark upon the offensive.

In its subsequent campaigns the Haganah was assisted not only by the Irgun and the Sternists but also by a remarkable organization called the *Palmach* (the abbreviation for *Plugot Ha'Machatz,* or Shock Troops). This commando force, which used guerrilla tactics to spearhead Haganah attacks, was an unofficial, stand-by army made up of kibbutz members, farmers-in-training ready to be mustered into action at a moment's notice, like the Minutemen of the American Revolution. The Palmach was the elite corps of the Jewish military forces, but its outlook was resolutely egalitarian, and it eschewed ranks and the trappings of military conventions. Being independent, it was not easily subjected to the authority of the Haganah and the Jewish Agency Executive. At the outbreak of hostilities it consisted of some 5,000 members, mostly in their late teens and early twenties, about a fourth of them young women.

The Haganah's first major operation took place in early April, when the troops of Fawzi al-Kawukji, one of the leaders of the Palestine Arab revolt in 1936–1939, laid siege to the Jewish settle-ment of Mishmar ha'Emek. This village guards the entranceway into the Valley of Jezreel, the heartland of Jewish agricultural settlement. The Haganah arrived with two battalions, the largest combat units it had ever used, and forced the Arabs to withdraw after four days of fighting. A few days later the Haganah launched its first major offensive, "Operation Jephtha," the purpose of which was to clear all enemy forces out of large stretches of the Galilee. It was in the course of this campaign that the sudden mass flight of the Palestine Arab community began.

The exodus had begun in late March and early April when thousands of Arabs living in communities on the Sharon coastal plain had evacuated to the Arab strongholds in the hills. But the first of the sudden and wholesale flights of entire communities took place in Tiberias on April 18. The British evacuated the city on that day, and the Haganah, moving in to control it as part of Operation Jephtha, found that all of the 6,000 Arabs living there had fled. In Haifa, on April 21, the Jews launched an offensive from their quarter on top of Mount Carmel, descending into the Arab part of the city; the next day the Arab commander in Haifa fled, and the remaining Arab leaders asked the British to aid them in evacuating the Arab population of the city. Both British and Jewish commanders urged them not to do this, but in the next few days all 70,000 Arabs of Haifa had left their homes. On May 13 the Arab city of Jaffa surrendered to the Haganah, and once again its entire population fled.

The reasons for this mass flight are still not fully understood. It seems to have begun with the urging on the part of some of the Arab leaders that the various Arab populations in potential combat areas take shelter elsewhere. This advice was based upon the assumption that the Arab armies would soon be victorious in these areas, so that the evacuees would quickly be able to return to their homes. The transformation of this evacuation into a mass flight was no doubt largely the result of the Deir Yassin atrocity, which took place on April 8 or 9. This occurred during the Jewish campaign to clear the Tel-Aviv-Jerusalem road, in which the fiercest and most desperate fighting of the war took place. Members of the Irgun and the Stern Gang occupied the Arab village of Deir Yassin, near Jerusalem, and massacred its entire population, 254 men, women and children. Menahem Begin later claimed that Irgun troops had first broadcast a warning to the civilian population of the village that they take shelter; the fighting for the town was so severe, he said, that it entailed house-to-house combat, and these civilians who remained in their homes "suffered inevitable casualties."[3] No such attempt at justification of the act was made by the Jewish Agency leadership, who promptly sent a message of apology to King Abdullah of Transjordan. There were no other such incidents, but this one was sufficient to cause panic among the Arabs of Palestine. Certain sectors of the Palestine Arab population remained notably unshaken, such as the community living in and around Nazareth, but these were exceptional. By the end of May some 200,000 Palestinian Arabs had fled their homes; at the end of 1948 this figure had reached to between 500,000 and 600,000.

The last major Haganah operation before the termination of the Mandate involved the defense of Jerusalem. This city contained one of the major concentrations of Jewish population in Palestine, but it stood in an isolated enclave far from the large contiguous area of Jewish settlement on the coast. It was connected with the coast by a road that was flanked by two almost unbroken strings of Arab towns and villages. From the Bab-el-Wad, the point at which it begins

[3] Menahem Begin, *The Revolt* (New York, 1951), pp. 163–164.

ascending from the coastal plain into the Judaean Hills, almost to Jerusalem itself, this road is surrounded by steep hills, and therefore highly susceptible to ambush. But Jewish Jerusalem's life was dependent upon the supply convoys that could be got to it from the coast. The Haganah's "Operation Nahshon" was therefore aimed at clearing the heights around the road to Jerusalem, and placing them under Jewish control. A particularly fierce battle was fought for the commanding hilltop of Qastel for a period of ten days ending on April 9: control of the village passed back and forth between the contenders several times before the Jews were finally victorious.

With great difficulty this lifeline between Jerusalem and the coast was preserved, but the situation of the northern, eastern and southern sides of the city was far more problematical and ultimately hopeless. Mount Scopus, somewhat to the north of the main part of the city, on which stood the Hebrew University and the Hadassah Hospital, was an isolated enclave separated from the main body of Jewish Jerusalem by Arab suburbs. It was on the road between Mount Scopus and the Jewish part of Jerusalem that the Arabs staged a reprisal for Deir Yassin on April 12. A convoy of seventy-seven doctors, nurses, professors and students, traveling to the hospital and the university under the Red Cross insignia, was ambushed, and all of them were killed. Directly to the east of Jewish Jerusalem was the Old City. This had been the city of King David and of the First and Second Temples, but it was now a walled Arab fortress containing a small and helpless enclave of ultrareligious Jews. This latter population ultimately had to be evacuated. It was to the south of Jerusalem that the last major battle before the termination of the Mandate took place, in and around the Jewish settlement of Kfar Etzion. This, too, was an isolated enclave, and ultimately indefensible. On April 28 the British aided in the evacuation of the Jewish population of the "Etzion Bloc," where, in weeks of fierce fighting seventy-five Jewish lives had been lost.

On May 14 the British, to the surprise of many in Palestine, proved true to their word: at 9 A.M. Sir Alan Cunningham, the last High Commissioner, departed from Haifa. On the afternoon of that same day the political leaders of the Yishuv convened in the art museum of Tel-Aviv, and heard a proclamation read to them by David Ben-Gurion. He declared the independent state of Israel to be now in existence; many of his listeners were hearing for the first time the name that was to be borne by the state for which they had been

fighting all their lives. The news of the proclamation was radioed to
Washington, and in a few minutes a message was returned, inform-
ing the new government of Israel that it had been awarded de facto
recognition by the government of the United States of America.
President Truman's swift decision took many of his own policy
makers by surprise; Professor Philip Jessup, the American Ambassa-
dor to the UN, made a personal telephone call to the White House to
make sure that the news he had just received was correct, and then
made the announcement to a stunned General Assembly. In four
days the Soviet Union followed suit. The state of Israel was now a
reality, but its borders and its very survival were still in question. On
May 15, the day after the British withdrawal and the proclamation,
the armies of the Arab League were entering Palestine from all sides.

At this time the Israeli population numbered some 600,000 and
were able, by a kind of total mustering of resources, to put about
60,000 troops into the field. The Arab League states engaged in war
against Israel had a combined population of about 30 million, and
marshaled some 70,000 or 80,000 troops. The most formidable among
these were the powerful Egyptian army, which came up from the
south, and the Arab Legion of Jordan, an elite army that had been
organized and trained by the British, and that was still largely under
the command of British officers during the Arab-Israeli War. These
two armies, along with the troops of Iraq, Syria and Lebanon, all
better armed at the outbreak of the war than the Israelis were, made
a formidable opposition for the fledgling Jewish state. But, against
them, the Israelis enjoyed one major advantage, if it can be called
such: unlike the Arabs, they were fighting for their very existence.
They had either to repel the invaders or literally to be pushed into
the sea. The Hebrew words Ein Brera (No Alternative) became the
Israeli battle cry in this period.

The first phase of the open all-out war between the Arabs and the
Israelis, which began on May 15 and ended with the first United
Nations truce on June 11, was not favorable to the Israelis, although
it ended on a promising note for them. The Egyptian forces pushed
up from the south and occupied virtually all of the Negev, leaving
only isolated Jewish settlements to form pockets of resistance. They
reached the outskirts of the southern part of Jerusalem, where they
were finally stopped at the settlement of Ramat Rachel, which today

still forms the southern boundary of the Jerusalem pocket of Israel. The Israelis made an attempt to break into the Old City of Jerusalem, but they failed, and the Jewish population of that sector had to be evacuated. The Arab Legion not only gained control of the Old City and almost all the non-Jewish suburbs surrounding Jerusalem, but they also established a solid foothold at key points on the slopes overlooking the Tel-Aviv-Jerusalem road. At Latrun, one of the commanding points of the road, the Israelis attempted a series of assaults against the Arab Legion position, using unseasoned troops in a brave but reckless manner, and suffering hundreds of casualties. By the time of the truce Latrun was still in Arab hands, and the Israelis had constructed an alternate route to Jerusalem through the hills, which they called the "Burma Road." Throughout the entire war the problem of getting convoys through to besieged Jerusalem was a major one, and many lives were lost in this hazardous enterprise. The brightest spot for the Israelis in this period before the first truce was the successful campaign in the Western Galilee led by Colonel Moshe Carmel, who had commanded the capture of Haifa. He captured Acre after a three-day siege and moved up the coast to the Lebanese border. This was the first time that Israeli forces had moved well into an area that was not allotted to them by the UN partition plan. At this time it was not necessarily understood that the Israelis could lay claim to Palestinian land outside of their partition boundaries if they occupied it, but by the end of the war such had become the aim of Israeli policy.

On May 20 the UN appointed Count Folke Bernadotte, president of the Swedish Red Cross and a member of Sweden's royal family, as its mediator in Palestine. A British resolution calling for a cease-fire in Palestine was passed in the UN on May 29, but Count Bernadotte did not succeed in getting both sides to agree to it until the 11th of June. The Arabs were slow to accept the truce, but the Israelis were rather amenable to it, since it gave them needed time to add to their still inadequate store of weapons and to consolidate their fledgling and somewhat chaotic military organization. It was only on May 28 that the Haganah was reconstituted as the National Defense Army of Israel. Organizations such as the Palmach and the Irgun were granted separate brigade status within the framework of the Israeli army, but Prime Minister Ben-Gurion was not content until he had put an end to the separatist tendencies of both these groups. There was a great

deal of romantic nostalgia surrounding the Palmach in particular, but
Ben-Gurion was determined that even this group subordinate itself to
the prosaic task of being part of a nation. He eventually dealt with
this matter with characteristically single-minded and even ruthless
vigor. It was while the Palmach battalion was engaged in its most
glorious undertaking, the recapture of the Negev in October, that he
dissolved the Palmach headquarters in Tel-Aviv.

But his most vexing quarrel was with the Irgun. This organization
had, in typical cavalier fashion, denounced the truce when it was
signed. Even though the Irgun had become, technically, a brigade of
the Haganah as far back as April 27, its leaders continued to formulate their own independent policy. In contrast with their own
conception of themselves, however, Ben-Gurion considered the Irgun
to have been dissolved. During the week in which the cease-fire went
into effect a ship hired by the Irgun and stocked with ammunition
left a port in southern France, bound for Israel. The ship was called
the *Altalena*, Jabotinsky's old pen name. According to Menahem
Begin, it contained 5,000 rifles, 4 million rounds of ammunition, 300
Bren guns, 150 spandaus, 5 caterpillar armed vehicles and thousands
of air-combat bombs, as well as 900 troops[4]—a tribute to the fund-
raising talents of friends of the Irgun in Western Europe and in the
United States. This store would have been of enormous benefit to
weapons-starved Israel. But this unauthorized and ill-concealed act
would have constituted an open defiance of the truce had the ship
landed. Furthermore, the Irgun was offering the National Defense
Army only half the arms and ammunition aboard, intending to use
the rest itself. Ben-Gurion insisted that all arms be turned over to the
National Defense Army. When this command, made in the name of
the law and order of a state that was only just constituting itself out
of the chaos of illegitimacy, was not heeded, Ben-Gurion ordered
Israeli troops to prevent the landing of the ship. At about midnight
on the 22nd of June, firing began upon the *Altalena* from the beach
at Tel-Aviv. The ship was set afire, and it sank with its entire arsenal.
The Irgun organization was promptly broken up, and on June 28 its
leaders took the oath of allegiance to the National Defense Army.

The first truce came to an end on July 9, and the ensuing phase of
the war lasted ten days. By this time the Israeli forces were better
organized and equipped, and were on the offensive throughout this
entire period until the second truce. In the north Israeli forces were

[4] Begin, *op. cit.*, p. 155.

able to take most of the Galilee. In the Jerusalem Corridor the Palmach was brought in to pit themselves against the Arab Legion. They were able to capture Lydda and Ramleh, two major positions surrounding the Tel-Aviv-Jerusalem road, and they succeeded in encircling Latrun, but the second truce came into effect before they could attempt to capture it. But the convoys could now bypass Latrun, since the Burma Road was in full operation, and a new permanent route to Jerusalem was being built. In Jerusalem itself a new attempt at organizing a capture of the Old City was delayed, and the truce intervened before it could get under way.

The second truce began at 5:30 P.M. on July 18. Count Bernadotte hoped to turn this into a permanent armistice, but it was never more than an uneasy cease-fire. There were frequent exchanges of shots in Jerusalem, and the Arabs blew up the Latrun pumping station on August 12. On September 16 Count Bernadotte presented a set of proposals for a settlement in Palestine. It was a partition plan considerably less favorable to the Israelis than the November, 1947, UN plan had been. Although it gave the entire Galilee to the Israelis, it gave all of the Negev to the Arabs and established Haifa as a free port. Jerusalem, once again, was to be under international administration. The plan was unacceptable to the Israelis. It was also looked upon with some disapproval by the Arab League, among whom dissensions were arising. Many of the League's members were growing wary of King Abdullah's ambitions, and considered that the Bernadotte plan gave too much to him.

Bernadotte, who had never been popular with the Israelis, was now looked upon by them with considerable hostility. On September 17, the day after he presented his armistice proposals, he was shot and killed while riding through the streets of Jerusalem. The assassination was clearly the work of the Stern Gang, but the Israeli government did not begin rounding up the leaders of that organization until some twenty-four hours after the assassination, and this fact, along with the rather lenient way in which the Sternist prisoners were treated, caused considerable criticism of the Israelis throughout the world. A quick settlement of the Arab-Israeli dispute was now desired everywhere. The Israelis, their stock of favorable world opinion now at an ebb, were left to their own resources to determine the outcome.

They seized the initiative on October 15, when, in the name of retaliation against the Egyptian forces for attacking one of the convoys to the surrounded Israeli settlements in the Negev, they began an all-out Negev campaign. With a fine sense of the poetry of history, this campaign, directed against the Egyptians, was called "Operation Ten Plagues." The task was turned over once again to the Palmach Brigade, which was now at the peak of its form under the command of Colonel Yigal Allon. By October 20 Allon had broken through the Egyptian lines and on the 21st Israeli forces captured Beersheba. By the end of October the Negev, with the exception of the Gaza Strip and a pocket in the area of Faluja, had been cleared of Egyptian forces. Later the Israelis continued their advance right into the Sinai Desert, but the British government demanded that they withdraw. During this same period Colonel Carmel directed a final campaign against the forces of Fawzi al-Kawukji in the Galilee. By October 31 the Israelis were on the Lebanese side of the border. These final actions determined the outlines of the Israel of today.

The armistice agreements were signed separately: with Egypt on February 24, with Lebanon on March 23, with Jordan on April 3, and with Syria on July 20, 1949. Iraq, the one other Arab nation whose troops fought against the Israelis, did not share a border with the new Jewish state, and refused to enter into negotiations with it. The state of Israel now occupied something considerably less than all of Palestine, but it was a larger and more viable entity than the state proposed in the UN partition scheme of November, 1947. Unlike the partition state, it comprised all of the Galilee, all of the Negev except the Gaza Strip, and the entire New City of Jerusalem with a reasonably broad corridor leading to it from the coastal area. The Israelis had also managed to retain the besieged Mount Scopus, but since this enclave was separated from the main body of Israeli Jerusalem by a stretch of Jordanian territory, the Hebrew University and Hadassah Hospital buildings on top of it were no longer usable. Today, both these institutions have been rebuilt in the hills to the west of Israeli Jerusalem. Originally, according to a UN resolution passed after the 1949 armistice agreements, both the Israel-held and Jordan-held parts of Jerusalem were to be placed under the administration of a single UN Trusteeship Council. But this resolution, received with hostility both in Israel and in Jordan, was never effectuated. Instead, on December 26, 1949, the Israel parliament transferred itself from Tel-Aviv to Jerusalem, and the seat of King David became once again the capital of a Jewish state.

PART THREE:

Society and Politics in Zion

CHAPTER 5

Growth of a National Community

I

DURING the Arab riots of 1936 the fourteen families who made up the entire Jewish population of the village of Pekiin in the upper Galilee fled their homes for safety. This act was the final break in the continuity of the ancient Jewish commonwealth, for, according to tradition, the Jews of Pekiin had been living there since before the destruction of the Temple by the Romans. The Roman conquest did not immediately put an end to Jewish national life in Palestine. The religious court presided over by Johanan ben Zakkai became the representative political body of the Jews of Palestine in the eyes of the Romans, and Johanan's successors in the presidency of the court eventually assumed the official title of Patriarch. But after its support of the unsuccessful uprising led by the pseudo Messiah Bar Kochba in 135 C.E., the patriarchate steadily lost political power and came to an end altogether in 425. From then on, the effective spiritual leadership of world Jewry was in Babylonia, which was in turn succeeded in this position by Spain, and then by other countries of the Diaspora. Palestine became a mere backwater of Jewish life, despite the immense emotional significance Jewry continued to accord it as a place, or as a dream. The Byzantine and Arab rulers allowed Jews to live in Jerusalem, as the Roman emperors had not after 73 C.E., but this only gave the Jews of seventh-century Jerusalem the privilege of watching a Muslim shrine, the Dome of the Rock, being built on the site of the Temple. In 1099 the Crusaders, another

conquering army from the west, expelled the Jews from Jerusalem
once again, along with the Muslim infidels.

For most of the two centuries that followed, the Jewish population
of Palestine was at the lowest ebb in its history, confined to a few
small outposts of settlement in the Galilee, such as Pekiin. When the
Jewish population of Palestine began to grow again after this period,
the growth was the phenomenon of a *returning* population. Jewish
life in Palestine was now no longer the natural continuity of an
indigenous community, but was the product of an effort of religious
and national self-consciousness—of a kind of crusade, which was
perhaps partly a response to the Christian crusade that had destroyed
the older Jewish national life in the Holy Land. It is appropriate that
the first powerful longings for a return to Zion of the modern
type—that is to say, longings of the type that readily transformed
itself into action—came from Spain of the Jewish Golden Age, the
greatest spiritual epoch in the history of the Diaspora. The two
greatest men of that epoch, the poet Judah Halevi (ca. 1086-ca.
1141) and the philosopher Moses Maimonides (1135-1204), both
made journeys to Palestine. It was under the leadership of the
Spanish-Jewish Philosopher Nahmanides that the Jewish community
of Jerusalem was re-established. In these men, the very height of the
creativity of the Diaspora induced a sense of the tragic condition of
exile, and a response to it. Furthermore, at this time a growing
crusade in Spain was moving toward the ultimate destruction of
Jewish national life there.

Kabbalism, also of Spanish-Jewish origin, lent new magnetism to
the soil of Palestine, and the establishment of Kabbalistic communities in Palestine restored its importance as a living Jewish spiritual
center. The center of this movement was in Safed, where Isaac Luria
lived in the sixteenth century. Standing at the top of a mountain in
the Galilee, this city is blurred in a unique haze of sunlight which,
even today, is capable of imparting mystical intimations to even the
most rational of minds. Safed, along with the three other holy cities
of Jewish medieval tradition—Tiberias, Hebron and Jerusalem—
gradually became the center of a small but growing Jewish population, made up largely of Kabbalists, Hasidim, and pious old men and
women who had come to end their lives on holy ground and be
buried in the Mount of Olives. By the nineteenth century this
religious community was largely of Eastern European origin. Except

for the fact that its members married and had children, the community had some of the qualities of a monastic brotherhood. Pious activity was considered to be its sole purpose, both by itself and by its kinsmen abroad. Its members were usually not economically productive, and their major or sole source of sustenance was the regular charitable contribution—the *halukah*—made by those Jews in the Diaspora whose piety was both tempered and buttressed by a greater talent for worldly acquisition. With rare exceptions, this community was either indifferent or hostile toward its more secular brethren from Eastern Europe who arrived to rebuild the country at the end of the nineteenth century.

But even before the Zionists arrived, the Jewish community of Palestine was supplemented by more worldly elements. These were the Jews who came into the country from the surrounding communities of the Middle East, mostly in search of new centers for trade. For these non-European Jews, whose activities ranged from peddling in the streets to presiding over large and prosperous commercial enterprises (often enough they went from one to the other in the course of a single lifetime), living in Palestine was as much a normal outgrowth of the regional social and economic life of which they were a part as it was a matter of piety. Originating in such major centers of Jewish life as Baghdad and Damascus, they were at least in part the direct descendants of the great ancient community of Babylonia. But by this time many of the Jews of the Levant were also in part or wholly descended from Spanish-Jewish refugees who had scattered throughout the Mediterranean area from the time of their expulsion from Spain in 1492. The cultural influence of these Spanish, or Sephardic (*Sepharad* is the Hebrew word for Spain), Jews was strong enough to achieve predominance throughout the Mediterranean littoral and to leave a permanent Sephardic imprint upon most of the Jewish communities of this area, even when they were not necessarily of Spanish-Jewish origin. This influence is manifest in the character of the synagogue ritual, in the pronounciation of Hebrew, and in the prevalence throughout the area of Ladino, a Hispanic patois which is the Sephardic equivalent of Yiddish, and is written, like the latter, in Hebrew characters. As a result of this widespread Sephardic influence, the term "Sephardim" is often applied even to Middle Eastern Jews who are not necessarily of Sephardic extraction at all.

The first efforts at quickening the Palestinian-Jewish community—

the Yishuv—into an authentic national life were, in effect, a Sephardic enterprise. This is to speak not only of the economic activities of Sephardic merchants from other countries in the Middle East,
but also of the charitable efforts of the British Sir Moses Montefiore
and the American Judah Touro, both Jews of Sephardic extraction. It
was the initiative of Sir Moses and the money of Judah Touro that
built for the Jews of Jerusalem, in 1860, the first quarter to stand outside the dank walls of the Old City, in the sunlight of the surrounding
hills. This was the first step in the building of the New City, the
present Israeli Jerusalem, a process which did not, however, achieve a
rapid pace until after 1900, in the Zionist period. Yet even in this
latter period, when the development of the country was dominated
by Jews from Northeastern Europe, culturally very different from the
Sephardim, the growing Jerusalem maintained a largely Middle Eastern, Arabic and Sephardic Jewish character, as did Tiberias. In other
words, these cities maintained a kind of Oriental continuity. The
sharp break with Palestine's Oriental past and the sudden departure
into the atmosphere of contemporary Eastern Europe took place in
the new rural settlements created by the Zionists out of nothing, and
in the new urban community of Tel-Aviv, founded in 1909 on the
sandy beach just north of Jaffa.

Zionism was a wholly Ashkenazic[1] conception, uniquely a product
of European culture. In particular the second wave of Zionist immigration into Palestine, which began in 1904, was the beginning of the
influx of an element which was as utterly Eastern European in
character as was the old ultrareligious community, for all of its
apparent differences from the latter. In both the new Zionist type
and the old religious type of Eastern European settler there was a
spiritual tension, a passion for abstract and even ideological commitments of the spirit, that was not at all characteristic of the more
graceful Sephardim. It is perhaps significant that the gap between the
old religious and the new ideological form of colonization was
spanned by a group of orthodox Jerusalem Jews of Eastern European

---

1 This word, the traditional counterpart to "Sephardic," refers to those Jewish communities who trace their ancestry more or less directly to the medieval
communities of the Rhineland (Ashkenaz is an old Hebrew word for Germany)
rather than of Spain. Generally speaking, the traditional communities of Northern Europe, particularly of Germany, Poland and Russia, are considered to be
Ashkenazic (the use of any of the forms of the Judaeo-German dialect or Yiddish
language is what distinguishes them).

origin, who founded the colony of Petah Tikva in 1878, under the influence of the agrarian ideals of the Alliance Israélite Universelle and its Mikveh Israel agricultural school. Even the Bilu pioneers of 1882, the first of the new type of settlers to arrive directly from Eastern Europe, were not impervious to religious feelings, and some of them became absorbed in the religious life of Petah Tikva. Like the kibbutzim of the next generation, this and other early pioneering settlements became outposts of Eastern European culture on the soil of Palestine.

But in the first wave of Zionist immigration from 1882 to 1904—known as the First *Aliyah*[2]—there was also a widespread romantic sentiment which favored orientalization and absorption into the indigenous cultural life of the Middle East. The young pioneers of this period, many of them educated in secular Russian schools and universities, were still under the influence of the old revolutionary mood of the *Narodniki* (literally: "Populists"). The young men and women who made up the Narodniki were intellectuals who sought messianic regeneration for the Russian peasantry and for their own souls by adopting rural dress, going into the villages, and attempting to become peasants themselves. This poetic enterprise—which was at its height in the 1860's and 1870's—failed not only because it was ultimately impossible for the urban intellectual to transform himself so radically, but because the naturally conservative instincts of the Russian peasants caused the latter to look with great suspicion upon these odd intruders in their midst. By the 1880's Narodnism had passed out of the mainstream of the Russian revolutionary movement, although it achieved its most splendid manifestation only later, in the old age of Tolstoy (who had not been a Narodnik), when he endeavored to live and work as a peasant on his own estate.

The romantic Narodnism of the First Aliyah generation found one of its outlets in a passion for the Arab way of life. Some of the rural settlers of this period strove for the ability to ride horseback and shoot in the Arab manner, and the most accomplished in these skills were held in a high esteem that was contrary to an Eastern European Jewish tradition which had always frowned on such things. One of the foremost writers of the First Aliyah, Moshe Smilansky, wove the

[2] This Hebrew word literally means "ascent," but it is the standard word for immigration to Israel.

indigenous folklore of the Palestinian Arabs into romantic tales about them—in Hebrew. The urban settlers of this generation found their Oriental appetites satisfied mainly by identification with the Sephardic Jews. Eliezer Ben-Yehuda, the man primarily responsible for the transformation of Hebrew into the spoken language of Israel today, wore the robes and turbans of an Oriental Jew for a time, even though he was himself born in Lithuania; he subsequently saw to it that the Sephardic rather than the Ashkenazic pronunciation of Hebrew became the dialect of Palestinian Jewry, as it is to this day.

But, for all the poetry of its spirit, the generation of the First Aliyah lacked the organizational rigor needed in the revolutionary task of creating a Palestinian Jewish nation. Their efforts were diffuse, and tended—with the exception of the cultural work of Ben-Yehuda and his circle in Jerusalem—to scatter themselves into mere isolated corners of Palestinian social and economic life. They had set out instinctively recognizing that the first step toward creating a real national community was that of transforming themselves into a landed Jewish agricultural working class. But like the Narodniki before them, their intentions outreached their methods. They approached their task using the classic American method of individualistic pioneering, but the conditions in Palestine were very different from those of the American frontier. The land was harsh and the climate extremely difficult for Europeans, especially for a group of Europeans mainly accustomed to urban occupations. Furthermore, a large native mass of cheap labor was temptingly at hand. As a result, many of the First Aliyah settlers in time simply became landlords, employing Arab labor and often turning away Jewish workers on the grounds that they were more expensive and less efficient than the Arabs. Yet, despite this concern with cost accounting, few of the settlements were able to achieve economic self-sufficiency in this period. The settlers' lack of experience in running farms was compounded by their slowness in adjusting agricultural conceptions developed in Russia to the special physical conditions of Palestine. By the 1890's, they had come largely to rely on the charitable subsidies of Baron Edmond de Rothschild in France—a new version of the halukah, as Ahad Ha-Am scathingly observed.

These problems were overcome by the more rigorous and conscientiously ideological approach of the Second Aliyah, the wave of immigration which began in 1904 after the Kishinev pogroms and ended with the outbreak of the First World War. The tough-minded members of the Second Aliyah generation were the product of the changes that had taken place in Russia since the gentler days of the Bilu pioneers. Even as far back as 1881, the end of the Narodnik type of idealism as a central element in the Russian revolutionary movement was foretold by the sudden outburst of terrorism in the activities of the Narodnaya Volya organization, which succeeded in assassinating Tsar Alexander II on March 1 of that year. In the years that followed, Narodnism was steadily displaced by a grimmer and more determined mood which, after 1883, increasingly found its outlet in Marxism. Many Jewish intellectuals had been attracted to Narodnism, and had been willing to identify themselves with the culture of a Russian peasantry, even though it was alien and hostile to the Jews. But after the pogroms of 1881, in which the beloved peasant rose up and became a murderer of Jews, the Jewish intelligentsia in Russia had to find another form of cultural identification for its radicalism. Marxist universalism, which focused upon an urban proletariat that included an infinite number of cultural groups, including the Jews, and which regarded the peasantry with some scorn, became a far more satisfactory outlet for Jewish radicalism than Narodnism had been, and Jews joined the revolutionary movement in increasing numbers.

The Jewish Socialist Federation, or Bund, which gave the Russian-Jewish radicals a cultural vehicle of their own within the general Russian Marxist movement, was formed in 1897, the year in which the first Zionist Congress took place in Basel. This began an epoch in which young Russian-Jewish intellectuals found themselves confronted with the two great alternatives of socialism and Zionism, one of which had to be chosen upon entering maturity. Many of them passed from one commitment to the other during the course of their lives, in one direction or the other. Both Chaim Weizmann and Vladimir Jabotinsky made something of a specialty, in their young manhood, out of gaining entry into the meetings of Jewish social democratic student organizations and winning converts to Zionism. The two ideologies appealed equally to the messianic impulse of the Jewish intellectual, and to his desire to achieve Jewish emancipation. The choice between them was separated only by an emotional hairsbreadth in many cases, but the fervor of rivalry between the two movements was immense, and they were considered by their respective adherents to be diametrically opposed.

In particular, the seemingly narrow choice between Bundism and

Labor Zionism, both socialist and both concerned with Jewish culture, revolved around a single point: the sense of one's own relationship as a Jew (and, incidentally, as an intellectual) to the proletariat. To the adherents of both movements it was clear that the Jews on the whole, for all the poverty and oppression under which they suffered, were not, properly speaking, a proletariat. In the eyes of Bundist and Labor Zionist alike, this was a failing that had to be overcome. The Bundist achieved his solution vicariously, by identifying Jewish suffering with that of the proletariat at large; this is parallel to the way in which the socialist intellectual in general seeks to transcend his middle-class situation through vicarious identification with the workers. For the Labor Zionists, on the other hand, the only solution was to transform themselves into a proletariat through a personal and direct act of will. This is what they set out to do in Palestine; in the meantime, their intimate contact and rivalry with Russian Marxism had taught them something about the organizational techniques and attitudes for the kind of revolutionary task they had chosen for themselves.

The twofold program of the Second Aliyah pioneers in Palestine—the establishment of self-supporting Jewish agricultural enterprises and the transformation of themselves into a laboring class—called for the use of cooperative methods from the outset. Even their initial task of gaining employment on the Jewish farms upon arrival demanded cooperation. The Jewish laborers had to live collectively on the farms in order to keep their living costs low enough to enable them to compete with Arab wage levels; in time, their groups functioned as unions, which bargained collectively with the Jewish employers and occasionally used the weapon of the strike. These new settlers were mainly very young men and women, many of them not yet twenty years old at the time of their arrival in Palestine, and the method of communal living helped them emotionally and physically to bridge their way into a new and difficult life. Furthermore, organizing themselves was the way in which they coped with a new danger that arose out of their growing success on the labor market: Arab attacks upon them.

Only a few years after the start of the Second Aliyah, the Jewish settlements in Palestine were brimming over with cooperative schemes and experiments. In 1908, at Sejera, a training farm in the Western Galilee run by the Zionist movement, a group of young

Jewish workers undertook to administer and work a portion of the estate entirely by themselves for one year. They were able not only to show a profit but also to learn numerous skills in the process, including that of defending themselves against Arab attacks. It was here that the first Jewish self-defense organization in Palestine, Ha'Shomer, was created, largely under the leadership of the young David Green, soon to become known as Ben-Gurion. In the following year, at Kinneret on the shore of the Sea of Galilee, a more permanent farm was established on land bought by the Jewish National Fund. Here the official proprietor and employer was not some private owner but the Zionist organization itself. This was envisioned as a way of overcoming the difficulties that the young pioneers had encountered in trying to find work at the old Rothschild-supported Jewish plantations near the Mediterranean coast. The Kinneret farm naturally favored Jewish labor and cooperation among the workers, but unfortunately these latter continued to be treated as employees. Although they received an equal wage among themselves, as they wanted, they were placed under the supervision of appointed farm managers, older men whose outlooks were different from those of the workers and who received higher salaries. Friction soon developed between managers and workers. The managers began seeking profitable arrangements in the same way as any traditional landholder, and even resorted to hiring Arab labor. The workers responded by staging a strike in the fall of 1909. The latter had still not found the formula for the cooperative method of production toward which they were groping, but they were now clear in their own minds about what they did not want, and had developed a strong sense of solidarity among themselves.

In December, 1909, a historic step was taken by a group of the Kinneret workers. A portion of the Kinneret estate stood on the eastern bank of the Jordan, separated by the river from the main body of the farm. Because of its location, this stretch of land, called Um Juni after the Arab village adjoining it, was not easily comprised within the general administration of the estate. Therefore, a group of workers at Kinneret asked Dr. Arthur Ruppin, the director of the Zionist Organization office in Jerusalem, who was particularly concerned with the agrarian experiments, for permission to cultivate Um Juni entirely under their own auspices for a year. Ruppin agreed to this, and six young men and one woman established themselves there at the beginning of 1910 as a completely collective community. They kept a household in common, over which the young woman presided, and distributed no cash payments among themselves. At the end of the year the Um Juni group showed a profit, while the rest of Kinneret did not. Ruppin was therefore quite willing to see a permanent independent collective established at Um Juni. The original seven workers were not inclined to do this permanently, but another group of ten men and two women at Kinneret, who called themselves the "Romny group" after the town in the Ukraine from which most of them had come, had already agreed among themselves to seek to live and work somewhere as a permanent labor collective, and volunteered to settle at Um Juni. They called their settlement "Deganiah" (cornflower). Now a prosperous settlement watching its third generation reach maturity, Deganiah is generally considered to be the first of the kibbutzim.

The cooperative method of founding villages developed by the Second Aliyah was used for the founding of urban communities as well. Tel-Aviv was as characteristic a product of this generation as Deganiah was. At the turn of the century, the ancient city of Jaffa was the major port of Palestine and was therefore an important commercial center, but the increasing numbers of Jewish settlers there found themselves uncomfortable in its cramped and dirty streets, and among its vast Arab majority. In 1907 a cooperative society was formed by a group of Jaffa Jews for the purpose of building a garden suburb on the sandy wastes north of the city. By the summer of 1909 the society had obtained financial help from the Jewish National Fund, and building was begun. This was followed by the formation of other such cooperative building societies, and the suburb rapidly grew; by 1914 it had a population of about 1,500. Its name was taken from the title of Nachum Sokolow's Hebrew translation of Herzl's Old–New Land. The name of an ancient Babylonian locale mentioned in Ezekiel 3:15, "Tel-Aviv" literally signifies in Hebrew "mound of spring"—"mound" in the sense of an archaeological site made up of a heap of ancient ruins. Hence Sokolow chose this name from the Bible as conveying, even more richly than Herzl's title, the sense of "old–new." The aptness of the name for the first all-Jewish city of modern times is clear. At the same time the departure of the Jewish community of Jaffa, and the formation of a separate Jewish city to the north of it, was a complete rupture from the Palestinian past. Unlike Jerusalem, there is scarcely anything Oriental about Tel-Aviv. Architecturally it is Mediterranean, but the texture of its everyday life and of its mood is that of a fragment of Eastern or Central Europe placed upon the Mediterranean littoral.

The end of the First World War brought a new wave of immigration into Palestine, and a new quickening of settlement activity. The Third Aliyah, which took place from 1919 to 1923, was a step further than its predecessors in the direction of firm ideological commitment. The Second Aliyah had moved beyond the vague romanticism of the First, but it nevertheless had had to work its way through tentativeness and an initial lack of clarity in its aims. By contrast, the Third Aliyah had a clear institutional base in Palestine—the work of its predecessors—upon which to build. Furthermore, this new generation had inherited the zealot mood bequeathed to Europe by the upheavals of the First World War and the Russian Revolution. The militant spirit was based upon a resurgent faith in the power of the will to reclaim man from the cravenness of urban middle-class life. It found one of its most characteristic expressions in the emergence of youth movements all over Europe, from the quasi-military "Young Germany" to the more blandly Anglo-Saxon institution of the Boy Scouts. These were early manifestations of that revolt of the lower middle class against itself, the white-collar lunge toward a vision of heroism, which has produced many of the major events, both good and ill, of this century. Zionism, which was itself in some respects such a lower-middle-class revolt from the beginning, was naturally susceptible to this new mood.

Its first important manifestation in Palestine was in the formation of work gangs, which roamed the country to take part in large-scale projects, such as road building and swamp drainage, rather than in the immediate founding of permanent settlements. Many of the new kibbutzim of the 1920's evolved only gradually out of the work camps that were established for these projects. There was a certain restlessness afoot in this period which had not been characteristic of the earlier generations of pioneers. But this was exactly the spirit that now was needed; its crowning achievement was the clearing of an entire swampy region, the Valley of Jezreel, which had been bought from an Arab landlord by the Jewish National Fund. Today, the Valley of Jezreel is a rich and fertile area, the heartland of agricultural settlement in Israel.

Much of this activity was organized under the quasi-military work force, the *G'dud Ha'avodah* (Legion of Labor), which had been founded in Russia by Joseph Trumpeldor, and which served as the framework for the eventual formation of the Haganah. This organization made its headquarters in a kibbutz named Ein Harod, which it had established in the eastern Jezreel Valley in 1921. Among those who established themselves in Ein Harod, the early mood of restlessness began to subside. In time they began to favor their own autonomy as against the organizational and ideological demands that the G'dud Ha'avodah was making upon them. In 1923 Ein Harod broke with the G'dud altogether. But its legacy of large-scale activity made it into the center of a newly developing kibbutz ideology, which arose in opposition to the ideal of a very small community held by Deganiah. The settlers of Deganiah had, in fact, always used the feminine form *kvutzah*, rather than kibbutz, to describe their community (both words signify a collective community, and are today considered to be interchangeable, although the feminine form is now only rarely used in this context), because it carries a certain connotation of diminutiveness. In their view the *kvutzah* was to be something on the order of an expanded family, and they thought at first that a group of about twenty persons was an optimum beyond which they would not go. In time they enlarged this figure, but their determination to limit their numbers was so firm that, in order to accommodate a number of new arrivals, they established Deganiah B, an adjacent but separate settlement, in 1921.

The Ein Harod group, on the other hand, came to envision a community of a much larger size; in fact, they considered that there did not have to be any set limits in principle to the size of a kibbutz. This was a conception more in keeping with the revolutionary vision of a generation that had been weaned on the events taking place in Eastern Europe from 1917 to 1920. In a sense, they were picturing a future Jewish Palestine as a vast and contiguous chain of workers' communities, a completely socialist society. The Deganiah group, on the other hand, belonged more to the nineteenth-century utopian tradition; they were satisfied to have a small socialist community of their own, and made few demands upon the surrounding world or upon history. Of course, whatever their underlying sentiments, the Deganiah and Ein Harod groups were both upholding an implicit notion of what the society of Jewish Palestine was to become. Hence their rivalry did not remain restricted to themselves, but took on a broadly ideological character and formed itself into two quasi-political movements. In 1927 an association of kibbutzim subscribing to the view propounded by Ein Harod was created under its leadership; called *Ha'kibbutz Ha'me'uhad* (The United Kibbutz), it was the first of several national kibbutz federations in Palestine. The small *kvutzot* (plural of *kvutzah*) did not hesitate to respond in kind; that same year they created their own federation, the *Hever Ha'kvutzot* (Society of Kvutzot). In the ensuing years these federations, along with others that subsequently came into being, served as sponsoring organizations for the founding of new kibbutzim. Although the federations tried to eschew specific identification with one or another of the national political parties, they eventually did become so identified. In later years this identification brought about a politicization of the kibbutzim that was in some ways detrimental to their spiritual health.

There was yet a third major national kibbutz movement which came into being in this period, the one that above all went on to become the model of militant ideological commitment. *Ha'shomer Ha'tza'ir* (The Young Guard) was formed in Poland in 1913 as a branch of the international Boy Scout movement, and drew its strength from the sons and daughters of Polish and Galician middle-class Jewish families, most of which were quite religious in outlook. Ha'shomer Ha'tza'ir became as militantly atheist as its members' parents were orthodox, and under the impact of the Russian Revolution it became firmly committed to a revolutionary Marxist ideology. Having originated in Poland, it did not have the firsthand experience of Bolshevik rule that led many Russian Zionists to become thoroughly disillusioned with Marxism. The Polish pogroms of that same period, which spurred the Ha'shomer youth on to settlement in Palestine, were looked upon by them as characteristic manifestations of a bourgeois society. The Ha'shomer kibbutzim in Palestine, for which a member was usually first rigorously prepared during a two-year period in a training camp in Poland, were considered the cells out of which the future proletarian socialist society would be generated. This group, then, became the far left of the kibbutz movement. As for the dispute over the optimum size of the kibbutz, Ha'shomer (which formed its own federation, the *Kibbutz Artzi*, in 1928) took up a position somewhere between those of the other two federations; in this matter, their view may be said to have been the triumphant

one, since none of the movements today regard as feasible either the
ideal group of about twenty that the *kvutzot* originally hoped to
maintain or the kibbutz consisting of thousands that the Ein Harod
leaders had envisioned. For the most part, the kibbutzim today have
memberships of from one hundred to three hundred, with total
populations ranging from about three hundred to a little over a
thousand, depending on the number of children and elderly parents
also attached to the community.

It was, then, during the period of the Third Aliyah and of the few
years that followed that the main outlines of kibbutz life and
ideology, still largely unchanged today, were established. It was also
in this period that a significant breach in the agrarian movement
occurred and a new type of rural collective was developed as an
alternative to the kibbutz. Among the fundamental ideals of the
kibbutz is not only that of a collective economy, but also that of a
collective way of life. The two go together: if the benefits of
production are to be shared freely, and no economic distinctions of
any sort are to arise between the members, then the individual should
not be expected to provide for himself and his family in a separate
household economy. The problem of the family has always been the
stumbling block of egalitarian socialist ideologies. Absolute equality
of distribution must always be qualified by consideration for varying
individual needs, and "to each according to his need" usually means
that a man with many children must receive a good deal more than
a man with few or none. But such an arrangement invariably makes
fecundity into a form of wealth, no more or no less justifiable than
the claims to wealth that individuals make within a capitalist system.
The kibbutz solution to this problem was to turn the entire community into a collective household, in which all individual needs, for
children and adults alike, were to be centrally provided for. At the
beginning, for example, all clothing was provided by the kibbutz; this
practice has been modified somewhat in the atmosphere of relative
"embourgeoisement" that has lately set in among the kibbutzim, and
members now usually receive clothing allowances with which they
can go to the towns and make their own purchases. As for the crucial
matter of the raising of children, the kibbutzim handle it collectively,
placing all the children in communal nurseries, at least during the
daytime hours. A few kibbutzim have the children sleep in their
parents' apartments at night, but most do not. The central element

Growth of a National Community 193

in this communal household structure has been and continues to be the large dining hall, in which all members take their meals.

In time, some of the founders of the kibbutz movement found that this communal atmosphere did not suit them. In particular, as their children were born and began to grow, they discovered in themselves a strong old-fashioned desire to have their own households and to gather their families around their own private dinner tables. At the same time they were still attached in principle to the ideal of collective or cooperative agriculture. In 1921 a group of men and women from various kibbutzim, including Deganiah, got together and founded a settlement in the Valley of Jezreel which was organized according to a new type of cooperative plan. Nahalal, as they called the new village, was the first *moshav ovdim*, or smallholders' cooperative settlement. In this type of settlement the members live, eat and sleep in separate cottages with their families, as do most farmers anywhere in the world. Furthermore, each cottager is allotted his own plot of land, to cultivate as he sees fit within certain general limits established by the community as a whole. Tractors and other heavy equipment and supplies are owned and used cooperatively by the entire village. The produce of each individual holding is turned over to a central village cooperative, which handles all processing and marketing. The profits of the central cooperative are then divided up among the villagers in proportion according to how much each of them produced. This method of smallholders' cooperation has become the major form of agricultural production in Israel today. It has had particular appeal to the type of immigrant who came to Israel in large numbers from Eastern Europe and from North Africa immediately after statehood. These new immigrants, mainly small tradesmen and artisans in their original homes, and generally more bound to traditions and less well educated than those who have been drawn to the kibbutz ideal, have found it perfectly satisfactory to transform themselves into agriculturists provided they can have their traditional family lives along with a system of mutual aid.

There are some technical disadvantages to this type of holding as compared with the kibbutz. The division of the land into small, separately cultivated parcels constitutes a less efficient system of production as compared with the large-scale cultivation practiced on the kibbutz. Furthermore, the parceling out of the land allows for far less flexibility in the admission and turnover of members than is possible in the kibbutz. For these and other reasons, a system midway between the kibbutz and the *moshav ovdim* has grown up in recent years—the *moshav shitufi*. Like the *moshav ovdim*, the *moshav shitufi* is made up of separate and independent households, which manage their affairs with money received from the division of the profits of the village as a whole. But here, unlike in the *moshav ovdim*, the profits are divided equally, because the land is cultivated in common, as a single large unit, as in the kibbutzim. This is a promising compromise arrangement between the two systems, although it has not as yet become a widespread form of settlement. But it can be said that both forms of *moshavim*, for all their resemblance to more traditional forms of village life, could not have come into being without the prior development of the kibbutz form. It was the radical kibbutz form that established the traditions of rural cooperation in Israel in the first place, and which developed both the methods of cultivation and the experienced agricultural class that were drawn upon for giving a start to these later forms of settlement.

It was also in the period of the Third Aliyah that the characteristic urban socialist institutions of the Yishuv were formed. In a conference held in December, 1920, the kibbutz and labor leaders of the Yishuv merged their forces into the creation of the *Histadrut*, or General Jewish Labor Federation in Palestine. Basically, the purpose of the Histadrut was to serve as a national federation of labor unions, like the AFL–CIO in the United States or the TUC in Britain. Under the special circumstances of the Yishuv, however, it was also intended for a larger historic role. The Jewish labor and socialist leaders of Palestine were creating a nation, and they therefore viewed their organization as a revolutionary medium for the creation of a labor commonwealth. The Histadrut was, in fact, in a unique historical situation; it had not only to serve as an instrument for organizing workers and as the creator of such welfare institutions as a system of socialized medicine but also had to be the medium for the development of an economy. In time the Histradut became as much an entrepreneur—and a large-scale one, at that—as it was an organizer of labor. From the point of view of Histadrut ideologists in the early days, this arrangement made the organization all the more a potential instrument for the creation of a society that would be socialist and worker-owned from the outset. It is only in recent years that contradictions have clearly emerged from the fact of being both a national labor union and the largest employer of labor in the country.

The formation of these rural and urban socialist institutions, which served as the major foundation stones of an emerging national community, was the work of a rather homogeneous group, which consisted almost entirely of Jews from Russia and Poland. Members of the old Oriental Jewish community of Palestine were scarcely to be found in its midst. A trickle of newer Oriental immigrants from Yemen and elsewhere became members of Histadrut unions, but their inferior educational backgrounds largely excluded them from positions among the leadership. As for the other major Ashkenazi group, the German Jews, they arrived late in Palestine and in relatively small numbers, and found themselves treated as a somewhat alien element by the Eastern European establishment. Furthermore, German Zionists tended to be more middle class in their outlook than the Eastern European pioneering elite, for whom socialism and Zionism were simply two aspects of a single ideal. To this day the dominant social and political establishment of Israel is mainly Eastern European and socialist, even in a society in which the private sector of the economy is at least as large as the socialist sector and in which the Eastern Europeans—indeed, the Ashkenazim in general—are no longer a majority of the population.

The first major modification in the homogeneity of the new Zionist immigration came with the so-called Fourth Aliyah, from 1924 to 1931. This wave of immigration, in contrast with its predecessors, was largely middle class in character. The reason for this sudden change was the closing of immigration to the United States in 1924; the major pole of attraction in the world for emigrating Eastern European Jews had virtually ceased to exist. Meanwhile, Palestine was undergoing a period of relative prosperity. It therefore came to seem a likely place for settlement in the eyes of a type of man who was older than most of the Labor Zionists had been when they emigrated, and who, being the head of a family, was primarily concerned with matters of personal security. It was this wave of immigration that transformed Tel-Aviv into a metropolis and added some color to the hitherto Spartan life of the Zionist community with a proliferation of small shops and display windows filled with consumer goods.

The Fifth Aliyah, which began with the rise of nazism in 1932 and lasted until the war, brought further modifications in the composi-

tion of the growing Yishuv. It brought the first large numbers of
German Jews to Palestine, where they experienced a unique reversal
of the relationship that usually prevails between themselves and
Eastern European Jews in other parts of the world where the two
groups have settled. The German Jews of America, for example, had
not only come from a country in which they had been a part of
European middle-class civilization at a time when their Eastern
European counterparts were still virtually in a medieval ghetto, but
they were already a well-established and often upper-class part of
American life when the latter began arriving en masse. But in
Palestine social pre-eminence belonged to that almost exclusively
Eastern European elite which had given its youth to pioneering, and
which now had a firm grasp on the top positions in the institutional
structure it had created. The only institutional realm in Palestine in
which the German Jews were able to achieve predominance was that
traditional stronghold of German culture, higher education. But for a
long time the university was the only place in Palestine and Israel in
which the Central European passion for trappings of middle-class
respectability was not merely something to be mocked, defied or
ignored. It is said that the origin of the popular and ironic nickname
of the German Jew in Israel—yekke—is simply a corruption of the
German word Jacke (jacket), and refers to the decorous wearing of
this article of clothing in the midst of a society whose pioneers had
eschewed such things. (Today in their sixties and older, the Second
and Third Aliyah pioneers usually wear jackets in public, but the
tie—called a "herring" in Israeli slang—is still avoided as much as
possible by them.) To this day, the life style of the German-born
Israeli tends to be patterned upon that of a Central Europe which is
gone forever. He is a dignified reminder of old Frankfurt, Berlin or
Vienna, soberly making his way through a world dominated, both
from the top and from the bottom of the social scale, by less decorous
breeds of Jews from Eastern Europe, North Africa and the Middle
East.

Since the Fifth Aliyah was largely made up of people whose main
reason for emigrating was to escape imminent danger, it brought to
Palestine the first large numbers of Europeans—other than the old
ultraorthodox community, which was scarcely part of the general life
of the Yishuv—who were not committed to Zionism at all. (This
was, on the whole, more true of those who came from Eastern

Europe in this wave of immigration than of those who came from Germany.) These elements further buttressed the growing middle-class life of the Yishuv and would probably have brought about a rapid diminution of the ideological density of atmosphere in Palestine but for the nature of the historical events that were now taking place. The great disaster that was befalling the Jewish people, and the almost constant state of emergency which prevailed in Palestine for the next two decades, stood in for ideological commitment and drew together the various elements of the Yishuv into a mood of collective effort.

II

The new state of Israel began its history as a rescue operation. At the time of the Proclamation of Independence in May, 1948, the Jewish population of Palestine was about 650,000. By the end of that year more than a hundred thousand new immigrants had arrived; at the end of 1951, the original figure for May, 1948, had been doubled. The immediate effect of this enormous influx was, of course, a severe strain on the economy of the fledgling country. Even with the financial aid that came from the Jews of the United States and of other parts of the Diaspora, it took the better part of the decade of the 1950's for Israel to begin recovering the semblance of prosperity it had known under the Mandate.

The economic strains produced by the mass influx which followed Independence have proved to be less important in the long run than the social and cultural ones. For one thing, the strong middle-class tendencies introduced into the Yishuv by the Fourth and Fifth Aliyot were furthered considerably by the refugees from postwar Europe. Their lives torn up and reduced to a horror for the better part of a decade, these people wanted nothing more than to return to the quiet middle-class security that had been snatched from them. This desire was reinforced by a sort of Zionist mood that the war had imparted to many of them, who now felt that such security was no longer available to Jews anywhere in the world but in a Jewish state. But this feeling made them all the more hostile to a socialist ideology which seemed, in their eyes, to threaten to undermine the way of life they sought. Such antisocialist vehemence was especially strong among those who, having been caught up for a time in postwar Eastern

Europe, had tasted life under a communist regime. The more recent immigrants to Israel from East Central Europe, refugees from some two decades of communist government there, tend to be the country's strongest supporters of free enterprise. This is often true even of those who hold proletarian jobs.

Another source of strain—the most significant of all in Israel today—was introduced by the radical change in the ethnic character of immigration following statehood. In the course of the seven decades preceding 1948, the old Sephardic-Oriental character of the Yishuv had, except in a few areas, become almost entirely obscured by the cultural stamp of the European-Ashkenazi immigrants. Some Oriental immigrants arrived during the Mandate period, particularly from Yemen, but their numbers were too few to have any cultural impact upon the Palestinian Jewish milieu. But starting in the early 1950's, large numbers of immigrants began to arrive from the Arab countries of the Middle East and North Africa. As a result of the size of this new group, and of its higher birth rate as compared with Europeans, more than half the population of Israel today consists of Oriental families and their children. Their sudden appearance has caused an equally rapid transformation in the cultural atmosphere of the country, a phenomenon which has given rise to an alarmed reaction on the part of many members of the European-Ashkenazi population.

At first glance the communal tension in Israel seems to bear all the earmarks of a classic racial confrontation. A dominant European group watches a non-European influx into its midst, made up of a substantial number of people whose skin coloring is darker than that of the dominant group, and the latter reacts with manifestations of fear and prejudice. Even the most liberal European nations have been subject to failings of this sort, and European Jews are not very different from their Christian counterparts in this respect. The phenomenon of racism in Israel is uniquely disappointing to behold only because European Jews have themselves recently been its victims, and because the Oriental immigrants also are people who have suffered for being Jews and who have therefore taken refuge in their homeland.

To a certain extent, then, many European Israelis share in the general spiritual failing of color prejudice from which Western civilization suffers, and which must be worked out in common by all

Europeans and North Americans wherever they are. But it would be a mistake to formulate Israel's communal problems entirely in these terms. The color lines in Israel are extremely vague, and though some of the Ashkenazim may occasionally include a color response in their expression of hostility toward the Orientals, there is neither the obsession with color nor the racial fear that characterizes the attitude of whites toward Negroes in the United States. In the end, the thin veneer of racial attitudes is not the crux of the problem of Ashkenazi-Oriental relations in Israel.

The problem is, rather, primarily a cultural one. Israel is a country beset with an extreme cultural self-consciousness. Such a self-consciousness was essential for the revival of the Hebrew language after it had not been popularly used for some two millennia, and for the creation of a national frame of mind on a soil that had hitherto existed for most Jews only as a spiritual abstraction. But this self-transformation from *European Jew* into *Israeli* was not achieved without a certain accompanying anxiety, even by the most dedicated Zionist. The individual undergoing this process was aware of the fact that he was turning away from the mainstream of European civilization to take up a resolutely *provincial* cultural stance. He was perfectly happy to do this during the heroic age of national reconstruction in Palestine at the turn of the century, and, in fact, his attitude was in harmony with a general mood of spiritual retrenchment prevailing in Europe at about the same time, represented by the nostalgia for the provinces of a Maurice Barrès or of the French Impressionists.

But nowadays Israelis of European extraction tend to be troubled by the thought that they might be living in an extremely provincial cultural situation. Not only in the high arts themselves, but in such secondary cultural manifestations as dress designing and hotel management, there is usually an overwhelming obeisance to what is referred to as "international standards." This phenomenon has produced a certain divided consciousness: the European-Israelis, or "Ashkenazim," are both troubled by the ways in which they fall short of "international standards" and annoyed with themselves for the way in which they—in contrast with their pioneering days—now worry about such things. In broader terms, this is the major crisis now being undergone by those generations of Israelis who were involved in the War of Independence. Looking back with regret at a bygone heroic youth, they now chide themselves as they pursue everyday lives that are no more but also no less venal than those of "ordinary" people elsewhere.

The Oriental Jews have come forth into the midst of this spiritual crisis as a kind of emotional scapegoat. Although they are quite varied culturally, one quality that most of the Oriental groups share in common is a certain Mediterranean *aisance*; they are not inclined to the sort of spiritual rigor and puritanism that characterizes Northern Europeans. This quality has produced a significant paradox in their relationship to Israel: on the one hand, their spirits are alien to the ideological outlook that produced Zionism and, on the other hand, they have, in only a few years, rooted themselves in Zion with an emotional solidity and lack of ambivalence that few Ashkenazi Israelis are able to attain, even after two or three generations. Furthermore, the younger Oriental Jews take quite readily to the joys that modern life has to offer, without casting any regretful side glances at the passing of the kind of Spartan rigor that many Ashkenazim had held up as a national moral standard. Poverty was an ideal to which many of the older Ashkenazi settlers had dedicated their lives; and now they are generally prosperous. Today, it is mainly the Oriental Jews who are poor, and they are no more addicted to the ideal of poverty than are poor people anywhere else in the world.

The Oriental Jew has thus come to represent, in the eyes of many an Ashkenazi Israeli, an exaggerated form of what the latter sees in himself and professes not to want to become. This view has had a strong effect upon the cultural anxiety of the Ashkenazi. To the extent that he is troubled by not being able to meet "international standards" he senses impending cultural disaster in his already provincial country as a result of this large influx that is non-European and, on the whole, not very well-educated. And to the extent that he is troubled by his own excessive concern with "international standards" he sees the Oriental Jews, particularly the younger generation, as far too susceptible to the new international world of mass consumer goods and mass culture. The resentment that he often feels toward the Oriental Jews on these grounds has, furthermore, found its focus within a larger historical anxiety. Being European in origin, the Ashkenazi has not always made a complete emotional adjustment to the fact that he is now living in Asia. In particular, the conflict with the Arabs has induced a certain ambivalence of feeling toward the culture of the Middle East on the part of the Ashkenazi Israeli. Not that the old First Aliyah romance of the Bedouin chieftain and the Spartan virtues of the desert has been repudiated; it is still a very compelling image for some. But the image of the Middle East that seems most in evidence to Israelis—who are now as urbanized as any other Western people—is a very different one: it is that of the Levant, full of sleazy market places and people of all sorts of backgrounds gathered together at the ports of call of vagabond steamers. Geographically, Israel is very much in the Levant, which is all the more reason, apparently, why the term "Levantinization" is so persistently used as one of the more frightening catch phrases in the country. Many Ashkenazi Israelis fear that their country is in danger of becoming, as they put it, "just another Levantine state," in which the veneer of a dozen cultures will overlay the complete absence of an indigenous culture, or at least of an indigenous moral fiber. In all fairness, it should be pointed out that veteran Ashkenazim see signs of Levantinization in their own children—with the latter's fondness for discothèques and sports cars—just as much as in anyone else's; nevertheless, for many Ashkenazim the "Levantine" image finds a particular focus in the Oriental Jewish community.

These attitudes can too easily be viewed as simply those of the European toward the non-European, and hence interpreted as another manifestation of the imperialist spirit. Actually, what is going on is both less alarming and more fundamental. In a sense, what is at work is simply the old ambivalence felt by the north toward the south, the ambivalence of the chilly forest puritans of Northern Europe as they contemplate the sun-drenched shores of the Mediterranean with mingled envy and disapproval. For the Ashkenazi is as utterly a part of that Northern European culture amidst which he and his ancestors dwelt for a thousand years or more as the great majority of the Sephardim are part of the Mediterranean. More specifically, throughout the greater part of the nineteenth century and the early years of the twentieth, the predominant cultural style of the educated Jew of Continental Europe, no matter where he lived, was German. Since nazism this style has, of course, disintegrated, but its underlying feelings have not really disappeared entirely. Nowadays the cultured Ashkenazi has found another Western style with which to replace the old German one, and which bears some affinities with it. The new style is derived from that Anglo-American world within which the largest single portion of Jewry now lives. Like its German predecessor, this style represents a mood that is quasi-Protestant in character.

The Sephardic-Oriental Jews, on the other hand, tend to be quasi-Catholic in their cultural character. Now, generally speaking, one of the qualities that distinguishes the Catholic religious culture from the Protestant is that the former has a sacramental character, while the latter has not. By "sacramental" I mean a religious mood that establishes its relationship with the divinity, not on the basis of a constant and rigorous program applied to everyday life, as the Protestant-puritan spirit does, but rather through separate moments of extreme passionate communion. In the intervals between these moments of communion the sacramental spirit tends to be far more at ease than the puritan spirit ever is. This is why the confessional has such importance in the Catholic religion; it is a recurring ritual of regeneration from sins committed in the ordinary course of human life. The puritan tries terribly hard not to commit these sins in the first place. The sacramental spirit, though capable of occasional high flights in pursuit of a transcendent conception of morality, is generally more prone to aesthetic than to moral preoccupations. The puritan seeks the moral significance in every confrontation, and is suspicious of a beauty that lacks clear moral credentials. Generally speaking, then, the puritan spirit tends to look with a certain envious disapproval upon the sacramental one and to regard it as essentially frivolous. This was, for example, largely the attitude throughout the nineteenth century of Protestant Germany toward Catholic France.

The old German outlook toward France is not at all irrelevant to the present communal confrontation in Israel. Among the Sephardic-Oriental population in Israel today, the largest group stems from North Africa, particularly Morocco, where the French cultural influence has been of some importance. This fact manifests itself on various levels in the lives of the North African Jews of Israel. On the level of the simplest religious piety, it emerges as a kind of quasi-Catholic religiosity quite different from the puritan rigor of orthodox Ashkenazim. Generally speaking, an Ashkenazi is either an observer of Talmudic law or he is not, and if he is going to live a life observant of some laws and not of others then he is likely to work out the distinctions and limits in his behavior rather carefully. But a pious Moroccan Jew, for example, is much more likely to be careless about

many details of observance while performing others with a sacramental awe, without having any grounds for these distinctions in his
behavior other than his spontaneous feelings. There are deeply
religious Moroccan-Jewish ladies, for example, who ride to work every
Saturday, but who would not dare light their stoves or turn on an
electric switch on that day. Technically, working and riding on the
Sabbath are as forbidden to an observant Jew as igniting a fire or an
electric current, as these ladies well know. But there is simply an
emotional significance to lighting a fire which for these ladies makes
it foremost among the things that must not be done on the Sabbath.
This is an attitude which lies deeper than religious law, at the very
sources of the religious experience.

Among the more sophisticated members of the North African
communities in Israel, the French influence manifests itself in a great
passion for French language and culture. Now, this is an aspect of
Israeli cultural life that has been rather brusquely shunted aside by
the dominant cultural milieu of the country. For the most part, the
educational and cultural policy of the Ashkenazi establishment, in its
response to the vast, heterogeneous influx of new immigrants, has
been assimilative. Israelis were once fond of saying that their country
was not just an American-style "melting pot," but a rather more
intense "pressure cooker." This was a way of expressing the old
Zionist ideal, whereby the Jews were to return from the traditional
"seventy lands" of the dispersion, and re-create themselves into a
single, Hebrew culture. Such a program could scarcely afford the
luxury of cultural pluralism.

But this program succeeded brilliantly only in part. What it did do
well was revive the Hebrew language and make it the overwhelming
unitary cultural force in Israel today, embraced with as much passion
by the simplest immigrant as by the philologist dedicated to a
lifetime of studying the beauties of its root system. But a distinct and
unique Hebrew culture is hardly discernible. Rather, the dominant
cultural style in Israel today is, as I have said, Ashkenazi and
Northern European, with very strong leanings toward the Anglo-
Saxon world. Indeed, now that spoken Hebrew is an accomplished
historic fact, these leanings are so strong that today many Israeli
parents are as eager to have their children learn to speak English as
they once were to have them know Hebrew. English is not only an
important—and often indispensable—tool for personal advancement

in Israel; it is also, by common consent, the country's chief medium of contact with the broader culture of the West.

This is, of course, something like the plight of any small country in the world at a time when English is rapidly becoming the predominant lingua franca of the age. But there is a particular zeal to the passion for English that prevails among Ashkenazi Israelis, which stems in part from the cultural reasons I have given as well as, in part, from the influence of the Mandate, but which also receives a particular psychological confirmation from the fact that millions of Jews, the vast majority of them Ashkenazi in origin, today live in the English-speaking countries. Now, these countries happen to form the main economic and political center of gravity in the contemporary world so that such intimate cultural links with them on the part of the predominant social group in Israel tend to give that group a subtle but definite confirmation of its status. On the other hand, a group in Israel suffering from feelings of social and cultural inferiority and identifying with French civilization—which has also had its historic claims to universality—might, in the present situation, find grounds for the same sort of resentment that France herself tends to feel today toward the Anglo-Saxon world.

In any case, though Hebrew should be—and is—the universal language of Israel, there is no reason why the quasi-Protestant, quasi-Anglo-Saxon spirit of the majority of the Ashkenazim should form the country's sole subculture. Certainly a French ideal is no less capable than an Anglo-Germanic one of leading to the highest cultural standards. Setting aside the possible long-run political benefits of the flowering of a French subculture—a bridge toward possible ultimate friendship with the Maghrib, for example—such a development would greatly enrich the quality of life in Israel. It would further provide an important channel along which a good part of the Sephardic population could find its own unique cultural expression, and achieve greater eminence in Israeli society.

Israel, then, is at present in a difficult period of emotional transition. The severe morality of personal austerity and self-regeneration through labor which built the country is now no longer relevant to its needs. The old pioneering ideal of self-sacrifice for the sake of *kibbush avodah* (the conquest of labor) has been superseded by the results of its own success: labor has been "conquered," the foundations of a system of production have been laid, and the emphasis in the country's life is now beginning to shift, as in any fairly well-developed industrial society today, from the values of production to the values of consumption. Urban life in Israel, with its cars, shops, cafés, cinemas, theaters and places for more clandestine pleasures, is coming to look like urban life anywhere else in the world. City dwellers in Israel have, by and large, come to accept this fact, even if with occasional resentments and regrets. But the focus of the classic pioneering ideal was never in the city anyway. Rather, it was in the rural collective settlements; and it is in these places—above all, in the kibbutz—that the shock of this transformation is being felt most severely.

The kibbutzim are now confronting the problems of adjustment to middle age in two senses of the term. In general the kibbutz movement has passed its period of youthful vitality, when it was the spearhead of national development. Having achieved its fundamental goals, the kibbutz has now passed on the role of pre-eminence in the country's progress to other sectors of society. The kibbutzim now find their chief problems to be internal, revolving around such questions as what to do with their new-found prosperity. These problems are especially difficult because of the fact that the kibbutz movement, having founded its heroic youth upon a wave of ideological exuberance, is now still in the grip of undying ideological passions which have hardened themselves into fixed principles at a time when those principles have become less relevant than they once were to the conditions of life in Israel.

The other sense in which the kibbutzim are confronting middle age is that, quite simply, the vast majority of the founding generations of the kibbutzim have now reached or gone past middle age. Most of the kibbutzim were founded between 1930 and the early 1950's—many of them as tactical outposts in the growing Arab-Jewish conflict throughout that period; only a tiny number have been founded since then. Therefore, very few founders of kibbutzim are any longer young, and this fact is playing a very important role in the spiritual crisis that is now taking place among them. For many of the essential characteristics of the kibbutz movement, characteristics which were first developed on a pragmatic basis and have since become rigid ideological principles, were the outcome of the over-whelming youth of the participants.

The importance of youth in the formulation of the kibbutz ideal

206 SOCIETY AND POLITICS IN ZION

can be seen in the early history of the movement's parent settlement, Deganiah. The average age of the founding group of Deganiah in 1910 was about twenty; some were even younger. If these young people envisioned their community as a sort of extended family, this conception was aided by the fact that, at the very beginning, none of them were married. In some ways marriage is, after all, a discordant note in the harmony of the communal ideal; the wisest principle of communal organization was perhaps the celibacy of the Essenes and the medieval monasteries. At first some of the members of Deganiah maintained that they should never marry. But two of the founding members had been engaged to each other even before they came to Deganiah, and they did not let communal considerations interfere with their wedding plans. Soon after the wedding of Joseph and Miriam Baratz came that of Shmuel Dayan (the father of General Moshe Dayan), who had been the most vehement among the members in opposing the idea of marriage. In this matter, as in others that arose later, the life at Deganiah began to shape itself out of the tension between childhood visions and adult realities. But adult realities were always to be the major source of problems.

Idealistic young people in their late teens and early twenties tend to conceive of themselves as a separate class, immune to the weaknesses of their elders. Patterns imposed upon human beings by nothing less than the course of life itself seem to the young to be perfectly resistible by force of will, since the sense of utter freedom of choice is one of the luxuries youth provides. This was especially true of young people such as the group at Deganiah, who had actually performed an act of will remarkable at any age. Most of them had left behind their families and the sedentary occupations for which they had been destined, quite against the wishes of their parents. How, then, could they not have felt ambivalently, at the beginning, toward the traditional notions of marrying and raising families, when those aims were so deeply enmeshed in ways of life that they had repudiated? From the vantage point of their own childhood experience, the family was an utterly bourgeois institution, the foundation stone of the notion of mine and thine. It was completely alien to the spirit of their first few years at Deganiah, which were lived, in many ways, in the atmosphere of an extended camping trip. Even after getting married, there could have been no better way of warding off the bourgeois implications of this act than by taking meals together in the communal dining hall, and talking, singing and dancing there after dinner, sometimes until dawn.

This atmosphere of youthful freedom at Deganiah (as in most of the kibbutzim in their formative days), combined with the Russian revolutionary inspiration of the participants, also led to vigorously antitraditional notions about the role of women. The concept of woman's equality was beginning to reach fulfillment all over the Western world at this time, and nobody was in a better position to put it fully into practice than these young pioneers. There is very little that a strong-willed girl of twenty will allow that a man can do and she cannot, and these Zionist girl pioneers were nothing if not strong-willed. If the young settlers at Deganiah felt that they had emancipated themselves from the conventions of bourgeois family life, who more than the women were in a position to profit by such an emancipation?

At first, in Deganiah and in some of the settlements that preceded it, the girls had cooked and taken care of the household while the young men went out to work in the fields. But at Deganiah the women raised the claim that for them to be restricted to household chores was to place them in the traditional position of feminine subservience from which they had sought to escape. They wanted to share in the roster of field chores, along with the men. From its inception, the ideology of the kibbutz has placed a strong emphasis upon the performance of productive work, as distinguished from mere service occupations. This is the essence of the revolt against that middle-class life and its occupations which most kibbutzniks, themselves usually of middle-class origin, would have faced if they had remained in the outside world. Could the women regard themselves as having achieved perfect equality in the revolutionary kibbutz society if they were to remain restricted to household chores, or even if (what is a more moderate alternative) household chores were restricted exclusively to them? This problem has not been fully solved even today. At Deganiah the women won the right they sought of sharing in the field work. To prove her point in the argument, Miriam Baratz contrived secretly to take lessons in milking from the Arabs of a nearby village. She went on to become one of Israel's foremost experts in dairying. But, even though they now took turns doing field chores, the women continued to rotate kitchen work strictly among themselves.

The birth of the first children at Deganiah presented new challenges. Miriam Baratz, the first mother there, at first tried to minimize the difference that an infant made in her life. Even while nursing him she would bring him into the cowshed and place him in the hay while going about her chores. Some of the other members were more nervous about this arrangement than she was. When more children came, it was decided that child care would be placed on the roster of chores to be performed by the community, so that the mothers could leave their children in the kibbutz nursery while they went out to do their day's work. Naturally, the charge of the nursery was another duty that went exclusively to women, like the kitchen chores. In other words, as the numbers of new service chores increased and became fixed parts of kibbutz life, they tended to be filled by women. This development has constituted, for the most part, a return on the part of the women to traditional household occupations, despite ideological scruples to the contrary. But, when it first arose, the institution of group child care was seen as another means of emancipating the woman, of releasing her to pursue her occupational interests.

Nowadays it is particularly these questions of household and family, revolving around the basic problem of the role of the woman, that occupy the center of attention in discussions within the kibbutzim about their own changing needs. In this connection one of the kibbutz institutions most subject to scrutiny and to a new ambivalence of feelings is the communal dining hall. For many kibbutzniks this has been the central institution of kibbutz life, the *sine qua non* of a genuine collective settlement. In the early days no settlement could afford to build more than one large public room, and so the place in which the members ate was also the place in which they held kibbutz meetings, and it further served as the communal theater, cinema and dance hall. Since dinner was the occasion that brought everyone together at the end of the day, this meal became the cherished time for talking and lingering over coffee until well into the evening. The communal dining hall is a very attractive institution indeed for unmarried boys and girls. But when there are children to be tucked into bed after dinner, this evening communal ritual loses something of its magnetism. Furthermore, as one develops the appetite for tranquillity that inevitably comes with passing years, and as, meanwhile, the growing kibbutz population turns dinnertime more and more into something approaching a roaring crowd scene, the communal dining hall sometimes becomes a place that one wants to get out of as soon as possible.

At one time the desire to have even so much as a cup of coffee in the privacy of one's quarters was regarded in many of the kibbutzim as a kind of bourgeois heresy. The individual possession of a coffee pot or teapot was considered a violation of the canon against personal property. Today, the individual members of the kibbutzim have their own coffee pots (and many other private possessions besides, although within limits established by the community as a whole), and not only the late evening cup of coffee but also the four-o'clock tea which is a widespread custom in Israel are now cherished private routines among them. In some kibbutzim, the newest apartments are even equipped with small kitchenettes, making it possible to prepare an occasional meal in private: but this is still discouraged as a regular practice, except in the religious kibbutzim, where the Sabbath day meal is held at home. The question is naturally growing as to whether the practice of taking meals in common should continue at all; but the feeling is still strong throughout the settlements that if there is no communal dining hall there is simply no kibbutz.

The most urgent question about the organization of personal life being discussed today is that of the communal rearing of children. Deganiah, which founded the institution of the communal nursery, never carried the idea to the extreme of having the children sleep in the nursery at night. But today there are only a few kibbutzim in addition to Deganiah in which the children sleep in their parents' apartments. Most of them choose to have the principle of the communal nursery in operation twenty-four hours a day, with the exception of a few hours each afternoon when the children pass the time with their parents. Although the majority of kibbutz members continue to profess that they want this institution maintained, it has proved to be the most severe source of strain upon their commitment. This is especially true of the woman, who is in general the weak link of the kibbutz establishment. In the majority of cases of veteran couples who leave the kibbutz, this step has been taken primarily for the sake of the woman's desires. It is in response to her desires that a certain consumer orientation, so to speak, has recently arisen in the kibbutzim; an increasing availability of varied and attractive clothing, and even of cosmetics, has made the kibbutz woman virtually indistinguishable from the modest but up-to-date townswoman in outer appearance. But the traditional family instincts

which remain in her are not so easily placated, and they remain a
persistent source of difficulties. Perhaps she is a woman who fought
with the Palmach in the War of Independence when she was twenty,
but now that she is approaching forty and has spent years working in
the kitchen or in the nursery she may sometimes wonder why, if she
has reverted to these traditional household occupations, she is not
doing them just for her own family, where the satisfactions would be
as traditional as the chores.

It is in the separation from her children that she feels the strain of
kibbutz life most severely. The established ideological justification
given by the kibbutz movement for the separation of the children
from the parents at night is that it sets the parents, especially the
mother, free to pursue their own interests. This freedom, however, is
not only often not relished by the kibbutz mother, but it at times
positively afflicts her with a feeling of guilt about her children.[3] Such
a feeling can be seen, for example, in a certain strained quality which
often tinges the already sacrosanct atmosphere of the "children's
hour" at the end of each day. This is the period before dinner,
usually about two hours long, when the children are sent out from
the nurseries to pass the time at the apartments of their parents, who
have come in and washed after a day's work. The children's hour is
often pointed to by kibbutz spokesmen as the culminating moment
of the kibbutz way of life, when the parents, refreshed by the
freedom of a whole night and a day away from their children, are
ready now to give them unadulterated attention and love. But there
is often also a high degree of anxiety present on this occasion, a mood
that is ready to plunge into a depression at the slightest repudiation
of a caress, and that is often slightly frantic in its endeavor to extract
the maximum from every possible moment in a race against the
clock.

A good deal of the passion that is unsuccessfully rationalized into
this late-afternoon ritual becomes manifest in the moments when the
children are put to bed after dinner. The practice of the parents'
coming into the children's houses to put their own children to bed,
called hashkavah, has come to be regarded by the Ha'shomer Ha'-
tza'ir federation as still too much of a trace of bourgeois family life,
and it has been eliminated in this federation's kibbutzim. But for

[3] This point is well made in Melford E. Spiro's classic study, Children of the
Kibbutz (New York, 1958), p. 63.

many kibbutz parents, *hashkavah* is the indispensable link without which they would feel that they have lost the charge of their children altogether. Theoretically only a perfunctory chore requiring not more than a few minutes to perform, *hashkavah* often takes a half hour or more for each child. It is a time when the children exercise their imaginations to the fullest in finding devices that will make their parents stay on a few minutes longer, and when the parents strain their imaginations equally in finding reasons for being detained. Each night seems to have the quality of the ritual rebreaking of a cord, and no matter how often the act is performed, it is never without a twinge of pain.

But whatever their own personal misgivings, the majority of kib-butz parents still consider separate sleeping quarters to be the best possible arrangement for their children, if not necessarily for them-selves. Many of the institutions of kibbutz life are based upon just such a view; indeed, it can be said that the rearing of children is probably the central activity in the kibbutz today, the main focus of its moral aspirations. The kibbutz is seen by its members as, above all, the locale in which a new type of Jew, a new type of human being, is being produced: a person free of selfishness, dedicated to the ideal of community responsibility, positive in his sense of life.

There have certainly been some fine results to these aspirations. For one thing, expert observers generally agree that kibbutz children are, on the whole, remarkably free of the neuroses that best the average urban middle-class child today (with whom the kibbutz child is in many ways an equivalent, despite the rural setting of his life). They also have a highly developed sense of responsibility to the community, both in the kibbutz and in Israeli life at large, where kibbutz offspring form a notably large proportion of the public servants. But there are also considerable tensions present in the kibbutz system of child rearing and education. A high degree of imagination is, in a sense, an aberration in any social context in which it appears; the tendency in kibbutz education, which is radically egalitarian in its outlook, is not to favor any aberrations, including this one. Kibbutz education is highly normative—as, indeed, is kibbutz life in general—and has even been called "totalitarian" by some of its critics. This is an exaggeration, but one can say that kibbutz education does often veer into indoctrination.

Ideally, the founding generations in the kibbutzim want their children to be just like themselves within certain limits, to be an intelligentsia committed, with a high degree of spiritual fervor, to a nonintellectual way of life. But this remarkable distillation of traits was founded upon a moral tension which simply cannot be transferred to a generation that takes the kibbutz for granted as a way of life; furthermore, it constitutes a revolutionary frame of mind that the older kibbutz generation cannot wholeheartedly want to impart to its children. The kibbutz veteran is sometimes dismayed at his grown son's preference for diesel engines over Tolstoy novels as a major object of interest, but the son has in fact made the right choice for his future spiritual well-being if he intends to spend the rest of his life in the kibbutz. The young man who has been genuinely afflicted with the disease of the liberal arts may feel impelled to leave the kibbutz altogether, and seek out the intellectual life of the city. Therefore, in order to avoid inculcating in the children the kind of rebelliousness that governed the youth of the parents, the liberal arts course in the kibbutz is often tempered to fit securely within the limits of doctrine.

Thus, in many respects, the kibbutz has become for the present a conservative institution. Struggling with the internal problems of fixing practices once developed in a revolutionary situation into a permanent way of life, the kibbutzim have tended to turn their eyes inward and away from the new revolutionary needs that have emerged in the era of mass immigration. From the very beginning of the new type of immigration, immediately after statehood in 1948, the kibbutzim seemed somewhat hesitant to immerse themselves in its problems. At first they did help in the task of absorbing immigrants by providing training facilities and temporary jobs; but they soon became the object of criticism from government circles, who felt that the kibbutz federations were not bearing their share of responsibility in this major national effort. The kibbutzim, who have welcomed into their midst any new immigrants who have chosen to become members, have not gone out of their way to help in the settlement of those who have not so chosen. But the great majority of the "new immigrants" who have arrived since the establishment of the state are not at all inclined to the kibbutz way of life; they have settled either in towns or in moshavim. In the eyes of such a prominent critic as David Ben-Gurion, the kibbutzim have, in this respect, manifested a self-interest which has caused them to shirk their duty to the country at large.

In recent years this controversy has revolved mainly around the question of the use of hired labor in the kibbutzim. In many of the kibbutzim today, the hiring of outside help for all or part of the year is in fact a fixed routine; this is not only true of those kibbutzim which have developed manufacturing industries but also of some that simply do not have enough hands available among their permanent membership to perform pressing seasonal tasks when they arise. In many fairly remote parts of the country the kibbutzim have thus become important creators of jobs. Ben-Gurion has even suggested that they go a step further and open all kibbutz facilities—particularly the schools (the kibbutzim are still the only places in Israel in which a free secondary education is available)—to the hired workers and their families. But the official attitude of the kibbutz federations, particularly of Ha'shomer Ha'tza'ir, has been to regard hired labor as a cancer that must be removed. To function as an employing class is regarded by many kibbutz members as a violation of their egalitarian ideals, and the making of payments to hired workers is generally thought of as a restoration of that bourgeois "cash nexus" that the kibbutznik had sought to repudiate. At the same time it is felt that the constant presence of individuals with cash in their pockets, who can indulge their personal tastes by buying things in the cities, will have a detrimental effect upon the values of kibbutz children. These are the hard-earned proprieties of a class of people who have struggled to achieve a way of life remarkable for its high standards of austerity and self-restraint. However, such attitudes are also tinged with an elitism that is not entirely attuned to the needs of the country at large.

There is a striking irony in this confrontation between the kibbutznik and the new immigrant worker. In the eyes of the latter the kibbutznik, for all his renunciation of personal luxuries, can only seem to be the member of a relatively privileged class. He enjoys absolute economic security, his children receive a free secondary education, and his standard of living is in general well above the average in Israel today. In his attitude toward manual labor as a form of spiritual regeneration, he is not at all like the hired worker who does his job primarily to make a living. By making moral imperatives paramount in his working life, he clearly distinguishes himself from the working-class person, for whom the economic imperatives remain overwhelmingly in the ascendant. In the early days of Zionist settlement the aim of the agrarian pioneers was to transform themselves into a proletariat and thereby overcome the lack of Jewish labor then prevailing in Palestine. What they did succeed in becoming was a kind of laboring elite, a unique realization in the contemporary world of the Tolstoyan idea that a life of manual labor is a worthy fulfillment even for learned and sensitive spirits. But they are not really a proletariat—not in terms of the world at large—and some of the ideals out of which they formed themselves are now the very ones that lead many of them to look with a certain scorn upon the genuine proletarians working in their midst.

To a certain extent, this contradiction was inherent in the kibbutz movement even at its inception. The early founders of the kibbutz ideal, such as the Tolstoyan philosopher A. D. Gordon, consciously repudiated the Marxian social democracy that then was prominent in Europe, in favor of the older "utopian" socialist ideal. As Martin Buber pointed out, the kibbutz was the last and by far the most successful of the great utopian socialist experiments. But the major shortcoming of utopianism was always that, while it provided an ideal way of life to those who joined the utopian community, it offered no solution whatsoever to the problems of society at large. The alternative proposed to it by Marxism was that the task of Socialists, rather than being one of turning away from society at large to form elite communities, was to seek to work with the conditions of society itself to bring about its liberation. This, in the end, is the principle of social democracy, whether called "Marxist" or not, that has achieved dominance in the industrialized welfare states of the world, including Israel. In the early years of Zionist settlement the kibbutz had a vital role because it served as the cell in which the laboring class of a new society was being generated. But now that this task has been accomplished, the kibbutz is to a large extent nothing more than a utopian community. The kibbutzim today are faced with the tragic choice either of accepting a new conception of social responsibility at the cost of setting aside an old and cherished ideal or of gradually turning into a mere byway of Israeli life, a retreat for idealists of a certain kind.

III

JERUSALEM

Jerusalem, with a population under two hundred thousand and little industry to speak of, is smaller and less prosperous than either Tel-Aviv or Haifa, the two other major cities of Israel, but its symbolic importance is far greater than theirs. It is the city in which Mount Zion is located, and many a Jerusalemite lives in the conviction that his return to Zion would not have been complete if he had not come to dwell on its very slopes. Even to the foreign visitor the ride to Jerusalem can often seem like the culmination of his voyage. One discovers there a unique experience of light, stone and geographical contour, and cannot but recognize Jerusalem as one of the external sources of the biblical imagination. The city seems to become not just a place to the beholder but a metaphor for both the origins and the destiny of the Jewish spirit, as well as of the Christian one. The central meaning of the revival of Israel seems somehow to be located there.

It is the stoniness of the Judaean Hills that is among the first of the qualities of the region to become evident to the traveler as he goes up to Jerusalem from the Mediterranean coast; in less than an hour of riding, fertile plain suddenly gives way to huge rocky mounds that seem only reluctantly to admit patches of crude vegetation in their cracks. Not that the Judaean Hills form solid masses of rock like the much larger Rocky Mountains in America; they seem, rather, to be of earth glutted with stones, some of them loose, some lodged in the ground, as if they were still in the midst of being exuded by some fecund and petrifying womb. The result is an illusion of process: stones lie heaped about in an excitement of configurations that suggest movement to the eyes. In some places the work of man has contributed to the illusion, in the form of stone huts, or of the rock-lined terraces rising up the circumferences of hills like contour lines on a map. These rocks seem to stand for the paradox of the Creation itself, the outcome of an instantaneous sally by eternity into the dimension of time, from which it then recoiled.

Jerusalem is the distillation of the encounter between spirit and nature in this region. For a short time after the founding of the state, the new buildings of Israeli Jerusalem were being made of poured concrete, of spongy surfaces that crack and fade in the sun; but an old Mandate bylaw was revived, obliging Jerusalem builders to use stone—the Jerusalem stone that is quarried right in the area, or that is lodged in the very ground upon which the city has been built. The city thus possesses a unity of substance and a rare harmony with its environment; it seems to have grown out of the hills on which it stands. Not that this uniformity of substance precludes variety of surface: even the lightly amber-colored blocks which make up the greatest number of structures in Jerusalem vary considerably in size and cut, from convex and roughened to flat and smooth; some buildings are of gleaming institutional white, some are cobbled, some are dank and gray. Furthermore, the very fact that the underlying color scheme is monochromatic enables the merest touch of something bright—a smear of whitewash, a tangle of red-painted railings, or of trees and flowers—to stand forth as a dazzling punctuation of tone, transforming the entire scene. But the greatest variations of surface occur in time, through the course of the daily and annual interplay of stone, air and light that is more intense here than in perhaps any other city in the world. Under the rain of winter the stones darken like khaki, some of them glistening as though they had been polished, others turning porous and soggy. In the hot, rainless summer they glow white with an intensity that increases through the course of the day. But then, at sunset, the heat suddenly withdraws into the disk descending into the western hills, as if in re-enactment of the Kabbalistic *Tsimtsum*, whereby the Creator, recoiling into Himself, leaves the universe behind as His precipitate: the cool, now inanimate stone of Jerusalem at twilight is suddenly left behind in one corner of a universe that had seemed about to become a continuum of solar energy. For a final few moments the western faces of buildings glow in a strange yellow light. Then night comes, causing variation to subside a little, and partially restoring Jerusalem to the rocky earth from which it had been dragged up.

Not that there is no softness in Jerusalem. To the west of the city there is a place called the Valley of the Cross, so named for the Greek monastery that sits at the bottom of it, a gnarled, shapeless stone structure that looks more ancient than it really is, for antiquity is a quality of Jerusalem that defies the limitations of time. The valley itself is a great bowl of olive trees and grass; on top of it, and to the right as you face it from the road leading out to the university, are the shifting white cubes of the new museum, and to the rear, rising up the far side of the bowl, are the weightless-looking stone residences of Kiryat Shmuel, which seem to stand one on top of the other as they ascend the slope, like the huts of a Pueblo Indian village. The valley is more or less surrounded by city, although it does not seem to be, for one can often see a flock of sheep grazing there, a brown, lumpy texture scattered through some small part of the olive groves. When the sun sets behind the museum buildings, a purple haze descends like dew and fills the spaces between the trees, enriching the color of the trees themselves into an emerald tone. The grass, which is fresh in April, has become a parched brown by late spring, but at twilight its greenness is restored as if by magic. As darkness comes on, and the museum turns into a rhythm of dark rectangles on the heights, the monastery and the olive trees become mere intimations of things present in the black recess, and the lights of the houses on the far side and the homely bulbs of the solitary but rhythmically placed street lamps all go on, replacing the notion of horizon with that of flat, vertical planes punctuated by scattered dots and patches of light. The quiet hangs in the air like that milky way of lights: this is the softness of Jerusalem.

Actually, the nature of the city as it presents itself to the eye resides in a balance between the soft and the harsh, between stone and olive or evergreen tree. This is the feeling imparted by the panoramic view of Jerusalem obtained from the height of Ramat Rachel, far to the south of town, in which one sees the amber towers of the city rising airily from thick pinetops. A similar feeling is obtained from a height in Kiryat Ha'yovel, far to the west of town, where one looks down through olive groves at the lawns, church towers and monastery walls of Ein Karem (the birthplace of John the Baptist), colored by the red-tiled roofs of religious places and the blue and yellow roofs and doorways of formerly Arab dwellings whose present occupants have maintained the old color schemes.

The most graceful beauty of Jerusalem is usually in the Christian and Arab places, in the one case because aesthetic purpose is deeply embedded in the Christian, and especially the Catholic, religious sensibility, and in the other because the people who have lived in the place for some thirteen hundred years have naturally achieved a style harmonious with their environment. There are some quarters founded by Jews in which grace is beginning to be a noticeable quality but, for the most part, Jewish-built neighborhoods are characterized by a certain roughness—one is tempted to say *agitation*. At its best, this roughness achieves a kind of mottled beauty of its own, and does indeed answer to some similarly rough quality of the environment. It is as if the Jews, having in ancient times discovered something fundamental and unique in this setting, incorporated it into their spirit and kept its secret to themselves, to release it again only after returning from an exile of eighteen hundred years.

For it must be said that if there is a delicacy about Jerusalem, a miracle of substance that makes rock seem to soar lightly into the air, this is a quality that is reserved almost exclusively to distant objects and to panoramas. In the aggregate, Jerusalem seems to *transcend*; viewed *sub specie aeternitatis*, or from some perspective approximating that condition, it drifts in the direction of pure spirit; but the immediate, the proximate, experience of the place is one of harshness, of jagged surfaces that grip and scrape, of rough fields of bramble and rock that prick your ankles and scuff your shoes. In this respect, city and countryside are one in Jerusalem; indeed, it is impossible here to define an area that represents city as distinct from surrounding landscape: large fields separating various quarters give way imperceptibly to patches of open countryside. Built on sharply rising and falling hills, in steep rocky places that nature does not seem to have intended for a city, Jerusalem never really gathers itself up into a contiguous urban mass. It is more like an assemblage of near-villages, scattered and winding through the hills, so that, to the uninitiated walker, the city seems on countless occasions to disappear from view altogether. The Jerusalemite has a more intimate experience of nature than most city dwellers have, and the nature that he knows is stark, an almost palpable conspiracy of rock and sunlight against the feebleness and volatility of organic life. I remember walking through a great field once in June, the brushfire season, when after more than a month of glaring, rainless summer, pale stretches of grass suddenly begin bursting into flames at the slightest provocation. At first sight this field through which I was walking had apparently thus far been spared, when suddenly my eye was caught by smoke coming from one olive tree, scarcely noticeable amidst the foliage of the others. It was burning on the inside, but I could see the flame through two wide holes in the trunk, being drawn up with great force, as through a chimney. What was visible of the interior of the trunk was white and leprous, and I could not help thinking of flesh as I watched it slowly disintegrate. The next day I passed the same spot and saw that the trunk had crumbled, leaving only a charred and smoldering stump surrounded by the still green branches of the fallen upper part of the tree. The hot surrounding field glowed in a triumph of desolation; I had perhaps been the sole witness to this death. The scene would have been vivid proof of the frailty of organic life no matter where it had taken place, but there is something about the air of Judaea that makes the wager and the struggle seem more intense here.

The last few miles of the road into Jerusalem from Tel-Aviv are a spectacular ascent on steep grades and narrow roads, and around sharp curves at the edges of mountains, which provide sweeping views of valleys dotted with villages, trees, crops and accumulations of rock. Jerusalem first comes into view a few miles ahead as you round a sudden turn; it stands high at the rim of a distant hill, glistening white in the sun like some futuristic display. This is the jack-in-the-box image with which you are tantalized for some minutes as you wind along the highway, now watching it disappear from view, now watching it leap back up into the sky. Then suddenly you have entered the town, and are in the midst of an incredibly dreary stretch of gray stone façade, a double row of bleak garages and warehouses closing in upon you from either side of the narrow street, as though you had mistakenly detoured into some back alleyway. It is not an alleyway, however, but Jaffa Street, the main artery into the center of town. State visitors are usually turned onto a sudden detour just before this point, taking them along a beautiful but devious route through the western hills before they re-enter town at a more presentable spot farther on. But the private traveler is granted the right to see Jerusalem's underside at his very first encounter with the city, a right which most Jerusalemites would want him to have, because such an initial view is necessary to a proper understanding of the place. For there is a certain quality of Jerusalem that finds itself in back alleyways, a sudden plummeting from the midst of this world into medieval silence, into small cobblestoned ravines in which one discovers broken walls covered by tufts of grass or iron door knockers shaped like hands, and where the only sound is the rustling of cats among garbage cans, their fat, mean faces mottled by a lifetime of probing through shells and rinds, springing to attention at your footsteps. Nightfall is the signal for the cats to begin their wars or love affairs, and their howling breaks in at your windows.

For all the significance of its effect upon your spirit, this bleak stretch of Jaffa Street is really rather short, and after a few moments, as you come into the vicinity of the market place of Mahaneh Yehuda, the street widens and comes to life. You are now approaching the center of town; but you should not imagine that you are about to encounter a sudden transformation, from the dinginess of the first stretch of Jaffa Street, into the kind of slick "downtown" area that is to be found in any modern city from New York to Tel-Aviv, for Jerusalem is not like any modern city. Zion Square, the heart of the business and entertainment district, formed where Jaffa meets Ben-Yehuda Street, is perhaps the most ramshackle "downtown" to be found in any capital in the world. An occasional streamlined storefront stands as a concession to the international tourist trade, but these are a violation of the predominant spirit of this anarchical mélange of three- and four-story office buildings, their ground floors teeming with soda and fruit juice stands and tiny store entrances crowded together, absorbing and spilling out masses of people that pour over the edges of the narrow sidewalks. One can find a touch of European chic in the glittering décor of the cafés, and, indeed, you can often see inside them groups of high-shouldered girls and smoothly athletic young men sitting about in the same languidly knowledgeable way that they might in the nightclubs of Saint-Tropez; but their effect upon the atmosphere is nullified by the presence, at other tables, of tense-looking intellectuals of the old Labor Zionist variety, in short sleeves, their newspapers spread out and hanging over the edges of the absurdly small tabletops, crushing out cigarettes in trays already glutted with butts and ashes, or of clusters of quietly perspiring lawyers and newspapermen, their eyes charging the atmosphere with inquiry, waiting for something to turn up.

The character of Jerusalem life is reflected in the movements, irregular in their outbursts, sharply contrasting in their variety, that take place in the Zion Square area every day. Into this spurting mob comes together every conceivable ethnic type, each quietly refuting any notion that the Jews are a single racial stock. Tall, fair-haired bureaucrats in short sleeves and sandals carry their briefcases past squatting Gandhi-like Moroccan patriarchs, their thin hands extended in the classic beggar's pose of the Middle East. Hasidim in great black hats, sidelocks, beards and long gabardines rush past young hipsters with heavily brilliantined hair. The varieties are greater still among the women: young, dark-skinned girls of Oriental origin move with a sensuousness and dress with a sense of color more pronounced than that of the more angular Ashkenazi girls, both of them contrasting with their mothers, who are generally shorter in stature and who still often represent the styles of the parts of the world from which they have come. In general, the atmosphere is created out of a fusion of Middle East and Central Europe—a more successful fusion of these elements than is to be found in any other city in Israel—held together by the common component of agitation. But, also in the midst of this scene, are moving, serenely and incongruously, tall Ethiopian monks in black robes or little groups of nuns, with airy white wings stretching out from their wimpled heads. They are a faint, narrow current in the Jerusalem stream, winding distantly through the place like the barely discernible church bells that can be heard ringing on Christmas Eve.

Outside of a small number of Sephardic families that have been in Palestine for several generations, the old and socially dominant population of Jerusalem is Ashkenazi, comprising mainly an intelligentsia which serves the university and the seat of government. Since Jerusalem, by virtue both of its location in a mountainous region and the difficulties of the border situation there, is not naturally viable economically, it has virtually no commercial and industrial class to dominate its social and cultural life, as Tel-Aviv and Haifa have. Not that Tel-Aviv is lacking an intelligentsia; this city is, in fact, the most important center of belles-lettres in the country. But the Tel-Aviv intellectuals are quite different in character from their counterparts in Jerusalem. Tel-Aviv has a cultural life that revolves around its Bohemia; café and theater are two important germinating centers of creativity there. In other words, the classic play element of artistic creation is dominant in Tel-Aviv. Not so in Jerusalem, where the academic or government status of many of its intellectuals leads them to take a more solemn cultural stance. They speak and write as

arbiters of the national policy and character, as legislators of the
public morality. The Holy City is, in effect, still the place of rabbis
and prophets, even in secular form.

The public style of this dominant social element has placed its
distinct mark upon Jerusalem. Once, an American visitor to Israel
who had spent some weeks in Tel-Aviv before coming to Jerusalem,
remarked to me at the end of his first day there, "But here they stand
in line for the bus!" This British propensity for "queuing up" is not
present in every sector of the city's public life, but it is noteworthy
that this formality is lacking only either in places where newer
immigrant groups predominate (and even many of these adopt the
formality soon enough) or where there is a large element of non-
Jerusalemites, as at the university. The Jerusalem middle classes,
weaned in the city that was the seat of the Mandate, have to a large
extent taken on the traits of their former colonial governors, or have
at least taken on the kind of Britishness that many a cultivated
gentleman of Central Europe used to aspire to in the old days. For
the style and outlook of cultivated Jerusalemites, even though most
of them stem from Yiddish-speaking, Eastern European Jewry, is
mainly that of the now defunct *Mitteleuropa*: indeed, if this region,
or concept rather, still exists anywhere in the world today, its capital
must be Jerusalem. This is especially true of the Hebrew University,
which, once dominated by Jews of German origin, has now shifted in
the predominant ancestry of its faculty roughly in the direction of
Poland and Galicia, but which has remained none the less resolutely
German in its devotion to constricting academic attitudes.

The principal seat of this Anglo-Germanic way of life is Rehavia,
the "best" residential quarter in Jerusalem, where the stone dwellings, built by and for Jews, come the closest of any such structures to
matching the grace of the Christian and Arab buildings scattered
throughout Jerusalem and its environs. The shapes of Rehavia are
produced from configurations of lightly rose-colored blocks, each
stone having a calculatedly roughened surface which, in the aggregate, imparts a well-to-do warmth to houses that might otherwise be
inclined to seem too austere. The warmth is added to by an abun-
dance of evergreens and honeysuckles that fill the gardens surrounding almost every house, whether private residence or apartment
building. The tidiness of Rehavia, a concretization of one of the most
cherished spiritual ideals reigning there, would be remarkable anywhere, but it is particularly striking in a country that, for all its

Westernness of character, still often bears tattered physical traces of its Middle Eastern origins. At night one can walk from fragrance to fragrance through Rehavia's neat and winding streets, the moonlight glistening on the asphalt surfaces, and the street lamps casting a richly molded shading on the roughened stone faces of the buildings. The sound of the breeze passing through the high treetops is often broken by the playing of a flute or violin heard through an open window. Through almost any window that you pass you can glimpse abundant and orderly rows of books lining the walls. The life of the spirit is reconciled with worldly solidity in Rehavia.

But this foundation of virtually northern sobriety which underlies Jerusalem's life has now been subject to the challenge of a quiet invasion on the part of a more Mediterranean spirit. The result is a confrontation that will in time probably bring considerable and interesting changes in the character of Jerusalem. For the moment, however, these newcomers from the Middle East and North Africa stay in their own areas, chiefly the new housing developments built around the southwestern rim of the city. Their most representative sector within the city itself is the quarter surrounding the market place of Mahaneh Yehuda. The market itself, a network of teeming alleyways, filled by the shouts of hawkers and the murmur of bargaining shoppers, and covered by a crisscross of tattered burlap rags to keep off the sun, is a conjunction of dankness and gorgeous color. Standing out against the stink of crushed and rotting fruit on the pavement and barrels full of bloody chicken heads are corroded wooden stalls full of glowing lemons, carrots, green beans, plums and cucumbers, great corrugated lumps of color occasionally broken by the dull silver glow of cheap kitchenware and the more intricate color combinations of tables covered with razor blades, toothpaste, shoe-laces, combs and other fixed concomitants of this classic miscellany. The voices that fill the ears are so thick with Oriental gutturals that it almost sounds as if they are speaking Arabic. The peddlers are men with brown, creased faces and double-pointed beards of kinky gray, or women, sitting on the pavement, barefoot and dressed in long kerchiefs, black blouses embroidered with gold, and great red dresses that reach to their ankles and spread beneath them on the ground where they sit. Their daughters walk about testing the capacities of modern dress, a jangle of trinkets, their black eyes causing the very air to respond: these are the Jewesses painted by Delacroix.

The keener sense of color that prevails among Oriental Jews can also be perceived in the narrow streets that start behind the market place, an area that is basically as stony as any part of Jerusalem, but which by small touches—an entrance painted over in a brilliant blue or yellow pastel, a mass of many-colored flowers dangling through the delicately twisted railings of a second-story balcony—induces a rioting of the aesthetic sense not to be experienced in any other quarter of the city. Through narrow stone doorways one often sees courtyards that uniquely assemble a crowd of casement windows, stone stairs, flowers and broken pots into a ramshackle version of a Japanese miniature. There is to be found everywhere in this quarter a juxtaposition of both greater crudeness and greater delicacy that the Ashkenazi spirit is accustomed to, thereby adding strength to the notion of the latter group that it is witnessing the infiltration of an alien culture into its midst.

But if there is friction between Ashkenazi and Oriental, this is as nothing alongside the tense and sometimes violent family quarrel that goes on between the Ashkenazi middle classes and those living representatives of their own medieval past, the ultraorthodox Jews whose citadel is the Meah Shearim section of Jerusalem. In this quarter the battered stone surfaces are irregular, as they are in Mahaneh Yehuda, but they are without color. By some kind of unconscious craftsmanship, the inhabitants of Meah Shearim have wrought an ancient Eastern European ghetto out of a quarter that is still less than a hundred years old. Squashed tomatoes, browned by footsteps and the sun, ooze along the cracks in the cobblestoned street, scrawny iron railings leap high and dart at crazy angles along the sides of jagged buildings, bulging casements lean out over courtyards, the smell of chickens fills cold stone vestibules, the white feathers clinging to walls. There is even a noticeable presence of wood in this quarter, even though it is quite rare in Israel, forming grayed, sagging hut-like buildings and appendages, lacking only great flat tracts of mud surrounding them to complete the picture of Ruthenian desolation that they suggest.

This intimation of continuity with a more ancient past is above all achieved by the people themselves: by the great-bearded men in black coats and hats, who seem always to be rushing, always at odds with the worldly necessities that have pulled them away from their sacred books and out into the sunlight, and who nevertheless smoke their cigarettes with a strange, almost decadent-looking sophistication; by the shapeless, tired women, endlessly bulging like casements over courtyards, their colorless kerchiefs worn, unlike those of the dowagers of Mahaneh Yehuda, in such a way as to cover their heads entirely. The little boys, beardless, but with huge, limp sidelocks wisping down to their shoulders, look like comic imitations of their fathers. Only the little girls are different: bright-faced and impish, they bear no indications, other than their long opaque cotton stockings, that they are destined to be someday like their mothers. For this is a male world, built to culminate in the joyous shouts and the sweaty smells of crowds of dancing men that emanate from the windows at *Simchas Torah* (The Rejoicing in the Law). It is a world meant to breed patriarchs, as in the apparition that suddenly arose to me one night through a ground-floor window, of an incredibly aged man, all white beard with glasses straddling the tip of his nose, surrounded by a limitless clutter of massive and crumbling books, reading by the dim light of a bare bulb that needed only to have been a candle to have transformed this scene into the incarnation of a seventeenth-century engraving, depicting some *gaon* of the epoch.

As if built on the Tablets of the Law themselves, this quarter seems the very quintessence of stone. Stones sometimes even serve here as weapons, in the hands of young religious zealots who throw them at passing violators of feminine modesty (a woman wearing short sleeves in this neighborhood is in possible danger) or at Sabbath motorists who are imprudent enough to drive in or near Meah Shearim. This latter situation is sometimes a considerable problem, since Meah Shearim is adjacent to the Mandelbaum Gate, the sole border crossing between Israeli and Jordanian Jerusalem. Many Christian pilgrims wish to pass through the Gate on Saturday in order to be on hand in the Old City for Sunday services. Those zealots who have on occasion thrown stones at busloads of such pilgrims have claimed that they were aiming at the Jewish drivers of the buses. But was there not also in this gesture a touch of jealous anger at those who were about to enter that part of the Holy City which contains the last relic of the Temple, and which is banned to the pietists of Meah Shearim, as to all Israelis?

The best view of the Old City possible from the Israel side is obtained on a secluded hilltop in the formerly Arab quarter of Abu Tor, in a courtyard cluttered with goats and chickens. The "Old

City"—ancient Jerusalem, now in Jordan—is on the next hill or group of hills, not more than half a mile away, but separated from the viewer as if by eternity. The valley that descends before you and rises to the Old City wall is the Vale of Hinnom, the Gai-Hinnom or Gehenna that is the Inferno of Jewish tradition. Surrounded by the great fortress wall built in the sixteenth century by Suleiman the Magnificent on the remains of walls whose segments mark the epochs of Jerusalem's history back to the time of the Jebusites, the entire city slopes away and upward in front of you, crowding together bulbous turrets, church steeples, minarets, and the great golden surface of the Dome of the Rock, one of the most sacred shrines of the Muslim world, built nearly twelve hundred years ago on the spot where the Temple of Solomon once stood. Additional walls jut out from the main one and zigzag up and down the hillside in such a way that an over-all flattening of perspective takes place; the effect to the eyes is of a foreshortened, boxed-in city of exactly the sort depicted in a typical medieval bas-relief or tapestry. Perhaps European art prior to Giotto was more faithful to the realities of perspective as people then saw them than we generally imagine. If so, life answered well to the exigencies of religious vision: this little walled nest of a city is like a living representation of the notion of man's infinite smallness in the face of eternity. This picture must even more so suggest a great Craftsman's hand when viewed from the top of the Mount of Olives, which rises high above the city on the opposite side from where I am standing, over which the Crusaders came and, seeing the Holy City beneath them, fell astonished to their knees.

I try to imagine what this view was like prior to 1948, when accessibility was among the conditions of one's perceptions. What was once a ten-minute walk from one hill to another is now a stretch of deserted field upon which, at some indiscernible point, there is a barrier marked by the threat of death. I remember the time when a young Swiss tourist, a Catholic, was shot and killed near here by a Jordanian rifleman, because he had committed the indiscretion of coming too close to the border at a particularly sensitive spot. Strange to think that this young man might, on some other day, have made his pilgrimage through the Mandelbaum Gate to be received as a welcome guest of the Kingdom of Jordan, protected by the very soldier whose rifle shot him down. The Mandelbaum Gate is hardly more than two sheds and a canopy of bars, yet the abstractions of politics have made it, by a kind of magic, the one corridor by which you may pass from the Jewish to the Arab city and live. Its only distinction to the senses is the awesome stillness that surrounds it; there are countless other places along the border at which I can look across and watch the rush of traffic, hear the honking of horns, see Jordanian children playing and their mothers hanging out the wash, the moment's passing mood almost distinguishable in their faces. They must see me too, exchanging glances with me across the frontier of eternity. What if I should wave to them one of these times, and try to start a shouted conversation? Are such intimacies permitted across a murderous frontier, or would a shot from a nearby rooftop put an end to my experiments? In Jerusalem a certain terror sometimes bears down upon one's contemplation of even the most trivial human gestures: does this also contribute to the holiness of a city?

The frontier becomes more imposing to the eyes in the vicinity of the former commercial center of the New City, just below and south of Mamilla Road, the once-busy street that winds up eastward to the looming wall of the Old City and enters it through the Jaffa Gate. It was through the Jaffa Gate and along this now desolate artery that rioting Arab mobs rushed with the outbreak of hostilities in 1947, smashing everything in sight. Walking about in this ghost quarter today, one sees the wreckage of a world that seems to have come to a stop in an instant. What had once been a Judaeo-Arab city came to be divided, in a sudden mitosis, into its two component parts along a line that stretches above and parallel to the eye level at this point, in the form of the remains of Mamilla Road, now nothing but a tangled hyphen of gutted buildings, broken walls and jagged fences. At the two extreme ends of this line are utterly contrasting scenes: to the left, in the distance, the imposing elegance of the King David Hotel; to the right, that massive gray wall of Suleiman the Magnificent, on top of which, behind a pile of sandbags and under the lean shadow of the "Tower of David" with its cardinal's-hat turret, stands the ever-watchful Jordanian rifleman, his head occasionally appearing into view, his rifle glistening in the sun. And standing strangely, just below him, halfway down the slope that rises sharply toward the Old City wall, in the middle of a stretch of no man's land covered with rocks, rusted oil cans and an assortment of indefinable scraps, is a lone, bent, but still unfaded bus-stop sign, as if unaware that it has long since been deprived of its function.

But this area is not completely unpopulated; just this side of the barbed-wire fence marking no man's land there are clotheslines filled with laundry. It is tempting to think that these are some sort of urban pioneers living here, staking out frontier posts like the soldier-founders of the strategic "Nahal" kibbutzim. In a sense, the people living here are, at least unconsciously, filling that sort of function; but the framework of their lives and purposes is very different from that of soldier-pioneeers. These are simply the poor of Jerusalem, mostly new immigrants from Oriental countries, living by a peculiar irony in physical circumstances that are as marginal as their place in society. A little girl sitting on a rock nearby has been staring at me for some time. Her lively and intelligent face contrasts with the faded old dress she is wearing, and the dusty pair of boys' high-ankled shoes, several sizes too large, that are on her feet. I begin talking to her. She tells me all about herself: she is Kurdish, she is eight years old, and she has just finished school for the day. I ask her why she is not playing. Pointing to a group of children some distance away, farther from the border, up the slope that leads toward the King David Hotel, she says that she sometimes goes up there to play with them, but that they never come down here, because they are afraid to. "Yes, you know, of course," I say to her, pointing in the other direction toward the sandbags on top of the Old City wall, rising so precipitously as almost to seem to be directly above our heads, "that there's a soldier up there staring down at us." "He's not a soldier, he's a watchman," she says with a well-deserved air of superiority. "And you mustn't point to him like that, or he'll shoot you." And of course there was something to what she said.

It is in the name of holiness of place that the possibility of sudden and violent death has here been made a part of the everyday life of small children. What can men mean when they call a place holy, that they should cause such things to come about? Jew and Arab today confront one another from opposite slopes, and Christians are scattered throughout the the hills on both sides of the border, all of them sifting through the holy dust of Jerusalem for the relics and sparks which glow with each one's own particular image of the divine. None of them knows where to draw the boundary lines of his claim. Fragments of the Jewish Temple lay buried under a sacred Muslim shrine, the site of Calvary has been determined on scarcely more than the word of a zealous queen-mother of the fourth century, the City

of David may have been on Mount Zion (now in Israel) or it may
have been on the Ophel (now in Jordan) farther to the southeast.
Almost all one knows with certainty is that it was somewhere in these
hills, about three thousand years ago, that King David established the
city that God was then said to have looked upon as the center of the
world, and that since that time two other great religions have come to
share in the idea of the holiness of Jerusalem, with the result that
countless wars and horrors have ensued in their rivalry for the
possession of it. For my own part, I would be glad to yield to the
grain of rationalist in myself and assert unequivocally that all these
abominations have been committed in the name of a delusion, of
some barbaric vanity in man that seizes upon stretches of barren
rocks and earth and makes them the vested interests of the human
soul; but I, like most men, am scarcely a rationalist at all. Knowing
nothing with certainty about the idea of God, I nevertheless must
acknowledge the weight of more than three thousand years of
collective human consciousness to be upon me. These rocks may
know nothing of their chosenness, but they cannot escape the burden
of my knowledge of them: I, like other victims of the human
imagination, look upon them as, somehow, holy. Does this mean
I must be a servant to the idea of continuing warfare among men?

But perhaps Jerusalem still has things to teach us. Out of the
ambiguous period following armistice settlements and United Nations resolutions, Jerusalem defied all the official plans and developed
according to certain tendencies inherent in her recent history. The
fact is that each of the three major groups concerned with Jerusalem
has now come to be in possession of what is really most important to
it: the Jews have the New City that they built, the city of their
future, contiguous with the rest of the state of Israel; the Muslims
have the Old City with the Dome of the Rock; and the Christians
retain sovereignty over their various holy places on both sides of the
Israel-Jordan frontier. Each religion has the shrines or plots that are
most appropriate to it, which is to say, in the case of the Jews, that
they now hold what has always been of greater import to their spirit
than scattered holy objects or special patches of consecrated ground:
they have the rocky horizons, glaring in the sun, that filled the eyes
and hearts of ancient Israel in its pursuit of a grandiose and restless
vision. It is the very indefinability of Palestinian landscapes that has
gone toward making this Land the clay as well as the mold of the

Jewish consciousness. The religion of Israel was founded in tents, not in a Temple built on a certain irreplaceable patch of ground. A restored Jewish Jerusalem could not have been built on anything but fresh new slopes. If, then, an appropriate proprietary division has arisen among the three peoples of Jerusalem, perhaps we should not be excessively troubled by the uniqueness of the situation that this division has brought about. Probably no city in history has been apportioned among different sovereignties in quite the way Jerusalem is today. But we are living in an era which is characterized by the breaking of precedents everywhere in the world and, besides, Jerusalem has always been unique. If, then, she were to find the way to become a crossroads at which the Jewish, Christian and Muslim worlds converge and live side by side in peace and mutual respect, she would certainly have achieved something befitting the sacred ideals her name has always evoked.

CHAPTER 6

Ideology and Politics

POLITICALLY as well as socially, Israel can be said to have first come into being largely as the product of a revolutionary ideology. In some respects, the movement which bore this ideology resembled other revolutionary movements in the political spawning ground of late nineteenth-century Europe—particularly Russia—from which it came. Like them, it was founded upon a set of ideals which served as powerful forces motivating human action and which established a broad and meaningful framework of purpose, but which were not necessarily geared to the realities of power. Socialism in general has long confronted this problem; both in the East and in the West, it has invariably risen to its noblest manifestations in opposition rather than in office. The Communist party in Russia did not recover easily from the shock of conversion from class movement to the governing power of an entire nation; the rough edges of the transition were smoothed over by the plane of Stalinist brutality. The slogan "from class to nation" was often used by David Ben-Gurion and other Labor Zionist leaders in the years prior to statehood. But once they had become the main governing power of a state, the Labor Zionists, unlike the Communists, then had to continue to function in the atmosphere of a liberal democracy. They not only had to confront an opposition that had existed even prior to statehood, but they also had to come to terms with the democratic will of a constantly and rapidly growing immigrant population. Israel is still, for the most part, governed by the same revolutionary coalition that brought the state into being—even, largely, by the same generation of leaders—which

has succeeded in obtaining a continuing mandate, through six national elections, from a free voting public. But this mandate, though
always a sizable plurality, has never come near to being a simple
majority. The labor group has therefore always had to seek support
from elements outside itself in order to form a governing coalition.

Yet this has not been the chief difficulty in the way of socialist
policies. For the most part, the labor coalition has gained a parliamentary majority by including in the Cabinet members of the
religious parties, who are willing to accept a socialist program as a
quid pro quo for Sabbath laws and other types of religious legislation.
This has brought about a situation in the country which sometimes
borders on theocracy, but it also means that the Socialists have been
able to govern without including in their midst elements from the
"bourgeois" opposition. Their chief difficulty, then, has not come so
much from this opposition as from the strong fissiparous tendencies
among themselves. These tendencies are perhaps in part a Jewish
cultural heritage; the old joke tells of a Jew stranded alone on a desert
island who builds two synagogues there—the one that he goes to and
the one that he would never go to. But they are primarily the legacy
of the extremely ideological atmosphere, largely Russian in character,
within which Labor Zionism was founded and developed. The Communist party of the Soviet Union dealt with the schismatic tendencies in its midst by a violent authoritarianism. The liberal atmosphere
of Israeli politics has enabled similar tendencies to develop to a
degree that sometimes seems to border on parliamentary anarchism.

Broadly speaking, Labor Zionism has always tended to divide into a
pragmatic, Fabian right and a more militantly ideological left. It
began, in fact, as two separate movements. The more left-wing of
these, the Poalei Zion (Workers of Zion), was strongly influenced by
the Bund—it even had something of a Yiddishist inclination in its
early years—and tried to conceive of its role in Marxian terms. This
was in some ways a remarkable feat, since in the Palestine of the early
years of the twentieth century there was not much of a capitalist
system to rail against. The major theoretician of the Poalei Zion
trend, Ber Borochow, maintained, in good Marxian fashion, that it
was the task of the Labor Zionists to cooperate in the building of a
capitalist Palestine, so that the country would then be ready for the
proletarian revolution. In any case, the vigorously anticapitalist frame
of mind of this group served it in good stead, helping it to form a

spirited opposition against the methods of the Jewish plantation owners and farm managers in the early days of Second Aliyah settlement.

The more right-wing Labor Zionist group, *Ha'poel Ha'tza'ir* (The Young Worker), was hostile to Marxism, and argued that the building of a socialist society had to begin not with a "class" but with the individual. This was considered above all to be a task of personal reconstruction, of *hagshamah atzmit* (self-realization), in the words of A. D. Gordon, who was the chief source of ideological inspiration for Ha'poel Ha'tza'ir. Gordon was a man who had worked as a clerk all his life when in 1904, at the age of forty-eight, he settled in Palestine and became an agricultural laborer. Despite the severe physical hardships that this entailed, he never again worked anywhere but in the fields, except at night, when he wrote his lyrical and philosophical essays about the reclamation of the human spirit and of the Jewish people through labor and intimate contact with nature. His ideals were derived primarily from Tolstoy, and indeed, he came to look like Tolstoy in his last years, a white-bearded prophet dressed in the clothing of a farm laborer. Recognizing the strong attraction that Marxism exerted upon Russian-Jewish intellectuals, Gordon vigorously opposed it, criticizing above all its repudiation of national-ist sentiments, which he considered to be a stress upon the head at the expense of the heart. His emphasis upon individual self-realiza-tion as opposed to a class orientation was absolutely essential to the adherents of both trends in Labor Zionism, most of whom, like Gordon, were converting themselves from sedentary occupations to lives of physical labor. It was Gordon who gave poetry to this austere undertaking. But his stress upon personal self-help has also been the source of a kind of moral elitism which prevails to this day, especially in the kibbutzim, and which does not always readily lend itself to the broadly social-democratic tasks of a modern welfare state.

The Poalei Zion and Ha'poel Ha'tza'ir—whose differences were always more discernible on the ideological than on the practical level—achieved a grudging alliance in the founding of the Histadrut in 1920. They continued, however, to identify themselves as separate political parties until 1929, when they merged in the founding of what is still the major socialist party of the country, Mapai (the abbreviation of *Mifleget Poalei Eretz Israel*—Israel Workers' party). But by this time, the most left-wing trend in Labor Zionism was no longer that of the Poalei Zion elements of Mapai, who were going, rather, in the direction of the pragmatic Marxian social democracy in Europe. Like the Mensheviks or the German Social Democrats of this period, they were being displaced on the left by a revolutionary Marxism more prone to the Bolshevik model. This left-wing movement, Ha'shomer Ha'tza'ir, could never have affiliated with the Communist international because of Moscow's anti-Zionism; on the other hand, it did at least find something of a social structure in Palestine against which to be militantly revolutionary, unlike the Labor Zionists of the previous generation.

The existence of a revolutionary Marxist party to the left did not put an end to the divisive tendencies in Mapai; rather, it encouraged such tendencies. By 1944 the moderate and pragmatic trend of the Mapai leadership was so pronounced that a left-wing faction broke away and formed a separate party, Ahdut Ha'avodah (Unity of Labor). Ahdut Ha'avodah had sought a bridge to closer relations with Ha'shomer Ha'tza'ir, a group vehemently opposed by the Mapai right wing. In 1948 Ahdut Ha'avodah carried its move to a logical conclusion, and joined with Ha'shomer Ha'tza'ir in the formation of a new political party, Mapam (the Hebrew abbreviation for United Workers' party). But this proved to be an uneasy alliance. In the years following the end of the Second World War, the period of the rise of the cold war between East and West, international relations became the main focus of the struggles between the labor parties in Israel. Mapai, though officially neutralist, tended toward affiliation with the West; Mapam—at least its Ha'shomer Ha'tza'ir element— was strongly pro-Soviet. The Ahdut Ha'avodah element grudgingly accepted this orientation, until the emerging anti-Semitism in the communist bloc during this period, culminating in the Slansky trial and the "Doctors' Plot," became too much for it to bear. In 1954 Ahdut Ha'avodah broke away from Mapam and became an independent party once again. From then on, it served regularly in Mapai-led coalitions, striving to maintain a moral influence upon its parent party in favor of a more traditional ideological approach. This collaboration has recently led to a new attempt at unifying Ahdut Ha'avodah and Mapai which will be considered further on.

The 1944 split between Mapai and Ahdut Ha'avodah was not a simple reversion to the old division between Poalei Zion and Ha'poel Ha'tza'ir, although it included some elements of this. The leader of the right-wing Mapai majority was David Ben-Gurion, who in his youth had been a member of the left-wing Poalei Zion. In some respects Ben-Gurion is still one of the most radical of all the socialist leaders—"radical" in the sense of the old Jacksonian democracy in America. He is a demagogue in both the favorable and the unfavorable meaning of the word: a man with genuinely popular instincts, who senses the needs of the masses, and a charismatic leader with strong authoritarian inclinations. This type of leader is rarely an adherent of some fixed program; hence, in the context of a socialist establishment, Ben-Gurion's anti-ideological and anti-establishment tendencies make him into a "right-wing" Socialist.

It is rather the left wing today which has, paradoxically, inherited certain attitudes from the old Ha'poel Ha'tza'ir. Socialist establishments in general are prone to an elitism in some ways more radical than that of any other kind of establishment. It is an elitism based upon pride in the moral superiority of the socialist institutions that one has helped to create and upon an unswerving loyalty to those institutions. Such attitudes are especially strong in Israel, where the institutions of the socialist establishment—the kibbutzim and the Histadrut—were the very foundation stones of the society and the state. But these institutions are now far from constituting Israeli society as a whole (they never did completely), and the Histadrut in particular is today an object against which popular discontent is directed as often as against any capitalist establishment. In other words, socialist orthodoxy in Israel is a kind of conservatism which seeks to protect certain elements in the institutional establishment of the country against assaults upon them by the popular will. There is in this more than a touch of the old Ha'poel Ha'tza'ir pride in "self-realization," which is, after all, a "bourgeois" ideal in some respects.

The stronghold of this type of conservatism is the kibbutz, where there is far less contact with the new social elements in Israel than there is in the Histadrut. During the Mandate period the kibbutzim remained relatively free of party politics. Ha'shomer Ha'tza'ir was the only kibbutz federation that was also a political movement from the outset, and it did not organize itself as a full-fledged party until the merger with Ahdut Ha'avodah and the formation of Mapam in 1948. The other two major federations were by and large nonpolitical in the Mandate period, although there was a naturally close association between the *Hever Ha'kvutzot*—the Deganiah federation—and Mapai. The Ein Harod federation, *Ha'kibbutz Ha'me'uhad,* conscientiously avoided any political identification and simply advocated labor unity. Its ideal of kibbutz autonomy, as well as its romantic conception of the kibbutz movement as a revolutionary force, was most fully manifested in the War of Independence, when its settlements became the strongholds of the Palmach.

In the period immediately following statehood, a rapid politicization of the kibbutzim took place, accompanied by considerable bitterness and strife. Unity of Labor (Ahdut Ha'avodah) was now not so much a broad ideal as a political faction, and its alliance with Ha'shomer Ha'tza'ir in the formation of Mapam received the tentative support of the Ha'kibbutz Ha'me'uhad settlements. But when the cold war conflict between Mapam and Mapai grew more intense in the early 1950's, members of the Ha'kibbutz Ha'me'uhad settlements began dividing into two factions supporting one party or the other. In some of the kibbutzim, opposition between these two factions became violent. There were fistfights at Ein Harod, and in 1951 its dining hall was divided into two sections, one for Mapam and one for Mapai. Finally, an election was held in each of the federation's kibbutzim to decide upon its political complexion. The losing minority in each kibbutz transferred themselves to one in which their tendency was in the majority. Ein Harod, like several of the other settlements, was evenly divided, and so it was split into two separate kibbutzim. The property was carefully divided between the two, a process which took some three or four years.

The effect of this tragedy was heightened by the fact that, in 1954, Ahdut Ha'avodah broke away from Mapam after all, and was supported in this by Ha'kibbutz Ha'me'uhad—or what remained of it. The pro-Mapai kibbutzim of this federation broke away from it and joined with the old Hever Ha'kvutzot in the formation of a new "Union of Kvutzot and Kibbutzim." This federation is, of course, closely identified with Mapai today, although it is still technically independent. Nowadays, popular usage simply refers to Mapai, Ahdut or Mapam kibbutzim, even though it is not strictly correct to do so. But in this widespread use of party labels instead of the federation names there is indeed more justification than the fact that the former are easier to pronounce.

Today, Mapai is the labor party least influenced by the kibbutzim, and the federation identified with it is the one least concerned with politics. Mapam and Ha'shomer Ha'tza'ir are virtually one and the same, and this group continues to be both militantly ideological and ardent in its stress upon the kibbutz as the keystone of society. Ahdut Ha'avodah, supported by the Ha'kibbutz Ha'me'uhad federation, has regularly held seats in the Cabinet, unlike Mapam, and is more attuned than the latter to political realities. Nevertheless, a strong ideological preoccupation with the traditional aims of Labor Zionism and the kibbutz still prevails in the ranks of Ahdut Ha'avodah, buttressed by a nostalgia for the Palmach. Former Palmach officers dominate the leadership of the party: Yigal Allon, for example, its Minister of Labor in a succession of Cabinets, was the commander of the Palmach Brigade in its brilliant Negev campaign of October, 1948. This fact has important repercussions in other respects: for Mapai lost a large number of its most talented young men, the leaders of the generation of the War of Independence, when Ahdut Ha'avodah broke away from it in the 1940's. Since then Mapai has been a party in search of a lost generation, especially now, at a time when that generation's leaders are reaching the prime age of political maturity.

Mapai is still led by a generation of patriarchs—by a Ben-Gurion, nearly eighty years old, and by a Levi Eshkol, now in his seventies—who are searching for a successor generation with considerable anxiety. In this quest Ben-Gurion, who retired from the Prime Ministry in early 1963, and Eshkol, whom he appointed as his successor, came to represent two distinct and increasingly antagonistic tendencies. Eshkol's approach, which was victorious in the general election of November, 1965, has focused upon the restoration of unity between Mapai and Ahdut Ha'avodah. The "Alignment"—the joint Mapai-Ahdut Ha'avodah ticket which ran in that election and won a substantial plurality—has meant to its supporters not only the recovery of the hitherto lost political generation for Mapai, but a first step toward a return to the ideal of complete labor unity (i.e., toward an entry on the part of Mapam into the more pragmatic world of the other two parties). In exchange for this return of Ahdut Ha'avodah to the fold, Mapai has had to show promise of a more ideological orientation than it has traditionally manifested and, in particular, of a greater concern with restoring the kibbutz to a central place in Israeli life.

Ben-Gurion's position has been at once less "socialist" and more radical. More concerned with such practical democratic programs as increasing the number of years of free, public education in Israel than with old-fashioned Labor Zionist ideologies, he has been resolutely opposed to Alignment with any of the parties to the left of Mapai. He is, however, strongly in favor of creating a single, large party of the left, which could achieve absolute majorities without coalitions— as is Eshkol. But in Ben-Gurion's eyes this is something to be achieved not through Alignment but through electoral reform. At present the Knesset (the Israeli parliament) is elected by a system of proportional representation, based upon the entire country as a single unit. Each party receives the same proportion of the Knesset's 120 seats that it obtained of the total national vote. As is well known to students of politics, this system provides a far more favorable climate for the proliferation of small parties than does the single-member constituency system of the United States or Great Britain. Since, under the latter system, each electoral subdivision of the country sends only one representative, elected by a simple majority, to the Congress or Parliament, minority parties tend to disappear alto-gether. But a party which obtains neither more nor less than 5 percent of the votes in every area, and which would therefore not gain a single seat in a single-member constituency system, would get 5 percent of the seats in a system of proportional representation such as that of Israel. Proportional representation is not the sole cause of a multiparty system as opposed to the two-party system of the United States, but it is a decidedly encouraging factor. Mr. Ben-Gurion believes that a single-member constituency system in Israel would bring a two-party system in its wake, consisting of Mapai on the left and some kind of middle-class, relatively conservative party on the right.

These are the trends, broadly stated, of the Ben-Gurion-Eshkol controversy. Some of the narrower issues upon which this controversy has focused have taken on an air of greater importance than they deserve, largely because of Ben-Gurion's remorseless will, marked authoritarian tendencies and charismatic personality. This is particu-larly true of the Lavon Affair. This case, which burdened the Israeli public for several years with a mass of loudly trumpeted accusations and counteraccusations, consisting of enormous intricacies piled upon still more enormous obscurities, concerns the degree of personal responsibility of Mr. Pinchas Lavon for a "security mishap" which took place in 1954, while he was Minister of Defense and while Mr. Ben-Gurion, who always served as his own Minister of Defense, was in temporary retirement. There were undoubtedly deep-lying personal issues underlying Ben-Gurion's obstinate refusal to allow Lavon to be absolved of responsibility in the matter, as well as political issues not intrinsically involved in the case. In any event, the Affair increasingly became more a political than a juridical controversy. Lavon, after his resignation from the Defense Ministry, became Secretary General of the Histadrut in 1955, and as such was one of the heads of a Labor Zionist establishment to which Ben-Gurion had become vehemently opposed. In particular, the vast structure of the Histadrut can be viewed as a kind of countersovereignty, a state-within-a-state, and Ben-Gurion has been one of Israel's most ardent advocates of the complete transcendence of state authority over the quasi-sovereign national institutions that preceded it (an outlook manifested, for example, by his summary dissolution of the Palmach in 1948). To a certain extent, then, Ben-Gurion's challenge to Lavon's personal integrity was also a challenge to the authority of the Histadrut and, by implication, of the whole Labor Zionist establishment.

This broader challenge led to a rallying of forces against Ben-Gurion, both in Mapai and in the parties further to the left, on the part of those who sought to defend Labor Zionist ideals against the assaults of what they called "statism." A group of university professors affiliated with Mapai gathered around the person of Pinchas Lavon in a political association called *Min Ha'yesod* (From the Ground Up). Lavon was a sort of Dreyfus for the Min Ha'yesod intellectuals, and, as with the Dreyfusards, many of them were less concerned with him than with the larger issues he represented to them. They saw the socialist ideals of the country as being threatened with extinction at the hands of a group of men—Ben-Gurion and some of his younger followers—who seemed to them less concerned with ideals than with the uses of state power. By gathering support in the Mapai kibbutzim, Min Ha'yesod became a lever which was eventually able to pry Mr. Eshkol and the bulk of Mapai into an open split with the Ben-Gurion faction in the spring of 1964. This was something that the party had hesitated to do, not only for sentimental reasons but because, even in retirement, Mr. Ben-Gurion was the biggest vote getter in the country.

Ben-Gurion continued to try to press for a judicial inquiry into the Lavon Affair, which he was sure would show Lavon to have been the responsible party in the 1954 "security mishap." But public opinion was becoming monumentally bored with the subject, and Ben-Gurion was losing support on this issue in the party ranks. As the November, 1965, general election approached, and Ben-Gurion found himself consistently repudiated by the party on the Lavon issue, he suddenly broke party discipline; in the summer of that year he and his followers formed a separate list for the election, called Rafi (abbreviation for the Hebrew of Israel Workers' List). He argued that this "list" was not a separate party, that those whose names figured on it were still members of Mapai, and that its purpose was simply to gather a mandate for those in the party who opposed the Alignment, which had been formed earlier in the year.

From then on, the Alignment very quickly came to the fore as the real issue, as, in a sense, it had been all along. It is a pity that the real questions involved in this issue had become obscured in endless months of haggling over the Lavon Affair, about which Mr. Ben-Gurion was thunderously obsessive. But despite its real lack of merits as a major political issue, the Affair had served as the catalyst which broke the party into its Ben-Gurionist and Alignment components. Rafi, which campaigned, among other things, on the issue of election reform, was a bid to form a new type of popular party as against the refurbished establishmentarianism of the Mapai-Ahdut Ha'avodah Alignment. To the extent that it stood for the principle of obtaining a new mass base of support among the electorate, Rafi seems at first glance not to have been successful in the 1965 election, since it obtained only 10 seats as opposed to 45 for the Alignment. The Rafi leaders had hoped for more, and of course they had grounds for such hopes in Ben-Gurion's still unrivaled vote-getting power; but, on the other hand, he had somewhat tarnished his political "image" in his long period of rage over a minor ten-year-old incident about which the public could hardly have cared less. Still, Rafi has made itself into an important lever against the Alignment, which did not succeed in obtaining as many seats as had been held in combination by Mapai and Ahdut Ha'avodah in the previous Knesset. Rafi may still prove to be an important new force in Israeli politics; this is particularly likely because, although most of the successor generation on the effective political left in Israel belongs to Ahdut Ha'avodah, as has been

mentioned, two of the most popular younger men in Israeli politics—
Shimon Peres, the talented former Assistant Minister of Defense,
and Moshe Dayan, celebrated for his leadership of the Sinai Campaign in 1956—are affiliated with Rafi.

A survey of the political left in Israel would not be complete
without a glance at the Communist party, or parties. Formed in the
1920's, *Maki* (Hebrew initials of Communist Party of Israel) has
never been more than a very minor force in the political life of the
country, because its policies are usually anti-Zionist. Not surprisingly,
it has always obtained its support primarily from Israeli Arabs;[1] but a
handful of the principal leaders of the party has always consisted of
Jews. In 1965, however, a split took place in the Maki leadership. It
turned out that certain of the Jewish leaders of the party did have
misgivings about advocating the extinction of the Jewish state, and
they began to stress, in the course of their still largely pro-Arab
statements, their view that any accommodations between the Arab
world and Israel would have to be based upon a recognition of the
latter's existence. In reaction to this "pro-Zionist" stance, a more
extreme faction broke away and formed a separate group, the New
Communist party. With one exception, the leaders of this new party
are Arabs, whereas the leadership of the more "Zionist" Maki is
almost exclusively Jewish. Maki won one seat in the 1965 election, as
against three won by the New Communists.

The political right in Israel held Cabinet portfolios only for a brief
period in the 1950's, and has otherwise functioned exclusively in
opposition. Its role as a revisionist and anti-establishment force in a
society that is socialist in origin is unique in comparison with that of
the right in most Western democracies, and has led to some unusual
manifestations. For the most part, the Israeli "right" has, quite
naturally, sought to encourage the growth of the private sector in the
national economy; but it has also advocated policies which are
paradoxically "socialist" in character. This is an outcome of its
opposition to the Histadrut; in seeking to divest that institution of
some of its powers, the right has called for the nationalization of
certain of its quasi-public facilities. The Histadruth's *Kupat Holim*,
for example, is in effect the national public health service of Israel.

[1] There is also a moderate Arab bloc in the Knesset, which regularly supports
Mapai. It won four seats in the 1965 election.

Since "socialized medicine" is therefore already an accomplished fact in the country, the right is only asking that it be socialized even more—that it be transferred to the state from an institution that is only quasi-public in character.

In some respects, then, the progressive wing of the Israeli right comes very close to the anti-Histadrut and "statist" position of the Ben-Gurion faction. Both of these groups perceive that the machinery of their new state has become, as in all the welfare states in the world today, the most powerful, the most viable, and the most genuinely *popular* social service institution in the nation. The old voluntaristic brotherhood of the Histadrut, already somewhat bruised by the contradictions of being both a workers' association and an employer of labor, has watched a world grow up around it, a "Second Israel" made up as much of proletarians as of capitalists, who see it simply as a privileged corporation—however cooperative its internal character—within the larger national community. The Histadrut bureaucracy often appears to the new immigrant as only a hierarchy of power which is closed to him; the mass democratic state is far more accessible to him. To a certain extent, the situation of the Histadrut in Israel today is something like that of the Church in the late Middle Ages, watching the new nation-states grow up around it. Once the sole instrument of public welfare, the Church came to be displaced by another instrument which, within the national territory, was ultimately more efficient and more *universal* in character.

In this respect, the progressive wing of the Israeli political right is potentially a highly democratic force in the country. Furthermore, its affinities with the Ben-Gurion group seem to suggest the possibility of some kind of progressive coalition of the center. This seems even more likely when one considers that, among Ben-Gurion's followers —most notably Moshe Dayan—there have been signs of a possible willingness to favor an increased development of the private sector in Israel's economy. The moderate right has, in fact, often dreamed of such a coalition, and the leading spokesman of its views, the independent newspaper *Ha'aretz*, called for an alliance between the right and Rafi during the 1965 election campaign. But Ben-Gurion has always had too much of the old socialist in him to agree to an alliance with any "bourgeois" party.

Part of the difficulty lies in the fact that the major grouping on the right—the old General Zionists, now the Liberal party—has been unable to decide whether its tendencies are to be a right-wing or a left-wing conservatism. In its origin, the General Zionist party was by nature something that could not be readily defined, least of all by itself; as its name indicates, it was simply a residue left over by the emergence of Labor Zionism, made up of all those who refused to "hyphenate" their Zionist commitment by any further ideological coloration. Resolutely ecumenical in character, its greatest strength prior to 1948 was always in the World Zionist Organization—in the Congresses—rather than in Palestine itself, where the Labor Zionists reigned supreme. Chaim Weizmann, for example, was a General Zionist, and the very model of what the term meant. Indeed, one major problem the party has faced since statehood has come from its natural desire not to be excessively influenced by its leaders outside the state of Israel. These are often men of world stature, and they naturally claim a great deal of moral authority. In the 1961 election, for example (when the General Zionists reconstituted themselves as the Liberal party), a good deal of controversy was aroused when Nahum Goldmann, President of the World Zionist Organization, entered the country and campaigned for the party list. Goldmann, who has since become an Israeli citizen, then still held American citizenship.

But within the broadly undefined conservative grouping that made up the General Zionist party, there was at the beginning one faction which held to a relatively clear ideological commitment. This group, which formed the left wing of General Zionism, was committed to the type of welfare-state liberalism of the old German Progressive party, or of the British Liberal party of today. In 1948 it broke away from the General Zionists and formed its own party, called the Progressives. Although often not easily distinguishable from the right wing of Mapai in ideological terms, the Progressive party was quite distinct in its social composition: it was made up primarily of academicians and professionals from Germany. But, standing alone, this party has not been able to be a viable political force. In the election year of 1961 it merged with the General Zionists once again, in the formation of a new Liberal party. However, this coalition broke up once again four years later, as a consequence of a swing toward the right on the part of the old General Zionist elements, a move which the old Progressives could not bring themselves to support.

This swing toward the right was in the direction of an alliance with the Herut (Freedom) party, which forms the extreme right wing of the Israeli political spectrum. Other than the fact that Herut is vehemently antisocialist—as are many of the General Zionists as well—the only grounds upon which it is to be designated as the extreme right is that of its past record of militant nationalism. Herut is the direct descendant of Vladimir Jabotinsky's Revisionists. When the Irgun Tzva'i Leumi was dissolved after the Altalena incident in 1948, it reconstituted itself, under the leadership of the energetic Menahem Begin, into the cadre of a newly formed Herut party. Since then, it has often managed to gain a substantial number of votes from that core of discontented people in any society who enjoy hearing the occasional sound of a rattling saber. Its roots in the martial trumpetings of Betar, in the terrorism of the Irgun, and in some occasional outstanding displays of irresponsibility even after statehood—such as its prominent role in the violent street demonstrations which accompanied the government's acceptance of German reparations in 1952—have led many of Herut's opponents to continue to use the term "fascist" among their invectives against it. But in recent years, as its core of old Irgunists has reached middle age and a reasonable degree of middle-class comfort, Herut has tended to become far less warlike than it once was, even in its pronouncements.

Herut's increasing moderation led the old General Zionist elements of the Liberal party to begin taking note of some of its virtues. In Menahem Begin, a man of considerable personal charm with a real flair for popular oratory, Herut possesses Ben-Gurion's nearest rival in the country as a vote getter and charismatic leader (both men have particular strength among Oriental immigrant voters, who often tend to favor politicians cast in the heroic mold). Until the formation of the Progressive-General Zionist alliance in 1961, Herut consistently held the largest bloc of seats in the Knesset after Mapai; even the unified Liberal party could do no better than equal Herut's 17 seats in that year's election. Therefore, with the formation of the left-wing Alignment in the election year of 1965, leaders of the Liberal and Herut parties decided to come together in the formation of an "alignment" of the right, called Gahal (from the initials of Gush—bloc—Herut-Liberal). But the centrist wing of the right—the old Progressives—could no more tolerate this "alignment" to the further-right than the centrist wing of the left—the Rafi group—could tolerate the Mapai Alignment with the further-left. This Progressive wing broke away once again and ran on a separate "Independent Liberal" ticket in the 1965 election. As usual, its showing as an independent group was small: 5 seats. But even had it remained with Gahal, which won 26 seats, the combined right would still have been substantially outnumbered by the Alignment total of 45 seats. Since it is the right that forms the only opposition bloc in the country (under the circumstances, Mapam, with its 8 seats, is merely a splinter on the left, without any political leverage), its defeat in November, 1965, must still—as always in the past—be considered one of landslide proportions.

This is a fact that would seem disastrous only if one looked upon the present arrangement in Israel as something like a two-party, or two-bloc, system. There is the distinct potentiality of such a system in Israel, and it would probably come out into the open under the single-member constituency system that Mr. Ben-Gurion advocates. But such a system is not likely to come into being in the foreseeable future, since the coalition entrenched in power by the present system is not going to exchange that system for another one less favorable to itself. At the present time, then, what exists in Israel is not the two-bloc system of Britain or the United States, but the traditional "third-force" system of France during the Third and Fourth Republics. Like its French counterpart, the Israeli third force is a more or less centrist coalition gathered up out of a complex spectrum of parties ranging from extreme left to extreme right. This system is the only viable one in a political framework which, like that of Israel or of France prior to de Gaulle, veers over into extremist parties; only countries like Britain and the United States, in which both sides are essentially moderate, can afford complete alternating shifts in the possession of power between the party of the left and the party of the right.

But there are, at present, significant differences between the French and Israeli systems. Although the French third force was always, essentially, hooked to the center of the political spectrum, there were nevertheless always shifts in the weight of the coalition, relatively to the right or to the left, from election to election and sometimes more frequently. In Israel, on the other hand, the weight has not shifted since the founding of the state. Israel's comparative political stability is to her advantage; the perishability of French governments under the Third and especially the Fourth Republic became legendary. But such alternation in the balance of governing is nevertheless essential to a healthy parliamentary system. Not that the alternations need take place as frequently as they must in two-party systems—indeed, they probably should not; but Israel today has reached a point at which such a shift might perhaps be in order. For close to two decades now the country has been governed by a coalition representing a two-part establishment: the Labor Zionist establishment and the religious one. The power of the religious parties is particularly irksome because they represent only a small fraction of the voting public. But their disproportionate power is due, precisely, to the resolute refusal of the governing coalition to think in terms of a third force. Since the First World War, the socialist parties of Western Europe have regularly joined forces with the "bourgeois" liberal parties in the formation of governments. In Israel, however, even the moderate Mapai has preferred to allow the partial theocratization of the country rather than enter into such an alliance.

This is where the formation of Rafi might prove to be of vital importance in the political future of Israel. If, in subsequent elections, Rafi can gain additional support from new generations of voters—young people free of sentimental attachments to the old pioneering establishment—without taking anything away from Mapai's base of support, then a Mapai-Rafi coalition could be formed. Such a coalition could perhaps even include the Independent Liberals; it could, in any case, dispense with the services of the religious parties. Then Israeli politics would at last be able to break through the crust of commitments which, though once noble and absolutely vital to the early growth of the nation, have now become somewhat stale.

PART FOUR:

Cultural and Spiritual Life

CHAPTER 7

Hebrew Language
and Literature

I

THE history of the relationship of the people of Israel to the
Hebrew language has been as much one of passion and vexation as
that of their relationship to their land. These two histories are
concurrent and intertwining, and have at times been virtually the
same. In the Jewish tradition, speaking the holy tongue has often
been considered to have a redemptive value equivalent to that of
dwelling in Zion, and both to live in the Land of Israel and to speak
Hebrew was once seen as a way of securing one's place among the
eternally blessed. This ideal makes it clear that the condition of
galut—of exile—has meant as much the linguistic as the physical
alienation; and, in fact, as was the case with the land, the alienation
from the language did not occur suddenly and without precedent at
the destruction of the Temple and the Jewish commonwealth by the
Romans in 70 C.E.

The linguistic, like the physical, galut began with the Babylonian
exile in the sixth century B.C.E. Not only the Jewish community that
remained in Babylonia, but even those Jews who returned to Palestine under the proclamation of Cyrus, had adopted Aramaic as their
normal everyday language by the end of that century. Hebrew
continued to be spoken in places and on occasions: one may conjec-

ture that it was retained primarily, on the one hand, by the learned and clerical elements—by the scribes and perhaps the priests—as the medium they reserved for elevated discourse and, on the other hand, by an utterly unlearned peasantry which, concentrated in the strongholds of Jewish settlement in the Galilee, had never gone out into exile in the first place. It was probably mainly the "middle" classes— the dealers in worldly goods on all economic levels—who had easily succumbed to the cultural influence of some three generations in Aramaic-speaking Babylonia. These were the elements to whom Ezra had to address himself with special vigor in order to bring Israel firmly back into the ways of the Law; and so a large part of his discourses to them was in Aramaic, and set down in that language in the book of Ezra. From then on, Aramaic—a Semitic language, closely related to Hebrew, but quite different from it in spirit—was probably the chief language spoken by the Jews of Palestine. Not only are there many Aramaic passages in the books of Ezra and of Daniel, written in this period, but even the Hebrew in them bears earmarks of the influence of that language. In other words, the beginning of the Second Commonwealth marks a major turning point in the history of Hebrew; from then on, until the end of the nineteenth century, it was approached from the standpoint of a consciousness at least partially formed in another language.

It was in the Hellenistic and Roman periods, when Aramaic had all but superseded Hebrew as the normal spoken language of the Jews of Palestine, and when the influence of Greek and Latin was in the air, that the prose language of the Mishna was formed. Mishnaic Hebrew, the vigorous medium of argumentation used by the Jewish sages of this period, develops its sentences according to the logic of any European language, and hence is the classical basis of modern Hebrew speech and prose. The poetic identity of Hebrew, on the other hand, continues to reside in the Bible. This is where its unique essence resides as well; no Israeli today, however, could speak the language of the Bible, perhaps the most beautiful literary instrument ever conceived, but scarcely amenable to the patterns of human speech and thought established in the West and its environs since Greco-Roman times.

Presumably the biblical mode of discourse was a highly "literary" one even in the epoch in which it was written. But we can never really know which biblical patterns were exclusively literary devices and which ones, however exotic to us, were faithful renderings of the plain language of the day. When we consider the remarkable vision with which the people of the Bible were struggling—a vision which seems, at least at times, to have derived its greatest strength from the passions of ordinary shepherds—then we must allow for the possibility of striking manifestations in the speech of even the humblest persons. Indeed, the greatest strength of biblical discourse often comes from a refinement of the most primitive way of understanding a thing. This is the case, for example, with the widely used rhythmic repetition of a word as both substantive and verb, as in the phrase, *mot tamut*, normally translated "thou shalt surely die," but literally being: "a death thou shalt die." The harsh poetry of this construction comes, precisely, from its etymological primitiveness: it is a repetition of the exact same stem, with only a prefix added to it the second time to make it into a verb. In English, we have many nouns and verbs which are exactly the same, and so we could duplicate this construction with phrases like "a cry thou shalt cry," "a fall thou shalt fall" and so on; but this would come through to our minds as mere tautology. Within the framework of the biblical consciousness, however, this construction has real import; it suggests a spirit just discovering how nouns become verbs, how stasis turns into motion, and thought into action. In biblical Hebrew the verb is not something taken for granted, as it is by ourselves. It is a primeval awakening, a sudden dislodgment from eternity, which from the instant of Creation in the opening words of the Bible, never throws off the jubilation of that discovery.

The biblical verb is not declined in tenses as we normally understand them today, but rather is formed simply in two aspects: perfect and imperfect. There is no past, present or future in the Hebrew of the Bible (the "tense" is known from the context), but only action completed and action not completed—only Being or Becoming. Thus, the opening sentence of the Bible, which is in the perfect, suggests pure Being, a primeval and timeless instant; when God created the heaven and the earth, this most fundamental of all creative acts could scarcely have been a process, but must have been completed in the moment that it was performed. On the other hand, when God subsequently creates light, He is now bringing into being one of the subsidiary and endlessly volatile manifestations of that state of process which is the unending burden of the Creation.

This is no longer primeval awakening into existence, but a mere particularizing of that which already exists, one of the endless offshoots of that Heraclitean fire which is nature: it is in the imperfect. The translation, "And God said, Let there be light: and there was light" loses the significance of the verb construction in the original, which is all in the imperfect, and in which the two forms used of the verb "to be," subjunctive and simple past, respectively, in the English translation, are both *exactly the same*. Va'yomer Elohim yehi or va'yehi or can roughly be rendered as: "And God saying there was light, there was light" ("was" to be taken here in the imperfective sense of "was being"). In this subsidiary act of Creation, taking place in time and not eternity, creation and process are now identical. Indeed, the Creator, who had preceded process and existed in an inscrutable eternity, is from now on understood in terms—more accessible to the human spirit—of Becoming, and is often represented as the essence of process itself. When He describes Himself to Moses by saying: "I am that I am," the phrase, once again, is in the imperfect; the meaning suggested is thus more like "I am being what I am being," or even "I become what I become."

In the more "Western" consciousness of the rabbis whose sayings are recorded in the Mishna, this rich but highly ambiguous (and hence all the richer) method of verb formation has been discarded in favor of standard tenses. The biblical imperfect becomes, in Mishnaic Hebrew, the future tense, and the perfect becomes the past. The present tense—which, according to one Jewish traditional view, is only an abstraction, a nonexistent infinitesimal point relating past and future—is an adjectival construction, closely related in conception to the English colloquial usage, "I am eating," "I am going," etc., which is really a kind of predicate adjective. These are the forms still in use in modern Hebrew. But there never has been, to this day, any verb form in Hebrew to stand in for the present tense of "to be"; where we use that verb in the present, Hebrew, like Russian, simply predicates. This, too, has a primeval quality to Western ears. Such lingering archaisms were an exception, however; for the most part, Hebrew was transformed in Mishnaic times into a discursive language as we understand the concept. Influenced by the Greek world view, Hebrew becomes in this period—the classical era of rabbinical interpretation—a vehicle for precise conceptualization and argument. Greek elements enter even into the grammar and the vocabulary. In general, there is a gain in suppleness and, as it were, modernity, but a loss in poetry.

Although Hebrew continued to be spoken in Palestine after the destruction of the Jewish commonwealth by the Romans, its use became highly restricted. Among those uneducated elements who continued to speak it, it no doubt quickly reduced itself to a dialect that was, in the end, easily absorbed by Aramaic and then by Arabic. Among the educated classes who continued to use it—at least for scholarly discourse if not for more practical purposes—it naturally tended to become something like Medieval Latin: an object, a prized vehicle for exalted purposes, a revered symbol of one's highest spiritual aspirations, but scarcely the pervasive and integrated part of a whole way of life that a living language is. Losing in robustness, gaining in spiritual significance, Hebrew was now entering upon a new and rarified phase of its existence.

By the eighth century c.e., as the Jews scattered throughout the world became increasingly absorbed, at least in part, into the multiplicity of cultures amidst which they were living, the sense of the imminent disappearance of Hebrew altogether led the Jewish editors of the Bible to begin introducing aids to pronunciation into the text. In particular, their task was to fix the pronunciation of *vowels* for future generations of readers. Like all Semitic alphabets, the Hebrew one contains no vowels. Words are written only in consonants, and it is left to the reader to supply the vowel sounds when he pronounces them. Since, as can readily be imagined, the same group of consonants can have several possible pronunciations and hence several possible meanings, this traditional form of writing demands a degree of engagement on the part of the reader that is not assumed in Western cultures. The reader of Hebrew must know the word not merely from its own appearance but from the context. The foundation letters of the consonantal text line themselves up like the rocks of Judaea, imperishable and strong, but leaving subtlety and delicacy to be supplied to their interstices by the play of human sensibility upon them. In Hebrew, whole families of words are built up on a single rocklike paradigm of three consonants, amidst which are woven vowel variations that supply the different shades of meaning. The shade of meaning is to be found amidst the consonants, but they themselves do not supply it. There is in this process of writing and reading, then, an intense interweaving of thought and substance—the

substance of both the written and the spoken word—which again
suggests that close relationship, that perhaps total lack of distinction,
between spirit and nature which writers like Moses Hess and Ahad Ha-
Am have considered the essence of the Hebrew tradition. It is
significant that, in classical Hebrew, there is a single word—davar—
meaning both "word" and "thing," and that its consonants also form
the root of the verb "to speak."

Within a clearly established cultural milieu, such as in the Israel of
today, a standard, consonantal Hebrew text can be reasonably unambiguous. But in the eighth century c.e. the cultural milieu of the
biblical text was already only a memory. Furthermore, the Bible is so
full of variations and ambiguities of spelling that considerable famil-
iarity with the text had always been a necessary prerequisite for
correct pronunciation of it. The Masoretes—the biblical editors of
the early Middle Ages—feared, however, that a uniform cultural
tradition ensuring correct pronunciation of the Old Testament was
no longer possible under the conditions of the Diaspora. They
therefore decided to introduce unambiguous symbols for what they
considered to be the correct vocalization of every word. Considering
the extent to which Hebrew was subject to Western influence by this
time, it might have tended to follow the Greek and Roman pattern
of introducing vowels into its alphabet (indeed, even in biblical times
certain Hebrew consonants had virtually come to serve as vowels in
some contexts); but such a possibility was forestalled by the Jewish
traditional view that the biblical text was sacred down to every last
letter and punctuation mark. The Masoretes therefore could not
consider changing the spelling of the words themselves. Their only
alternative was to place vowel signs at the appropriate syllables above
or below the words of the text (both methods were tried, but it soon
became the fixed tradition to place the vowel signs below the words).
These vowel signs—or "dots," as they are called in Hebrew—are now
as fixed a part of the Hebrew text of the Bible as are the words
themselves; but they are no more a regular element in Hebrew
writing than they ever were, as many a student of the language learns
to his dismay. Other than the Bible, the only places in which dots are
used are in texts for beginning students of Hebrew (including Israeli
children) and in poetry, where the ambiguity would otherwise be too
great.

Hebrew underwent a new major phase in its development from
about the tenth to the thirteenth century. This was partly the work

of Rabbi Shlomo Yitzhak (called Rashi from his initials) of Troyes, the eleventh-century sage who was the greatest biblical commentator after the Talmudic epoch and whose works greatly enriched the vocabulary as well as the literary canon of Hebrew. It was even more so the work of the great scholars and thinkers of the Jewish Golden Age in Spain. This period was the pinnacle of a fruitful symbiosis between Jewish and Arabic cultures. Islam had founded itself upon Jewish religious and moral traditions; now Jewish tradition was in turn enriching itself from sources in Arabic language and thought. The highest expression of the age was the works of Moses Maimonides, who sought to reconcile the Jewish religious tradition with Aristotelian philosophy, of which Arab teachers were then the principal caretakers. In the realm of language, a science of Hebrew grammar was developed for the first time, under the influence of the Arab grammarians. The work of the Hebrew grammarians of Spain in this epoch made it possible, by isolating and classifying the structural principles of classical Hebrew, to continue the development of the language upon a confident and systematic base. Furthermore, the intimate presence of Arabic, a closely related Semitic language, provided a constant source of new words and constructions.

These developments took Hebrew further in the direction of being a vehicle of prose expression, separated by a widening gap from the lyricism of the Bible. It is significant that the great Hebrew poets of the age—such as Judah Halevi and Solomon ibn-Gabirol—wrote their prose works in Arabic. Even though Hebrew was then being made into a vehicle capable of handling their prose purposes, they seemed to prefer keeping it as a preserve of lyricism, its biblical purity undamaged. For with the new scientific advances in the language, a new self-consciousness—utterly unbiblical and unlyrical in character—was entering in as well. It is in this era that a word for "Judaism"—*Yahadut*—makes an appearance for the first time in the history of the language; in ancient times such a self-distinguishing concept did not exist. In the earlier books of the Bible there is not even a word for "religion"; when such a word (*dat*) finally appears in the late books of Ezra, Esther and Daniel, it is of Persian origin. It is only from then on that there grows gradually, through the ages, a manner of conceptualizing that serves not only to distinguish the Jewish tradition from its neighbors but also to explain it to itself. This is the linguistic expression of a growing sense of exile.

From the dispersion of Spanish Jewry at the end of the fifteenth

century until the Hebrew renaissance at the beginning of the nineteenth, Hebrew literature and language underwent a severe decline.
Throughout this period the language was scarcely used for any but
the most scholastic religious purposes and the drawing up of legal
documents in the Jewish communities. In Eastern Europe it became
the custom to carry on discussions of the Talmud and the Pentateuch
in Yiddish. Religious Eastern Europeans came to consider it blas-
phemous to use Hebrew for ordinary profane purposes. If ever the
continuity of a more or less living Hebrew tradition was lost entirely,
it was in this period. Even the advances made by the medieval
grammarians were now largely lost, and left to be recovered by the
philological researches of later generations.

The modern Hebrew revival began first in an isolated appearance
with the mystic and pseudo Messiah Moses Haim Luzzato of eighteenth-century Padua, and then in a stream with the Haskalah writers
of Galicia and Russia in the nineteenth century. These writers found
themselves confronted with a task of intellectual pioneering, since
the vocabulary of Hebrew was at that time not at all adequate to the
nineteenth-century European civilization they sought to embrace.
Even many of the words that tradition had once made available had
now become lost. Therefore, in a way scarcely known to the Anglo-
Saxon or the French tradition, but well known to the German and
Russian ones (which were the predominant external cultures influ-
encing nineteenth-century European Jewry), philology became a
central form of activity for patriots. But this scholarly return to
sources on the part of the Hebraists differed from the German and
Russian models in one important respect: the Hebraists had no
villages to go to, in which they could hear the spontaneous utterances
of a folk. Among Jews, this was an advantage reserved to Yiddishists.
The Hebraists had to reconstruct their folk sources in their own
imaginations: aged Hebrew volumes were their peasantry.

This pursuit sometimes took considerable imagination indeed. One
can take as an example the discovery of the present Hebrew word for
"electricity," the achievement of the Haskalah poet, Judah Leib
Gordon (1830–1892). It would have been quite the normal pattern
to have dipped into the German language, as Jewish writers of the
time were prone to do, and laden this concept unknown to the
Hebraists of former times with the name *elektritzitet*; misfortunes of
this nature have crept into Hebrew, and survive to this day. But

Gordon found an alternative through philological ingenuity, a thorough acquaintance with the Bible, and a certain interest in Greek. The latter language is important for Old Testament scholars because of the Septuagint Bible, the Greek translation made in Alexandria in the second century B.C.E. Gordon discovered that the Septuagint translators had used the word *electron*—the etymological source of our word "electricity"—to translate the mysterious Old Testament word *hashmal*. It is not certain what the word *hashmal* really meant. *Electron* means "amber," and the translators of the King James Version followed the lead of the Septuagint in this respect. Thus the English version of Ezekiel 1:4 reads:

> And I looked, and, behold, a whirlwind came out of the north, a great cloud, and a fire infolding itself, and a brightness was about it, and out of the midst thereof as the colour of amber, out of the midst of the fire.

The "amber" of this passage, the *electron* of the Septuagint, is *hashmal*. Gordon's whole method is perhaps questionable, but the suggestion of ineffable brightness and power in *hashmal* and the extraordinary beauty of the word (the initial "h" sound is the guttural *het*, not to be found in the Western languages) outweigh all other considerations. The great lexicographer of modern Hebrew, Eliezer Ben-Yehuda, admitted the word into his dictionary with some reluctance—but he admitted it, and it is the Hebrew word for "electricity" to this day.

Eliezer Ben-Yehuda, born Perlman (1858–1922), was the greatest single force in the creation of a modern, spoken Hebrew vernacular. Born in a small town in Lithuania, he was exposed in childhood to the worldly pietism of the *Habad* movement in Hasidism. The Habad school (the word is constructed from the initials of *Hochmah*, *Binah* and *Da'at*—Wisdom, Understanding and Knowledge), was a reconciliation of the more rationalistic and practical spirit of Lithuanian Jewry with the Hasidism that came to it from the less cultured south. As a young Talmud student, Eliezer Perlman boarded at the home of a Habad Hasid, a man of thoroughly modern inclinations under whose influence the boy turned to the reading of European literature. For Perlman, as for his mentor, reading of this sort was never a divergence into the profane; it was always infused with higher and at least quasi-religious significance. It was the reading of George Eliot's *Daniel Deronda*, for example, that converted Perlman to

Zionism. This spiritual legacy would have been a great enough gift
for Shlomo Yonas to have given Perlman; but in the sequel, he gave
him two of his daughters as well. Ben-Yehuda's first wife, Deborah,
had been his teacher of French when he boarded in her father's
home. When she died a few years after the couple had settled in
Palestine, Ben-Yehuda married her young sister Hemda, who had
been a child when he lived in the Yonas house. Both women were
deeply devoted to him, learned Hebrew for his sake, suffered lives of
hardship in the primitive Jerusalem of that day, and helped him in
his work.

There is an air of fanaticism to Ben-Yehuda's career, much like
that of A. D. Gordon in his willful self-regeneration. Basically, Ben-
Yehuda was simply a Hebrew teacher and a man of letters, who went
to practice his craft in the Land of Israel itself, and eventually to edit
his own Hebrew-language journal there. In most other men, this
might simply have been an isolated act of pietism, performed with
the hope that others would do the same, and that there would
eventually be a Hebrew literary circle in Jerusalem. But Ben-Yehuda
was on a mission, to preach and to instill the gospel of a linguistic
revival. A circle of Hebrew teachers and writers—which eventually
did grow up around him—was not sufficient in his eyes to do what
had to be done: to make Hebrew the mother tongue of a restored
Palestinian Jewry, spoken by them as Frenchmen speak French. This
was far more than a merely literary task, a continuation of the
Russian-Jewish Hebrew revival on the soil of the Holy Land. The
Hebrew writers of the day did not usually converse in Hebrew, and
some of them, like Ahad Ha-Am, preferred to avoid speaking it
altogether. Hebrew conversation, when it came up among the Hebraist intelligentsia, was usually a mere ornament, a stilted exercise. It
lacked the vigor that necessity usually imposes upon human speech.

In Palestine there was at least one external element, as Ben-
Yehuda discovered, that imposed a touch of necessity upon his
inclination to use Hebrew in everyday conversation. This was the fact
that, outside of the ultrareligious and anti-Zionist Ashkenazi community, in which Ben-Yehuda had no interest, the Jews in Palestine
were almost entirely Sephardim from the Middle Eastern countries.
Hebrew was the only common language for communication between
Ben-Yehuda and these Arabic-speaking Jews. This fact, and a certain
romanticism about the Orient, led Ben-Yehuda to absorb himself in

the life of the Sephardim of Jerusalem, to the extent of even affecting the Oriental style of dress for a time. It was this intercourse with the Sephardim that enabled him to develop a fluency and a style of Hebrew speech. Eager to shake off all intimations of an Eastern European ghetto past, Ben-Yehuda romantically embraced the Sephardic pronunciation of Hebrew, which has subsequently, with only minor variations, become the standard correct pronunciation in Israel today. This was a historic turning point; though the more traditional synagogues in Europe and America still lean to the Ashkenazic pronunciation, it is now gradually being replaced there by the Sephardic even for purely religious purposes.

One of the fundamental differences between the two dialects is in the syllable that is stressed; in the Sephardic pronunciation the accent is almost always on the final syllable, whereas in the Ashkenazic it is usually on the penultimate. Hence, the Sephardic Kab-bal-*lah* is the Ashkenazic Kab-*bal*-lah. Of the two, the Ashkenazic stress is more akin to that of the European languages. The exotic Sephardic Hebrew stress comes across with a striking vigor, capable of taking on even a lyric fierceness, as syllable after syllable explodes forth; the effect is indeed biblical. It may or may not be closer to the pronunciation of biblical times than the Ashkenazic, but it is much truer to a Zionist conception of what that pronunciation should have been. The softness of Diaspora Judaism here fades away. This effect of a sudden leap into strength is added to by certain vowel and consonantal changes, the most significant of which is the changing of the soft *tav* (or *thav*) to the modified "t" sound of Sephardic and Israeli Hebrew, in contrast with the Ashkenazic sounding of it, which is like an "s." Hence the Sephardic-Israeli *galut* (exile), with the accent on the second syllable, was the Ashkenazic *golos*, with the accent on the first. To many a Jew of Eastern European origin, this transformation has a virtually metaphysical quality. *Golos* perhaps belongs even more to its stepmother Yiddish than to the Hebrew in which it originated. In Yiddish it rings with the despair of exile, with the eternal plight of suffering Jewry, accepted with a philosophical shrug of the shoulder. But the Israeli *galut*, sharp and unrelenting, comes down from the heights of Zion with a certain scorn for those Jews throughout the world who have not seen fit to come home. A transformation of this sort was the spiritual music of the self-regeneration that the Zionists aspired to.

Ben-Yehuda's linguistic program began to show its edge of fanaticism when he came to insist, even among his Ashkenazi friends, that they speak only Hebrew to him. Yet even this must have come to seem reasonable to his associates when, as the birth of his first child approached, he announced that this would be the first Hebrew-speaking child of modern times. He proposed that no language but Hebrew be spoken in the presence of the infant. For this purpose he gave Hebrew instruction to his wife, and, after the baby boy was born, carefully screened all visitors to the household before admitting them to the child's room. Nurses were restricted either to silence or to whatever Hebrew words they knew. Even those among Ben-Yehuda's friends who were most dedicated to his ideals urged him to abandon this project, warning him that he would turn his child into an idiot. The situation grew quite tense, since, as it happened, the boy did not speak a word until well into his third year. Ben-Zion Ben-Yehuda's first utterances were awaited with the eagerness and sense of destiny of King Psammetichus listening for news of what had been spoken by the child whom he had ordered isolated in a cave at birth, in order to discover from its first words what would therefore have to be considered the most primeval and hence the most ancient of the languages of mankind. At last young Ben-Zion spoke, and the Hebrew revival had begun.

Eliezer Ben-Yehuda lived to watch the spread of Hebrew as the spoken language of Palestinian Jewry. The young pioneers of the Second Aliyah, with characteristic vigor, resolutely spoke only Hebrew among themselves in their settlements and corrected one another's mistakes, thereby remaking themselves into Hebrews as decisively as they were remaking themselves into farmers. In their case, the linguistic program was given the force of more than a mere exercise by the fact that it was a decisive aid in the psychological transformation they were undergoing and had to undergo if they were both to stay in Palestine and to survive. In the meantime, through the efforts of Ben-Yehuda and the circle of Hebrew teachers surrounding him, Hebrew became the language of instruction in the primary and secondary schools founded specifically by the Zionist movement. A generation was growing up using Hebrew as its mother tongue.

One last threat to the imminent supremacy of Hebrew in the Yishuv was overcome in 1914. In the decade just preceding the outbreak of the First World War, German-Jewish philanthropy suddenly became a powerful force in Palestine, surpassing that of the English and rivaling that of the French. The philanthropic enterprises in Palestine were still quite independent of the Zionist ones, and were not even necessarily inclined to cooperate with Zionist aspirations. The chain of schools run by the Alliance Israélite Universelle used French as their language of instruction, and sought to achieve French cultural supremacy in Palestine. The Evelina de Rothschild school in Jerusalem represented similar aspirations for English language and culture. And so, when the *Hilfsverein der Deutschen Juden* sent its first emissaries to Palestine in 1903 it did so as part of the general German bid for cultural and political supremacy that was taking place in the world at that time. German became the language of instruction in the Hilfsverein schools in Palestine, although during their first few years they were at least prone, unlike the French, to give Hebrew a prominent role in the curriculum. Even today the modern Hebrew vernacular bears some of the earmarks of that stage in its formation when it was rather heavily under German influence. But by 1913 German nationalist feelings were swelling with the growing world crisis, and Hebrew disappeared from the curriculum of the Hilfsverein schools.

It was in that year that a brewing cultural controversy reached its head. It arose over questions concerning the curriculum of the first Yishuv institution of higher learning—the technological institute of Haifa, now known as the Technion, which was then nearing completion. Contributions for the erection of this institute had been raised among Jewish communities all over the world, but it was the members of the Hilfsverein who made their influence felt among the new school's board of governors. The announcement suddenly was made that the institute's language of instruction would not be Hebrew but German. The reaction in the Yishuv was pronounced; protest demonstrations were held throughout the country. The three Zionist members of the board of governors, one of whom was Ahad Ha-Am, submitted their resignations. It was argued by the Germans that the Hebrew language was not yet adequate to cope with modern technological subjects. This was a delicate issue; Hebrew philologists had dedicated themselves with particular zeal to the pursuit of scientific terminology, knowing that this realm was the Achilles heel of their aspirations. They felt that the language was now ready for

such things. It was finally the protests of contributors throughout the
world that convinced the board of governors to reverse its decision. It
was agreed that, at first, only mathematics and physics would be
taught in Hebrew (in the other subjects, time was needed for the
instructors to gain competence in the language) but that Hebrew
would subsequently be the language of the entire curriculum, as it is
today. Higher learning in Hebrew was now a reality. On July 24,
1918, the cornerstone was laid for the Hebrew University in Jerusalem, the institution which was to be from the very outset the major
world center of Hebrew language and learning.

Ben-Yehuda crowned his life's efforts with a monumental project:
his dictionary of the Hebrew language. By the time of his death in
1922 he had completed five large volumes, and had left notes for
most of the remainder. The task of completing the dictionary from
his notes was left to a committee, which published the sixteenth and
last volume in 1958. This huge lexicon provides for each word a
definition in Hebrew, equivalents in German, French and English,
and a summary history of the word, with quotes from its major
sources for each epoch in the history of the Hebrew language. A mark
next to the word indicates whether its earliest origin is biblical,
Mishnaic, medieval or modern. Among the words of modern origin,
Ben-Yehuda distinguishes his own coinages from those of other
scholars and writers. One of his own coinages was the word for
"dictionary" itself: *milon* is made up of the word *milah* (word) and
an ancient suffix of agent, and has a ring of venerable authenticity.
He followed the lead of the old Spanish grammarians in drawing
upon Arabic, and when he had to resort to a European word, he
often turned to the form of it that had been incorporated into that
language. The present Hebrew word for "brush"—*mivreshet* (a slight
variant of Ben-Yehuda's own *mivrashah*)—clearly originates in our
own word. Ben-Yehuda, however, finds the pedigree for it in the
Arabic root *brsh*, which he vocalizes as *brosh*. He only adds the sly
comment: "But this is possibly not a Semitic root."

Ben-Yehuda's task of recovering and coining words in accordance
with learned precedents was carried on after his death by an official
linguistic establishment, embodied under the Mandate as the Language Council and since statehood as the Hebrew Language Academy. But such a body, although it has a counterpart of long standing
in the Académie Française, is in some ways now an anachronism; for

Hebrew is now a popularly spoken language once again, developing as a living organism. This fact is perhaps the greatest single achievement of Zionism other than the Jewish state itself, the very essence of that crystallization and revival of a way of life which had for two thousand years been simply an abstraction, frozen into the collective memory of the people. The Hebrew revival has often been looked upon as a model by linguistic revival movements in other parts of the world, such as the Gaelic movement in Ireland. But whatever are the possibilities for the ultimate success of the Gaelic movement or any other like it, the fact is that none of these possesses the special combination of qualities which has been responsible for the success of the Hebrew one.

The great source of strength on the part of Hebrew in its efforts at revival was the fact that it was the language of a transcendent literary source, a book which has had overwhelming spiritual power among Western men in general and among Jews in particular. Whatever other languages the Bible was translated into, it always remained best known to the more traditional Jewish communities—such as the Eastern European one in which the Zionist cultural revival originated —in the original Hebrew. In the orthodox religious environment of Eastern Europe, the passion for the Bible had declined somewhat in relation to the stress upon the Talmud by the nineteenth century; therefore, when the Zionists from this area reacted against the Diaspora mentality as they understood it, and sought a return to a more natural and earthbound identification of their Jewishness than the Talmud had seemed to represent in their eyes, they reached out for the spirit of the Bible—and the language which is the embodiment of that spirit—with a special fervor. The success of this endeavor on their part was furthermore helped by the fact that they were uprooting and transferring themselves to a new and challenging environment, in which they were cut off from the normal patterns of their lives, patterns which had been the containers of their linguistic habits. Harsh as this new environment was, it at least became familiar, more accessible and less terrifying to them to the extent that it was associated with biblical memories; this also reinforced their inclination to weave a fabric of Hebrew consciousness around their lives. In other words, this linguistic transformation was enabled to succeed by the fact that it was part of a total program of self-transformation, made concrete above all by the physical change in

one's environment. The Gaelic movement has had no such external
buttresses to strengthen and dramatize the subjective task.

Furthermore, the Gaelic movement suffers the immense disadvantage of having to ward off English, an advanced Western language. It
is above all the great fortune of the Hebrew movement that its
counterpoise was Yiddish, a tongue that was reaching linguistic
maturity only in the moment when the civilization upon which it was
founded was entering a final stage of decay, and when the vast
majority of Eastern European Jews were turning to other languages.
The assimilationists in Russia and Poland who were turning to the
Slavic tongues spoken there, the emigrants to the West who were
turning to English or French, and the Zionists turning to Hebrew
were all shaking off a mother tongue fraught with associations that
they were eager to be rid of for good. But if English—a language
representing the heights of the kind of cultural advancement all Jews,
including Hebraists, were aspiring to in renouncing Yiddish—had
been the language of Palestine when the Zionists arrived there, the
Hebrew revival would probably not have taken place.

Now that Hebrew has succeeded in becoming a spoken language,
and is therefore no longer exclusively in the hands of the tradition of
scholarship responsible for its survival and ultimate rebirth, a conflict
has emerged between the learned establishment and the living language it had fostered. It is ironic, as well as indicative of the central
problem modern Hebrew still has to confront, that one can often
hear visiting Hebrew scholars in Israel—men whose own medium of
everyday discourse is English or some other European language—
remark with horror that Israelis are ruining the ancestral Jewish
tongue. No doubt Roman emissaries in Gaul felt much the same way
when they first heard the corrupt Latin that was eventually to
become the language of Racine. But the Hebrew emissaries of today
have less to fear than their Roman counterparts. The whole meaning
of the Hebrew renaissance would be lost if the language spoken in
Israel today were simply to evolve into a different one from that of
the Bible and the Mishna. Not that the spontaneous popular will in
Israel is necessarily subject to such considerations as "the meaning of
the Hebrew renaissance"; but, unlike Latin in Roman-dominated
Gaul, the Hebrew language in Israel is developing in an era in which
instantaneous communication, mass literacy, and the flood of words
in print all conspire to impose linguistic uniformity. Such uniformity

is especially likely in a very small country in which, on the one hand, all the public arbiters of the language are more or less committed to its classical identity and, on the other hand, there are no regions or native dialects.

This lack of native dialects is not entirely an advantage, however. For modern Hebrew has still not discovered its own authenticity; it is still not a language springing from the earth of the country, but rather is one that has filtered down from the top and served as a homogenizing medium for absorbing newcomers. It is not so much the national language as the national lingua franca. In English, for example, there is just as much authenticity in the language of a Cockney as in that of a Shakespeare: indeed, there is an intimate relationship between the two. But there is no Israeli Cockney. This fact even became a matter of public attention in the winter of 1964, when a Hebrew version of *My Fair Lady*, the musical comedy adaptation of Shaw's *Pygmalion*, made its premiere on the Tel-Aviv stage. The ingenuity of the translators was justly praised, particularly for the way in which they had constructed, as an equivalent to the Cockney speech which has such a central role in the play, a Hebrew lower-class dialect. Although Israeli civilization has now advanced far enough that there were some sources to draw upon, this was mainly a work of the translators' imagination.

Dialects in Israel today are reflections of foreign national origin rather than of region. The result is that, if there is anything like a correlation of class and dialect there, it is the reverse of that which is to be found anywhere else in the world. A predominant segment of the Israeli lower classes of today is of Middle Eastern or North African origin. Having been weaned on Arabic, this group tends to pronounce the uniquely Semitic gutturals in Hebrew better than the more upper-class Ashkenazim do, including the native born. On the other hand, the most elite of Israeli accents is the utterly un-Semitic Russian one of the Second and Third Aliyah aristocracy. Tel-Aviv, the stronghold of this elite, is sometimes jokingly referred to as "Tel-Avyov." *Habimah*, the Israel National Theater, has made this thick Russian accent into a trademark, the symbol of Hebrew classical pronunciation equivalent to that of the Old Vic in the English-speaking world. Actually, the Hebrew of both Habimah and the Oriental Jews has a beauty superior to any native speech in Israel today. The only existing "high" standard for the native-born is that of *Kol Yisrael* ("The Voice of Israel"), the national radio service, whose conscientiously polished syllables are far more exasperatingly neutral than those of the BBC, which has served it as a source of inspiration. In dialect as in grammar, Israeli Hebrew is still partly under the sway of academicism.

But there is now, as I have said, a spontaneous language in the country at large growing in defiance of the academicians. In the corner of an Oriental market place one can hear a vigor of expression far removed from the artificial literary language of the Haskalah. There are, to be sure, certain dangers to which this development is exposed—particularly those coming from that very twentieth-century atmosphere which assures that modern Hebrew will not completely abandon the identity of the classical language. For there is a kind of international jargon coming into the world today, full of the vocabulary of a technologized way of life, streamlined in accordance with the spirit of that life, and English to a very large extent. Its effects are pervasive everywhere, but they are particularly strong in a country like Israel, whose society is very largely a technological construct, a quintessential product of the era. Furthermore, as a language only just emerging from antiquity, Hebrew still has to make efforts to come abreast of the twentieth century. Foreign words, especially English ones, therefore pour into the language at a sometimes alarming rate. On the popular level, this influx has created a whole vocabulary for sports, entertainment, automobiles, and a wide range of mass-consumed goods. On the technical and academic level, it is even more overwhelming, particularly in a field like sociology, racing ever onward with American-made concepts and terms. It is therefore a moment of historic import when a philologist can discover a new but perfectly Hebrew word like *iyur* (derived from *ir*—city) to replace the previously current *urbanizatsiya*.

This is not a problem to be handled by philologists, however; it is mainly one for poets. Poetry has, in fact, a more prominent role in Israel than in perhaps any other country in the world at the present time. It is the poet alone who combines the proprieties of the philologist with an ear for the music of spontaneous folk utterance. It is he alone, then, who will juxtapose the most exalted Hebrew phrasing with a term like *luna-park* (the standard Israeli word for amusement park). In the hands of the best poets, the over-all effect of such a combination is, in fact, astonishingly biblical. For somehow, in the perceptible folk rhythms of Israel today, with all its baggage of jet-age terminology, there distinctly tends to be a return from the spirit of the Mishna to that of the Bible. The starkly monosyllabic speech of the new immigrant may be mainly due to ignorance of the language, but it is nevertheless resonant with qualities that go beyond the occasion to the very essence of Hebrew. Maybe the return of an Oriental spirit to the mainstream of the Hebrew tradition is just what that tradition needs to refresh itself with some of the qualities of its own sources. In any case, the poets, too, are making their way back to a tone which is in some respects primitive, but which is no less profound for being free of the quality of abstraction that had marked Hebrew discourse for two thousand years. Amid the clang of twentieth-century dissonances one can sense the beginnings of a return to the spirit of the language of the prophets, even of Deborah, chanting her primeval song of victory over Sisera.

II

One of the major tasks of Hebrew literature in modern Israel, then, has been to bridge the long-standing gap in the language established by the biblical and Mishnaic traditions, the gap between poetry and prose. In the works of some of the Haskalah writers of the early nineteenth century, this problem was solved through recourse to a false prose style, a flowery form of rhetoric called *melitzah*, which consisted mainly of biblical phrases strung together without too much regard for either the logic or the lucidity of the context that was thereby created. It is one of the principal achievements of Ahad Ha-Am to have put the ghost of *melitzah* to rest once and for all and to have created a truly modern Hebrew prose style, vigorous, spare and lucid. His style is a model for Hebrew prose writing today, although there is often a danger that, when it is imitated by lesser hands, the results will merely read like a Western language literally translated—a kind of Esperanto. This comes back to the central problem of the Hebrew language today: that of finding its identity while being reborn under the influence of languages which, though alien to it in principle, are superior to it as modern instruments of expression and exert an often irresistible pull upon the predominantly European cultural outlook of Israelis.

Poetry has been far more successful than prose in finding its own

idiom. The resistance of the biblical mode to modern discourse is far
less strong in poetry than in prose. In fact, the history of modern
Hebrew poetry has to some extent been that of a return to a more
biblical identity from a poetic tradition that originated in the conventions of medieval and modern European literature. Modernism has
played a role in Hebrew literature in some respects opposite to the
one it has played elsewhere, in that it has brought about a return to
the most traditional sources. This is particularly true in the case of
meters. From the Middle Ages until the beginning of the twentieth
century, Hebrew poets usually followed the metric forms used in the
European literatures. Biblical poetry, on the other hand, is written in
something more like free verse, in which, if anything like meter is
discernible at all, it is in prose stresses rather than in the accentual or
syllabic patterns that have constituted the basis of Western meters
since Greek and Roman times. In other words, the feeling of biblical
poetic forms is highly "modern."

But it was not merely the awakening of a modernist outlook that
brought about this turning point in Hebrew metric conventions; the
issue was also forced, suddenly and precipitately, by an event. This
was the founding of a spoken Hebrew idiom in Palestine, pronounced *in the Sephardic accent*. For, throughout the nineteenth
century, the major world center for Hebrew poetry had of course
been Eastern Europe, where the pronunciation was Ashkenazic. This
had been a largely scholastic tradition, like Latin poetry in the Renaissance. But as spoken Hebrew gradually became a reality in Palestine,
and that country grew into the focus and then the real center of
Hebrew literary activity, the poets were faced with the necessity of
making their muses sing to them into a different rhythm. The
Sephardic rhythms not only call for different meters; they are in some
ways not readily susceptible to meter at all. The almost unvarying
stress on the final syllable tends, in combination with meters, to have
an overly staccato effect. Nor was this the only aspect of the change
of accent which encouraged a departure from metric conventions. In
the ears of a generation which grew up speaking Palestinian Hebrew,
the meters of nineteenth-century Hebrew poetry were not easily
discernible. Unless they forced themselves to pronounce the poems in
a manner unnatural to them, the young Palestinians were more likely
to hear their "biblical" rhythms, and to desire to imitate these.
Young Israelis writing in free verse are responding to the music of

tradition in the form in which it has most naturally come down to them.

This turning point—signaled not only by the shifting of the stress but also by the very emergence of a folk voice where none had existed before—was the central experience of what can be called the "classical" generation of modern Hebrew literature. For the writers of this generation, the creation of a Hebrew-speaking Jewish community in Palestine was not only a step forward, a fulfillment of the logic of their convictions, but was also a major crisis which shook and sometimes even destroyed the basis of their convictions. Some poets succeeded quite well in making the transition to the new pronunciation, and even "translated" their Ashkenazic poems into the Sephardic. One of them, Uri Zvi Greenberg, wrote some poems in which he used the Ashkenazic pronunciation when he spoke in his own voice and the Sephardic when he reproduced the dialogue of Palestinian workers. But the greatest of them all, Chaim Nachman Bialik, generally considered to be the foremost Hebrew poet since the epoch of Judah Halevi, became silent. During the last decade of his life, when he had finally settled in Palestine, he wrote prose works, but his few poems, always resolutely written in the Ashkenazic stress, were almost exclusively pastiche—folk ballads and children's verse. This loss of poetic energy on his part was not, of course, merely a matter of the change in Hebrew rhythms; the latter was, rather, part of a larger crisis. Bialik's flow of poems had reduced itself to a trickle nearly twenty years before he settled in Palestine, while he was still only in his thirties. At that moment a crisis of historic and personal developments conspired to break down the tension upon which his creativity had been founded—a tension made up of a combined longing for Zion and a nostalgia for the Diaspora.

Bialik's role as the poet laureate of the Hebrew national renaissance was always really an ambivalent one. He was the heir to that nineteenth-century tradition—especially strong in Eastern Europe— of poets whose personal visions and aspirations were so bound up with a crucial historic moment in the lives of their peoples that they came to be considered the embodiment of their nations in rebirth. The tradition began with Byron in England and Hugo in France, although neither of these men was a national poet in the way of the Eastern Europeans whom they inspired—of Pushkin, of the Polish Adam Mickiewicz, or of the Hungarian Sandor Petöfi. Hugo may be the greatest lyric poet in the history of French literature, but he is certainly not the greatest single poet France has produced, and of course Byron is far from being that in England. But both men played out with singular vigor (and, as with all the poets of this tradition, their lives were as significant as their works) the role of prophet in the revolutionary epoch of the early nineteenth century. As such, they became models for poets in Eastern Europe—where political and cultural passions are more closely intertwined than they are in the West—whose place at the moment when their languages were arriving at a tardy maturity made them the Shakespeares of their nations as well as the Byrons and the Hugos. In a historic moment of great intensity these men were the representatives both of literary renaissance and of revolution. There was a remarkable conformity between their inner sufferings and the external plight of their nations. The romantic longings which a Keats could project no further than onto the image of a nightingale, found their "objective-correlative" for the equally romantic Adam Mickiewicz in the historic sufferings and hopes of the Polish people.

Eastern European in birth and upbringing, romantic in temperament, Bialik was readily susceptible to the mood of this tradition, which was appropriate to the moment of the national renaissance of his own people. But Bialik, like Zionism itself, did not belong to that more innocent generation of the early nineteenth century, with its fresh outburst of revolutionary enthusiasm. Born in 1873, he was rather a part of that era when the European romantic spirit was giving way to the mood of decadence and modernism. To be sure, there has usually been, until quite recently, a time lapse between general European literature, on the one hand, and Hebrew and Yiddish literature, on the other; like other literary currents, romanticism made its way into these Jewish literatures about two generations after its first appearance in Europe. To some extent, then, Bialik's spirit developed in an atmosphere in which the romantic mood was still relatively fresh. But the traditional time lapse was disappearing in this era when the cultural walls separating Eastern European Jewry from the rest of Europe were breaking down, and the former was now more susceptible than it had been to immediate external influences. Bialik felt the bleak and complex mood prevailing in the Russian and the German literature of his day. This created undercurrents in his work that are not to be found in the earlier generation of great "national" poets. But, for that matter, there were also qualities of the Jewish experience in general which were not to be found among the other reviving nationalities of Eastern Europe. The former was patently more complex, more ambivalent. It is one of the most remarkable qualities of Bialik's poetic achievement that, just as the great national poets of the early nineteenth century were able to project their personal and romantic longings in terms of the aspirations of their peoples, so also was Bialik able to project the ambivalences of the modern spirit and of his own consciousness in terms of the Jewish history of his epoch.

Whatever the purely personal source of the unfulfilled longings in Bialik's work—including the rather nonnational love poems he often wrote—its specifically Jewish expression was a certain nostalgia for the suffering ghetto Jew which was in some respects irreconcilable with his desire for national regeneration. Zionism was, as we have seen, a Jewish counterpart to that desire for self-transcendence through the will that struck the generation of late-nineteenth-century Europe in reaction to the decadence of the times, and that manifested itself in some cases as a heightened passion for a return to national roots. Maurice Barrès, for example, sought to recover a relationship with the soil and with a kind of peasant simplicity that was not at all aspired to by the more abstract and, in a sense, cosmopolitan nationalism of Victor Hugo. Bialik shared many of Barrès' feelings, but the different situations of their respective peoples made for a striking difference in the ways each of these two men expressed his nationalist outlook. For Barrès, there was a direct link between the life of the simple folk he admired and the institutions of a powerful state. From asserting that the strength of France is her peasantry to proclaiming that the glory of France is her military prowess is not a large step, and many nationalists in the Barrès tradition have taken it. But Bialik's simple folk—the simple folk of Mendele Moicher S'forim or of Sholom Aleichem—were not identified with a state at all; indeed, it was their glory, if also the bane of their lives, that they had no connection with political power. Bialik was fully aware of this trait in the Jewish people, and it was one of the qualities for which he loved them. But, loving them, he also wished for an end to their tragic plight, for them to be a people in their land like any other. This latter desire can also, of course, be construed as a return to roots; the Zionists did precisely this. Such a formulation, however, is based upon an abstraction, at least initially; there was no concrete Jewish relationship to the Palestinian soil until a group of people went there and established one. The poetic spirit is not easily drawn to abstractions, at least not since the latter part of the nineteenth century. For Bialik, the more concrete folk situation of the Jew was that of the ghetto; it attracted him and it made him despair.

This is the ambivalence that pervades Bialik's poems as his longings move, first in one direction, then in the other: now toward Zionism and the heroic mode, now toward the abject gentleness of the ghetto. In the earlier poems the Zionist aspiration seems straightforward, uncolored by the second thoughts that are to appear in later works. His first published poem, "To the Bird," reads like a Zionist rewriting of Keats's "To a Nightingale." As in the latter poem, the bird becomes a focus of longings for a freedom greater than men can ever know; but a specifically Jewish national focus is provided in Bialik's poem by his conjecture that the bird has flown over Palestine, and has seen there the poet's more fortunate brothers. Yet, for all this poetic tribute to the notion of salvation in Zion, Bialik himself did not settle there until 1924, when he was fifty-one years old, and then only because the Russian Revolution had forced him, as a "Zionist reactionary," to leave his native land for good. For all his central importance in the Hebrew renaissance which was increasingly finding Zion to be its main focus, Bialik wrote some of his most outstanding poems, not about Hebrew pioneers regenerating themselves in the land of the Bible but about the Yeshiva (the traditional Jewish religious school) and about pale students in gabardines poring over huge volumes of the Talmud. His most celebrated poem in this vein, Ha'matmid (literally "The Diligent One"—the traditional term for the dedicated Talmud student), is a long eulogy—though not without ironies—to these boys giving their youth to the darkness of the house of study, and to their painful ideal of Talmudic learning. The central quality celebrated in this poem—as in the works of many classic Jewish authors—is Jewish long-suffering; it is a rumination upon two thousand years of exile, and the infinitely patient wait for the return. But if this quality is seen as the principal source of a uniquely Jewish heroism, then is Zionism, a mere political movement, reason enough for rejecting the tradition of the Diaspora?

Yet if Bialik had simply sought to embrace wholeheartedly the qualities of the Diaspora, he could have gone the way of a Sholom

Aleichem or a Mendele and made Yiddish his medium of expression. Not that he did not write in Yiddish; he produced some fine works in that language, including a remarkable translation from the German of Heinrich Heine's "Rabbi of Bacharach." But he did not yield to the pull of Yiddish because, in spite of his doubts, he was seeking the way to the kind of self-transcendence that was represented by Zionism and the Hebrew revival. Two of his greatest poems—they might be described as two efforts in the creation of legends—"The Dead of the Desert" and "The Scroll of Fire"—are indeed thorough repudiations of the Diasporic spirit. The former is an evocation of the legend of the "desert generation"—of those Israelites who died in the wilderness of Sinai during the sojourn there with Moses, and whose remains are there to this day as a permanent reminder of the lot of an alienated people. One can scarcely find anything but contempt for the Diaspora in this poem.

The latter poem builds a legend of Palestine at the time of the destruction of the Temple, and goes even further than the mere ideal of a Jewish people in their land, into what has often been called a "Canaanite" conception of Jewish identity. Canaanitism was a popular Hebrew literary movement for a time, particularly among a group of militantly nationalist intellectuals during the final period of the struggle for statehood—the terrorist Abraham Stern had some links with the Canaanite movement, for example. It derives its views from the opinion of some scholars that only a small portion of the later Israelite nation entered Canaan with Joshua, and that the major part of this nation was made up of the indigenous pagan peoples whom Joshua's band found there and who were subsequently absorbed by the religion of Moses. From this point of view, the Canaanites were a people living in pagan innocence upon whom a stern and somewhat alien religiosity was imposed from the outside. For the foremost of the Canaanites, the nineteenth-century Hebrew writer Berditchevski, this conception led to an embracing of Nietzschean ideals and a celebration of the apparently somewhat Dionysian Canaanite cult which had preceded the Mosaic religion. Bialik plays with a Canaanite conception in "The Scroll of Fire"; the poem suggests a possible forthcoming departure on the part of the poet into a new conception of Jewish identity. But no such new departure came; instead, the poem turned out to be the prelude to a sudden plunge into relative silence.

These two works followed upon a historic event which not only had produced Bialik's greatest poem but had also begun the process leading to the complete collapse of the delicate ambivalence upon which his poetry had been tensely strung in the first place. In the spring of 1903 the Kishinev pogroms took place. Later that year a group of Russian-Jewish intellectuals formed a Historical Committee to investigate the pogroms, and Bialik was sent onto the scene as the group's representative. The poem that he was inspired to write by this experience, "In the City of Slaughter," is a long outburst of prophetic rage. It is not only God or the pogromists against whom his anger is directed, but the victims themselves, as he evokes image after image of Jews cringing and scurrying for their lives. This, then, is the final performance of the pale Talmud student, of the gentle Yiddish-ness that Bialik had continued to love despite his Hebraism. He wrote this poem in a Yiddish version as well, but this latter opens with a small though significant change from the original. Whereas the Hebrew poem begins "Come to the city of slaughter . . ." and goes right into its horrifying description of the scene, the Yiddish version has two lines prefixed to this opening, which read:

> From steel and iron, cold, hard and dumb,
> Forge yourself a heart, O man,—and come!

To the softer soul of Yiddish, so alien to rage, the poet must make an apology.

Zionist history is full of the biographies of men who read Bialik's "In the City of Slaughter" and promptly set out for Palestine. But Bialik himself remained in Russia for another twenty years. In that period his poetic output rapidly diminished, and he turned to literary activities of another sort, primarily as a publisher and a collector of Jewish legend and folklore. In 1916 the trickle of bleak lyrics from his pen came to a stop altogether. After he had settled in Palestine he was able to write poems for children and a kind of folkpastiche, many of them lovely creations which continue to serve today for the kind of folk song that the Hebrew tradition is otherwise almost entirely lacking. Today, Bialik is best known to a younger generation for these folk songs, which are sung around campfires.

The problems of transition from *galut* to Zion which Bialik and other poets suffered were also felt by a generation of writers of fiction. Hayim Hazaz, for example, one of the foremost of Israel's writers today, had originally found his literary subject matter in the

Jewish life of the Ukraine, where he was born in 1898. But, once Hazaz had settled in Palestine he recognized that the very convictions which had brought him there and which had, in fact, brought him to writing in Hebrew in the first place, could not brook a continuing literary preoccupation with Eastern European Jewry. In one of his short stories he has a kibbutznik say—not without a certain regret— "I am opposed to Jewish history." Hazaz recognized that this was what his generation, at any rate—the transitional generation—had to conclude if it was to come to terms with its own acts. But, like other writers of his generation, Hazaz did not easily adjust to a broadly Israeli milieu. Instead, he found a solution—and a highly successful one—by turning to a relatively secluded corner of Israeli life for his subject matter: the Yemenite Jews. The Yemenites provided him with a milieu which, for all its exoticism, resembles in its simple pietism and folkloric integrity the atmosphere of the Eastern European Jewish life he had previously written about. Other writers of his generation found a less successful solution in turning to some of the Palestinian fragments of Eastern European Jewish life, such as the Hasidic communities of Safed or of the Meah Shearim quarter in Jerusalem. This was less successful because such a focus implies a certain regression, a repudiation of the aspiration on the part of Zionism to reject such elements in its Eastern European background. Indeed, some of the writers who focused upon such subject matter intended precisely to demonstrate a certain ambivalence concerning Zion.

This is particularly true of the foremost prose writer of the transitional generation, Shmuel Yoseph Agnon. Born in Galicia in 1888, Agnon's spirit has suffered, along with the characteristic ambivalences of his generation, the further alienation that comes of being Galician in origin amidst a society whose elite is primarily Russo-Polish in character. The Galician stamp is always clearly upon Agnon's work. There is the intense atmosphere of southern Hasidism in his writings, alongside a distinct melancholy of a Central European stamp not to be found in the attitudes of most Yiddish-speaking Jews from the north and the east of Agnon's native region. Furthermore, his style— frequently obscure—is both enriched and marred by a characteristic elevation of language which comes from the solid tradition of Hebrew letters in Galicia, birthplace of the Haskalah, combined with the persisting German influence in that region. Agnon, in fact, lived in Germany for eleven years, and it is maintained by many readers that his complex Hebrew prose seems to translate better into German than into any other European language.

Agnon's best work—or at any rate, that part of his work whose virtues are least marred by obscurity—is in his earlier writings about the Hasidic life of early nineteenth-century Galicia. These works are idylls of a sort, in which a strong undercurrent of twentieth-century doubting that becomes more manifest in his later writings is here obscured by the haze of a pietistic utopia glimpsed through a great distance in time. The Bridal Canopy, which is the longest and most ambitious of these works,[1] is a sort of Hasidic Don Quixote, the knight of this story being an elderly Hasid who rides out into the world of the Galician villages seeking husbands for his three daughters, and the Sancho Panza his wagon driver. The world through which they ride can best be pictured in terms of the paintings of Marc Chagall; it is a world of objects which are perhaps not quite arranged in the conventional order, but it is vibrant with life in every unexpected corner, and the animals in it have as much on their minds as the human beings. The entire picture, though epic in conception, is somehow painted in miniature. Although there are many borrowings from Don Quixote in the book, such as the endless telling of long tales in wayside inns, the atmosphere differs radically from that of Cervantes' novel in being joyous and thoroughly infused with a piety that makes despair impossible. It takes up the same theme of Jewish long-suffering that preoccupied Bialik, but here endurance ends in success: at the end of his long odyssey, Reb Yudel finds husbands for his daughters and sets forth with his wife to spend his last years in Eretz Yisroel (the Land of Israel).

Agnon tells this story as if he were himself a Hasid of Reb Yudel's generation; his style is a kind of Hasidic singsong, heavily laden with pious allusions to the whole of Jewish religious literature—Bible, Talmud, Midrash, Zohar, and so on. This quality of rich allusiveness is the trademark of Agnon's writings: it is both the stamp of his particular genius and the element that turns his writing into so special a case in the world of secular literature—of which it is, after all, a part—that it is in danger of remaining only an admirable

[1] At this time it is also the only full-length novel by Agnon that has been published in an English translation (an excellent one, by I. M. Lask)—in 1937, by Doubleday, Doran & Co., New York.

literary curiosity, a byway of cultural history. This is true not only in an international perspective—Agnon's wordplays and allusions are notoriously unyielding to translation—but even in the perspective of Hebrew letters themselves. For Hebrew literature today is undergoing the same revolution that literature in general is undergoing in the democratic culture of the West. Today the literary audience in all the advanced countries of the world is larger and more heterogeneous than ever before in history. This is true not merely of the audience for the various kinds of subliteratures that mass literacy has produced, but also of readers who are prepared to respond to the finest writing. The audience for fine literature, therefore, can no longer be defined so easily as it once was in terms of a particular set of attitudes and predilections, or of a specific body of knowledge. The great literary spirits of the twentieth century, such as Camus and Silone, speak to any sensibility that is intelligent and serious, no matter what courses it has taken at school, or even if it has taken virtually none at all. In Israel today, as in all the Western democracies, an audience is emerging which is prepared to listen to writers who speak to thinking man in general and do not muffle their thoughts behind the parochialism of a special body of knowledge.

Now, such a development is a revolutionary departure from the aristocratic or elitist cultures of the past anywhere in the world; but it is particularly so in the case of the Hebrew literary tradition. Here was an extreme case of coterie literature, based on a common body of learning that was both specifically definable and voluminous, which was for nearly two thousand years almost the sole source of identity for the literary tradition. This, combined with the fact that the tradition was religious as well as national in character, gave it a cultural intensity that is in many ways enviable. A high degree of allusiveness is one of the pre-eminent characteristics of the entire Jewish literary tradition of the Diaspora. Even Yiddish literature, with its radically democratic impulses, could not avoid this convention; but some of the best manifestations of the convention in Yiddish literature come with a parody of it, as in the way in which Sholom Aleichem's simple workingmen constantly misquote their learned sources. In a way, the desire to parody the convention is of the very essence of the Yiddish impulse. But there is no such impulse in Agnon, who, after a few attempts at writing in Yiddish early in life, abandoned that language completely as a literary medium. In the same sense, he set aside a literary milieu which could draw its allusions more from life than from books, as a younger generation of Israeli writers, rooted in the soil of a Hebrew-speaking country, is now able to do. The fabric of Agnon's writing is a perfection of learned conventions, achieved by the monumental labors of a consummate artist; for those who are as learned as he in their Jewish sources, the experience of reading Agnon is filled with a richness perhaps unparalleled in contemporary world literature. But in another generation or two, even among those Israelis who are concerned with the highest literary values, those who are both learned enough to enjoy fully the experience Agnon has to provide and secular enough to be interested in reading him in the first place, will be very few indeed.

Agnon did not, however, remain solely in the world of nineteenth-century Hasidism for his literary material. There are, broadly speaking, two other settings in his writings: Eastern Europe in the late nineteenth or early twentieth century, when the traditional Jewish life was in decline, and an utterly "modern" world, most frequently described in terms of contemporary Jerusalem, where Agnon has lived most of his life. Although the painting-in-miniature, the pastiche, of such a work as *The Bridal Canopy* is what shows Agnon's literary skill at its best, he has been too much of an artist to confine himself to that idealized world. Choosing to chronicle in his writings the decline of pure faith since the days of Reb Yudel, Agnon changes his style noticeably in the transition from the Hasidic to the modern world. A highly personal and obscure mysticism replaces the more objective and conventionalized Hasidic variety, although the Hasidic and Kabbalistic foundations of the former are often clearly discernible; in the same way, a dense atmosphere of personal symbolism replaces the crowding of enchanted detail in the Hasidic miniature. The long personal quest of Reb Yudel is echoed in the more "modern" stories and novels, but the searching protagonist now suffers a loneliness and a threatening despair unknown to his Hasidic counterpart. Indeed, Agnon the modern, exiled in these later works from his nineteenth-century Galician utopia, suddenly takes on remarkable affinities with another Central European Jew of his generation, Franz Kafka.

This later development in Agnon is well characterized in his 1952 novel, *Temol Shilshum* (*Long Ago*). The hero of this tale, the

Galician Jew Isaac Kummer, is a descendant of Reb Yudel. Isaac, according to Agnon's opening sentence, "like the rest of our brothers, the men of our salvation, the sons of the Second Aliyah, left behind his country and birthplace and home town, and went up to Eretz Israel to rebuild it from its ruins and be rebuilt by it." This sounds very much, at first, as if Isaac is a true modern version of his ancestor; Agnon has combined in this sentence the classic rhetoric of Zionism with the flavor of his incantatory Hasidic style. But in the sequel the sentence proves to have been ironic. Even at the very beginning there are clear signs that the interval which separates Reb Yudel from Isaac Kummer, his descendant, is a valley into which pure faith has collapsed. Isaac's father, Shimeon, who does not approve of his son's impractical desire to go on Aliyah, is himself a businessman: "to Reb Yudel, who was full of faith, the Holy One Blessed Be He had given fulfillment[2] in accordance with that faith, whereas Shimeon his descendant placed his faith in business." Isaac is also looked upon with some scorn by his own contemporaries as they take up their worldly careers.

Once Isaac lands in Palestine, his Aliyah very quickly loses its purpose. He never becomes involved in the busy communal and political activities of most of the Second Aliyah pioneers. Here, the fact that he is Galician, and hence something of an outsider culturally, provides objective validation for Isaac's solitude; but, in fact, his alienation comes from a higher source, a genuine spiritual disturbance. Unlike that of the pioneers from Russia and northern Poland, his own Aliyah comes from an unconscious search for the faith of Reb Yudel, which has been lost to him. Instead of becoming the subject of the more classic Zionist history, Isaac increasingly wanders in the byways of the Yishuv, among an alienated intelligentsia sitting about in the cafés of Jaffa, a Bohemia in search of its soul not unlike its equivalent in any European capital (Agnon thus gives us a rare glimpse of this often unnoticed corner of life in Palestine during the epoch of the Second Aliyah). Isaac becomes involved in an utterly indecisive love affair, as his mind becomes increasingly preoccupied with memories of his childhood.

2 This is a characteristic Agnon wordplay. The "full" and the "fulfillment" of this passage are two forms of the Hebrew *shilem*, which also means "to pay." The "faith" of this passage is *bitahon*, which means "security," and also carries business connotations, like the English word.

Eventually Isaac more or less finds his own salvation in a further
"Aliyah" (literally "ascent"), when he goes up the hills to Jerusalem
and settles there. In Jerusalem he becomes involved in the life of the
Hasidim of Meah Shearim and marries a Hasidic girl. The Zion
which more or less saves him is thus a complete repudiation of
Second Aliyah ideals and a return to the pietism of Reb Yudel. But
even this salvation is a mixed one. The novel, which steadily re-
nounces all pretensions to realism as it moves onward, ends in an orgy
of symbolism. Shortly after his marriage Isaac is bitten and killed by a
mad dog, a creature which he had himself persecuted earlier in the
story. Throughout much of the last part of the book the wanderings
of this dog through the streets of Jerusalem is described in detail; he
seems to come to represent the classic wandering and suffering Jew of
the exile. His revenge upon Isaac at the end therefore seems to be a
final ironic confrontation between past and present. The book
suggests that there is no simple salvation through a return either to
Zion or to the pure faith of the "exile" that had been represented by
Reb Yudel. Galut becomes represented as a larger spiritual condition
of modern man, which has nothing to do with the mere physical fact
of being in Zion or in the Diaspora.

This novel is, to a large extent, a late fruition of the ambivalences
which had always been present in Agnon's literary generation, and
which had brought Bialik to stop writing altogether. But, appearing
as it did in the early 1950's, the book also signaled a forthcoming
change of climate in Israeli literature, particularly among a younger
generation of writers, over whom Agnon has had considerable influence. From the era of the Second Aliyah down to the first few years
after the founding of the state, Israeli writing was naturally dominated by a kind of "socialist realism," not imposed from the top as in
the Soviet Union, to be sure, but nonetheless firmly established due
to the overwhelming exuberance of the atmosphere of national
enterprise. For poets in particular, this epoch was in some ways the
fulfillment of a wish that most writers feel from time to time, of
being the makers of a poetry of exhortation, inspiring men to great
tasks. Nathan Alterman (b. 1910 in Warsaw) even managed to
produce some work of high literary quality in a weekly newspaper
column of poetry which, during the turbulent 1930's and 1940's,
actively engaged itself in the events of the day.

But, since after Homer at any rate, it has been among the foremost prerogatives of the writer to express doubt about the prevailing assumptions of the world around him; this is true even in the situation in which Israeli writers have found themselves. Even one of the foremost attempts to write a Zionist epic, Isaac Lamdan's (1900–1954) poem *Masada* includes a shade of doubt. Lamdan mingles autobiography with an epic image of pioneers ascending the slopes of the ancient zealot fortress; but standing victoriously atop Masada at the end, the poet is aware of a certain loneliness. David Maletz, another writer of Lamdan's generation, wrote novels about the kibbutz showing the ways in which some of the pioneers had not found personal salvation in these agrarian communities. But until 1948 these were merely scattered echoes of doubt in the epic poem the Jews of Palestine were living through.

In 1948 Moshe Shamir's novel, *He Walked Through the Fields,* made a sensation with its depiction of a kibbutznik and Haganah fighter as a heel and as a man filled with personal doubts. Shamir, who was born in Palestine in 1921, represented the first major arrival on the part of the young, Israeli-born generation which had been weaned on the struggle for statehood and the War of Independence. In the years that followed, this generation reached maturity and has now come to dominate the literary scene in Israel. For the most part, the writings of this generation have constituted a reflection upon its own central experience: the great struggle for national self-realization, followed by the inevitable disappointment of adjustment to the middle years of an ordinary life, both as a nation and as individuals. Caught up both by the spirit of modernism in literature and their frequent disapproval of what they have themselves become, these younger writers have often resorted to an iconoclasm even about the epic experiences of their youth. The outstanding manifestation of this feeling was in S. Yizhar's 1,200-page novel about the War of Independence, *The Days of Ziklag*, which appeared in 1958. This book was roundly condemned by many critics who said that it was a slur upon those who had fought and died in the struggle for independence, and this opposition prevented it from winning Israel's major literary award, the Bialik Prize, even though it is one of the most important novels to have appeared since statehood. What the book does is show soldiers in the War of Independence behaving like soldiers anywhere—eagerly anticipating their furloughs, complaining about their duties and sometimes trying to dodge them, and in general looking out for themselves. Few of them seem inspired by the glories of the national undertaking. The title is ironic: the group of soldiers upon which the novel focuses finds itself defending Tel Ziklag, the site of King David's ancient military headquarters. When they first arrive at the site and discover what it is, the following exchange takes place: " 'Look,' said Barzilai enthusiastically, 'isn't this great? . . . You can still make out an inscription! Don't you remember what happened at Ziklag? The wars of King David?' 'Big deal,' said Nahum, shrugging him off, and he turned away."[3]

Yizhar does not stop at this point in his criticisms; in this book, and elsewhere, his central concern is the moral problems involved in the treatment of Arabs by Israelis. "S. Yizhar" is the pen name of Yizhar Smilansky, who is a member of the Knesset and a nephew of the First Aliyah writer Moshe Smilansky. Yizhar's uncle was one of the great exponents of the ideal of a profound Arab-Jewish friendship; he had not only written romances about Arab life in Palestine, but was also eminently involved, along with Martin Buber and Judah Magnes, in the Ihud (Unity) movement of the 1940's, which advocated the establishment of a binational, Arab-Jewish state in Palestine. Yizhar has continued this family tradition by constantly seeking to awaken the conscience of Israeli Jews to the moments and ways in which they have not treated Arabs in a spirit true to the ideals of justice in the Jewish tradition.

Yizhar writes more as a reformer than most of his contemporaries do, but the mood he shares with them is one which tends to repudiate the Israeli ideal of the Jewish warrior, in favor of an image of gentleness and piety presented by a certain type of traditional Diaspora Jew, such as Reb Yudel. There is now a perceptible return on the part of this younger generation to the ambivalence of Bialik or Agnon concerning the Zionist destiny. Having re-emerged in the period following the Second World War, this mood is reinforced by a feeling of guilt concerning the destiny of the Jews of Europe under Hitler. Aharon Megged's short story, "The Name,"[4] focuses this mood upon a somewhat archetypal theme. For many Israelis, the changing of their names from Diasporic Jewish ones to purely

---

[3] S. Yizhar, Y'mei Ziklag (Tel-Aviv, 1958), p. 26.

[4] An English translation of this story, by Minna Givton, can be found in the volume entitled Israeli Stories, edited by Joel Blocker, with an introduction by Robert Alter (New York: Schocken Books, 1962).

Hebrew forms was a necessary symbolic representation of Zionist self-transformation, but this step has not always been taken without a certain sense of its tragic aspects. In Megged's story an old man hopes that his granddaughter will name her new, Israeli-born son after her cousin, who was killed in Russia by the Nazis. The name of this cousin, who had been the vehicle of his grandfather's hopes, was Mendele—a name as unacceptable to young Israelis as it generally is to young American Jews. The girl calls her young son Ehud, but this small act takes on tragic significance in the story; it is a sudden termination of two thousand years of suffering and hope.

The echo of the Holocaust heard in this story gives signs of growing more pronounced in the near future. The Holocaust was a central moment in Jewish history, immense in its tragic proportions, and also intimately related to the creation of the state of Israel. The younger generation of writers, confident of their Israeli identity in a way that Bialik's contemporaries were not, are increasingly inclined to seek the nature of that identity even in this most Diasporic of events, as their tragic sense heightens. In this pursuit they are being true to the essence of the Jewish literary vision—of the biblical vision itself—which is epic in character and tends to discover a fundamental identification between the personal sufferings and aspirations of the writer and the destiny of his people as a whole. Such a vision, formulated by the first generation for whom Hebrew is the spontaneous vehicle of their thoughts, seems to promise a return to the biblical mode in style as well as in mood. Such a biblical character is to be found, for example, in the major statement thus far written on the Eichmann Trial by an Israeli, Haim Guri's *The Glass Cage*.[5] Guri is a poet, who covered the trial for an Israeli newspaper. But this collection of his daily reports is not mere coverage; it is a form of classical drama in the French or Greco-Roman sense, in which the characters come forth to speak of great events which have taken place offstage. This particular drama is given its form by the consciousness of the poet, reacting to the proceedings in the courtroom. The themes themselves seem to be the source of the book's success in establishing a modern Hebrew prose diction in the biblical mode.

It may well be that, in the near future, the most important

[5] *Mul Ta Ha'zichuchit* (Tel-Aviv, 1962). There is a French translation, *La Cage de Verre*, published by Albin Michel in 1964. The title refers to the bulletproof glass booth in which Eichmann sat while in the courtroom.

advances in Israeli prose are to be made by poets, the focus of whose
work has regularly brought them to the noblest sources of the
language. The most distinguished novel yet written by a younger
Israeli, Yehuda Amihai's Lo Me'achshav Lo Mi'kan[6] (Not of This
Time, Not of This Place), is in fact the work of a man who
established his literary reputation as a poet. Amihai's poetry has
always been remarkable for its "metaphysical" character, its way of
yoking together images—ancient and modern, elevated and homely—
in entirely unexpected but often enlightening ways. This quality has
now been brought to bear in his novel, which he has made into a
vehicle uniting intense personal soul-searching with an epic vision of
modern Jewish history.

Unlike most Israeli writers of his generation, Amihai (b. 1924) was
born in Germany. Although he was still a child when he emigrated to
Palestine with his family, there remains an element of alienation in
his work which comes from his background, and which both provides
his language with a special vitality and enables him to formulate in
personal terms the tragic sense of Jewish destiny that is arising among
his contemporaries. At the same time he is very much a part of his
generation of Israelis, weaned into manhood, like them, by his
participation in the War of Independence. These various strands of
his own experience are woven together in his novel by the device of
creating a protagonist split into two parts—an "I" and a "he"—
whose complementary stories are told in alternating sections throughout the length of the book. The narrative begins in contemporary
Jerusalem, where the two-part protagonist, a professor of archaeology,
decides to spend his summer (1) staying in Jerusalem (as the "he"),
where he has a love affair which seems to reflect the purposelessness
his life has taken on in the years since his youthful participation in
the War of Independence, and (2) taking a trip back to his native
town in Germany (as the "I"), to confront both his origins and his
guilt concerning the fate of his townsmen. Both of these courses are
followed, and the two of them are thematically interwoven in such a
way as to provide a constant confrontation with various levels of the
Jewish and Zionist experience in this century. The novel therefore
becomes a comprehensive statement of all the themes which are
concerning the present generation of Israeli writers.

[6] Tel-Aviv, 1963. An English translation is to be published by Harper &
Row.

Amihai's work shares with that of Agnon a certain richness of literary fabric, a mood of ambivalence about Zion, and a quality of melancholy which finds its focus for both men in the theme of unrealizable love and its setting in the Jerusalem in which they both live. The differences between the younger writer and the older one who has influenced him are therefore significant. The allusive richness of Amihai's writing is founded not upon learned tradition as in Agnon but upon the objects of everyday life. Whereas Agnon is the product of the traditions of the Diaspora, Amihai writes as an Israeli to a generation for whom Zion is its natural environment. The younger man seems to represent, in other words, the appearance of a genuinely Israeli literature, one that is rooted in the Land of Israel for the first time in two millennia. It is therefore also a most favorable sign that, between these two men, one representing the end of an old tradition, and the other the beginning of a new one, there are elements of continuity. A genuinely Israeli literature must blossom both out of the land and out of the history of the Diaspora. To achieve this fusion of elements, Israel has had to undergo a period of growing pains that has been harsh and tragic in many ways; but the works of Amihai, Guri and others suggest that such pains are at last to find compensation in the flowering of a national literature that will be at once truly Hebrew and—if the irony may be allowed—truly Jewish.

CHAPTER 8

The Religion of Israel

ALTHOUGH nationalism has always existed in the Jewish tradition as a distinct current, it can never free itself entirely from involvement with the Jewish religion. For a time, during the antireligious reaction among Russian Jews at the turn of the century, both the Bundists and the Labor Zionists sought to substitute a myth of oppression for a religious tradition as the cultural basis for Jewish identity; but this aspiration has now largely run its course. Bundism, for all its power and richness in the lives of some two generations, has only succeeded in causing a third or fourth generation either to begin losing its Jewish identity or to search elsewhere for it. Zionism devoted all its energies to the task of creating a state, and then was flung upon one of the gravest crises a revolutionary movement can confront: success. From the time of the achievement of statehood, the energies that created Zionism have steadily moved on into a deepening query as to what their larger spiritual purposes had been. Many of those who had once said that their aspiration was to have Israel become simply "a state like any other" have now found it difficult to settle for this aim in practice: even amidst the rocks of Canaan, the sense of the uniqueness of Jewish history is too overbearing, the legacy of Diasporic self-consciousness which had been the chief force creating Zionism itself too powerful, to allow such a thing to happen.

A certain return to piety which is now taking place among many Israelis of previously secularist inclinations is, in some respects, simply a counterpart of the mild religious revival that is taking place among middle-class people throughout the Western world, upon whom relative prosperity and leisure have conspired, along with a sudden feeling of purposelessness, to induce a new curiosity about religion. Such a mood is, furthermore, often bound up with a fervor of nationalist feeling, a desire to root one's uncertain piety in the solid earth of the homeland. Now, this frame of mind is bound to produce a particularly intense spiritual experience for an Israeli, due to the unique inextricability of the religious from the national strands in his heritage. For an Israeli, the rational and emotional logic of the ideal of national revival leads almost inevitably to an at least partial recovery of religious roots. Moses Hess recognized this when he said that, "I myself, if I had a family, would not only actually have joined a pious Jewish congregation but would also regularly observe in my house all the fasts and feasts in order to keep alive in me and my descendants the Jewish folk traditions."[1] These are the words of a man who, as a young radical some twenty years earlier, had been denouncing all forms of "clericalism," Jewish and Christian alike. But this pattern of return is not at all unique to Moses Hess among Zionist-Socialists; some of the Labor Zionist kibbutzim, for example, are now beginning to set aside classroom time for an at least modified form of religious instruction for their children, and a few of them have even built synagogues—this would have been an unthinkable heresy thirty years ago. Perhaps this attitude was best expressed by a friend of mine in Jerusalem, himself a former kibbutznik and secularist radical, when he saw me trying to conceal my surprise as he took out skullcaps and prayer books with which to make a blessing over the Friday evening meal. "I want my son," he said, "to realize that he is a Jew."

The common element in all these manifestations is the desire to educate one's children, to keep alive in them traditions that are both religious and national at the same time. Not that this is the sole reason for all these revivals of piety. Clearly, an internal, personal confrontation with religion on the part of the parents is taking place as well, but the ultimate question of *belief* is being deferred by them, while a more palpable form of justification stands in for it. One may or may not find belief at the end of a personal path of inquiry, but mere doubts are not sufficient reason—in the eyes of Moses Hess or of my friend in Jerusalem—for putting an end to a tradition that has

[1] Moses Hess, *Rome and Jerusalem*, p. 51.

been handed down from father to son for at least three thousand years. This feeling on their part is the expression of a fundamentally and traditionally Jewish outlook in two ways. In the first place, it is another manifestation of the traditional Jewish appetite to survive as a national entity, to maintain the existence of a distinct Jewish people, for whatever reason and at whatever cost, down to the end of days. Among those Jews who maintain their traditional religious beliefs reasonably intact, this passion for survival is at least accounted for in terms of messianic purposes. But this passion often remains among Jews even when all other traces of their religious or cultural identity have been lost. It is simply a primeval Jewish appetite, the last one to disappear before an individual Jew becomes completely absorbed—in the Diaspora—into the culture surrounding him. The fact that it also persists in Israel demonstrates that this aspiration to maintain a national identity is not merely national in the usual sense of the word.

The second way in which one can perceive a traditionally Jewish impulse in this desire to maintain the continuity of religious traditions even when the foundations of one's belief are, at best, ambivalent can be characterized in terms of a celebrated essay by Ahad Ha-Am, called "Sacred and Profane." According to Ahad Ha-Am (who is here using the word rendered into English as "profane" in its meaning of "nonreligious" or "nonsacred," without any pejorative connotations), the essence of any profane doctrine is such that it can be understood and restated in a variety of forms. A philosophical work, unlike a poem, can be paraphrased without any essential loss of meaning. But in religious doctrine, as in poetry, the essence is in the form itself. The rituals and sacred texts of a religion are more fundamental than any ideas which they may be deemed to express; in fact, while the ideas may vary from one generation to the next, the fundamental forms of the religion do not. It is precisely the purpose of sacred tradition, according to Ahad Ha-Am, to provide a permanent and immutable receptacle for constantly changing ideas.

Now, a profound attachment to traditional forms is indeed to be found in any religion; but there is no other religious tradition in the West with so pronounced a tendency as Judaism to exclude theology from the central place of importance occupied by ritual and sacred text. Moses Maimonides is the only theologian who has had major doctrinal significance in Judaism, but even he did not address himself as St. Thomas Aquinas did, for example, to the question of the existence of God. This latter question has, in fact, no more relevance within a traditionally Jewish frame of reference than the question "Does a point exist?" would have to a student of Euclidian geometry. Within Judaism, the concept of God is axiomatic, the central datum upon which the entire system is founded. To someone emotionally rooted in the system, the merely rationalistic and endlessly evasive question of "existence" can have little or no relevance. To those whose roots in the Jewish religion have been partially but not completely torn up (and the uprooting is never complete so long as there is any persisting sense of "national" identity, however secularist it professes to be), personal doubts about the existence of God are often subsumed to a feeling of attachment—the product of three thousand years of waiting for the sublime to turn up—to a religious framework within which confidence about this question could, after all, return at some future date, either to a subsequent generation or even, perhaps, to one's self. Such a conception of things is another manifestation of the traditional Jewish resistance to the idea that there is any gap between thought and action. Religiosity of spirit is seen to consist, above all, in religiosity of acts; in the Hasidic tradition, at any rate, if these acts are performed fervently enough (with kavanah), then they themselves become the form of one's beliefs.

All this might seem to imply that the Jewish religious tradition is—as many of its detractors have maintained throughout history—a narrowly legalistic one, in which emphasis is placed upon the exacting performance of a vast array of ordinances to the detriment of the true cultivation of a higher morality. Indeed, Jewish religion can turn into this in its worst moments, as is the case in any religious tradition when piety turns into a mere priggish attachment to conventions. But, at its best, the Jewish tradition of Law is a constitutional one in the American sense, a constantly moving dialectic of regard for legal precedents and responsible extensions of them in the name of a large spiritual conception, which must ever adapt itself to the world in which it lives. This tradition has been extremely rich and varied at times, and does not necessarily belong to any single line of interpretation, such as the Eastern European Jewish orthodoxy which tends to monopolize religious institutional life in Israel today. Indeed, modern research into the civilization of the Jewish Second Commonwealth (the period in Palestine from the end of the Babylonian Exile to the destruction of the Second Temple by the Romans) has discovered its religious life to be so varied that there may not then have even existed anything like a "normative" Judaism such as prevailed among Ashkenazic Jewry before the nineteenth century. There was clearly a line, crossed by Samaritanism and then by Pauline Christianity, beyond which the departure from central traditions became something that was no longer Judaism at all; but within that frontier there were manifestations which went a long way from Pharisaism, even though it was the latter that became the exclusive prototype for the Judaism of the Diaspora. Pharisaism itself, for that matter, was broader and more flexible in its own day than the Eastern European orthodoxy which has descended from it.

There have always been clerical establishments throughout the history of the Diaspora, but their role has varied considerably in character and importance. The spiritual life of Judaism in medieval Spain, for example, seems to have been quite free of any domination on the part of a narrow clericalism. Since the Spanish Jews, even in the liberal religious atmosphere within which they lived, tended not to become absorbed into the surrounding culture (Islam never exerted the same powerful attraction upon Jews as Christianity has always done), the chief traditional justification for building a clerical ghetto was not present. In this respect, the situation was quite different in nineteenth-century Germany, the other major epoch prior to the twentieth century in which a Jewish community fully participated in the civilization surrounding it and also maintained its separate identity. As soon as the "Enlightenment" movement initiated by Moses Mendelssohn had begun to break down the barriers of clerical obscurantism that had hitherto surrounded them, large numbers of German Jews became susceptible to the pull of assimilation and conversion. In this atmosphere, the old clerical establishment was no longer adequate to cope with the situation created by the powerful attraction of a European culture it had traditionally repudiated, and a new, nonnormative clericalism came into being—Reform Judaism.

The Reform movement was a major challenge to the reign of an orthodoxy grown rigid, and although it tended at its worst to be dominated by an overweening passion for middle-class respectability and to eschew the more national elements of the Jewish identity, it nevertheless served as a spearhead into new areas of Jewish religious thought. As a result of the atmosphere created by Reform Judaism, it was no longer necessary for a Jew of modern but pious leanings to have to make a stark choice between a rigid Jewish orthodoxy, on the one hand, and Christianity, on the other. One could now find the path toward the formulation of a modern Judaism, cut off neither from tradition nor from general European civilization. Ultimately, the best such formulations were conceived in reaction to Reform; men like Moses Hess, Franz Rosenzweig, and Martin Buber formed their religious visions in opposition to its pallid bourgeois atmosphere. But even in the opposition that it created the Reform movement was dialectically responsible for a quickening of the religious atmosphere which even had a certain modernizing effect upon Jewish orthodoxy in Germany. In America, Reform played a similar dialectical role; the masses of Eastern European Jewish immigrants and their children were largely inclined to move out of the strict bounds of orthodoxy, but finding the established American Reform movement to be too nontraditional—and perhaps too German—for their taste, they were drawn in large numbers to the middle way of Conservative Judaism. Conservatism has in turn had a liberalizing influence upon one wing of Orthodox Judaism in America, with the result that the boundary lines between these two are not always readily discernible.

No such changes took place in the religious atmosphere of Judaism in Eastern Europe, which continued to be dominated by the narrow dogmatism of the old clerical establishment. Even Hasidism had run its course as a creative religious movement by the end of the nineteenth century, and the Hasidic sects tended by this time to be the most zealous of all in their dogmatism. It was rather the secularist movements, chiefly socialism and Zionism, which became the major outlets among Eastern European Jews for a creative impulse which was often quasi-religious in character. The climate of Zionism made it possible for men like Ahad Ha-Am and A. D. Gordon to work their way toward a vision which fused traditional Jewish religious values and practices with a modern outlook, but these were only isolated manifestations. Most Eastern European Zionists accepted the philosophical vision of these two men without its religious elements, while most religious Jews in Poland and Russia did not pay any attention to Gordon or Ahad Ha-Am at all. It is only in recent years that their unique fusion of Zionism and traditional religiosity has come to have importance in Israel; but this current of thought now faces the same

institutional obstacles it has always faced. For contemporary Israel
has inherited, among the elements of her large and varied legacy from
Eastern Europe, a traditionally rigid and powerful clerical establishment.

There are actually two principal groupings in Israel's religious
establishment today. One is descended from the old extremely religious communities which had settled in Palestine with no Zionist
commitment whatsoever, and is concentrated in certain quarters such
as the Meah Shearim section of Jerusalem. These communities were
often hostile to Zionism, and one sect in the Meah Shearim quarter,
the *Neturai Karta* (Defenders of the Citadel), still does not recognize the state of Israel. But these ultrareligious communities have, for
the most part, come to recognize that they must deal with the state
to maintain their own interests, and they have created their own
political parties, the *Agudat Israel* (Society of Israel) and *Poalei
Agudat Israel* (Workers of the Society of Israel), which together
hold six seats in the present Knesset.

The larger and more significant grouping is descended from the
religious Zionist movement. Even though Zionism was initially
founded by men and women whose impulses were secularist, there
was never anything in the Zionist idea intrinsically irreconcilable with
religious orthodoxy. The bulk of the Eastern European Jewish religious establishment opposed Zionism in its early days only because of
the secularist notions with which it was riddled, and because many of
the most spiritually ambitious of the Zionists seemed to be arrogating
to themselves a task of national redemption that, in the eyes of the
orthodox, could be performed only by the Messiah. Indeed, the
major architect of the reconciliation between religious orthodoxy and
Zionist aspirations, Rabbi Abraham Isaac Kook (1865–1935), the first
Chief Rabbi of Palestine under the Mandate, felt put upon to argue
that the Zionist pioneers, for all their religious heresy, could be
perceived as men and women divinely appointed to pave the way for
the coming of the Messiah. But even before Rabbi Kook there were
imaginative orthodox rabbis who were sufficiently inspired with the
Zionist idea to be willing to overlook their own reservations about
most Zionists. The foremost among these was Rabbi Samuel Mohi-
lever, who, in 1893, was authorized by the Hibbat Zion organization
in Odessa to form a separate office as a center for religious Zionism.
This office was called *Mizrahi*, which was an abbreviation of the

words *Merkaz Ruhani* (Spiritual Center), but which also means "Eastern," a word rich both with Zionist and traditional religious connotations. Following the schismatic trend of Zionism in general at that time, the Mizrahi became a political party in 1901. It even eventually gave rise to its own labor trend (as did the Agudat Israel), which became a separate party, *Ha'poel Ha'mizrahi* (The Labor Mizrahi), in 1922. But in 1955 this latter group merged with its parent organization once again to form the National Religious Party, which today holds eleven seats in the Knesset. Although the Mizrahi trend is primarily Ashkenazi in origin, leadership and outlook, it has received its principal support in recent years from pious Oriental Jews.

The distribution of seats among the competing parties in the Knesset has been such as to give extraordinary bargaining power to the religious bloc, which together holds seventeen seats. The Agudat Israel has not itself participated in any Cabinet, but its support has enabled the National Religious party to hold the portfolios of Religious Affairs, Social Welfare and the Interior with regularity. In exchange for supporting the Mapai-led coalitions, the religious bloc has been able to extend the power of clericalism in such matters as Sabbath restrictions and anti-pig-breeding laws, and to maintain the already well-entrenched position that the rabbinate had obtained in the realm of civil law under Turkish rule and the Mandate. It is in this latter area that the power of clericalism has been most severely felt in Israel, particularly in matters relating to marriage.

There are, in effect, two court systems in Israel today; one is the standard secular system to be found in any democratic state, the other is the religious court system. This arrangement is the legacy of the old *millet* system used by the Ottoman Empire to deal with the always complex matter of the religious complexion of the Levant. Under the *millet* system, an individual was given legal status in accordance with the religious group to which he was attached, and a large part of his affairs were officially conducted through the institutions of his religious group. Such an arrangement seems out of place in the liberal atmosphere we know in the West; but here, if an individual remains free of any religious affiliation, he still lives his life and dies largely like a Christian or Judaeo-Christian: the atmosphere is culturally homogeneous. In the old Ottoman Levant, on the other hand, the choice of one religious affiliation or another was the choice of the civilization with which one identified oneself. This system has passed on virtually without alteration into the state of Israel, in which the established Jewish, Muslim and Christian corporations are juridically equal. On the corporate level, the system is an entirely liberal one: the Jewish religion has no special privileges as compared with the others. But on the level of the individual person, Israel stands alongside Italy in one major departure from the practices of the other liberal democracies of the world: civil marriage, and hence marriage between two people of different faiths, does not take place there.

For the majority of Israelis this arrangement at least does not create the same restriction upon divorce as it does for the majority of Italians. In the Jewish tradition, a divorce has never been difficult to obtain if both parties consent to it. But in the strictly orthodox establishment which governs Jewish religious institutions in Israel there persist certain archaisms which are not easily tolerated by the modern sensibility. For example, a woman whose husband dies and leaves behind him an unmarried brother must receive the latter's consent if she wishes to marry someone other than he—a situation that usually leads to humiliation and often to flagrant abuse. A more widespread set of problems beset anyone bearing the name of Cohen, or some name manifestly derived from this word, which means "priest." The possession of the name is taken to designate direct descent from the Temple priesthood of antiquity, and so all sorts of restrictions attach to a Cohen, the import of which is to maintain him in the condition of purity appropriate to his priestly status. He cannot, for example, come into the presence of a dead body, which in ancient times was considered to be contaminating. Furthermore, he is not permitted to marry a divorced woman; the child of such a marriage would be considered a mamzer—a bastard—an outcast from the Jewish community.

These barbarisms, which represent a significant obstacle in the way of the complete realization of a modern democratic state, still only apply to relatively few instances. The problem which has much broader import—although still far more so in theory than in practice —is the question of intermarriage. It is over this issue—and questions related to it—that a major constitutional conflict has begun to emerge in the country between the secular and the religious court systems, which cannot easily establish the boundary lines between

The Religion of Israel

one another's jurisdictions. There is still no question of the performance of civil marriages in Israel; no authority has the power to do it. The problem, rather, revolves around the recognition of marriages performed outside the state of Israel. Many Jewish immigrants have entered the country with non-Jewish spouses. In recent years, increasing numbers of young Israelis have married non-Jews in civil marriages outside the country. All these marriages, like any marriage contracted within the country, must be officially entered at an office of the National Registry. Now, there have been cases in which the National Registry clerk has refused to enter the marriage, but the civil courts have directed him to do so every time. This means that these civil marriages contracted outside the country must at any rate be legally *registered;* the larger question of whether such a marriage is really considered to *exist,* in every legal and moral respect, by the community at large is still left unresolved. There are undoubtedly numerous clashes to come between the civil and rabbinical authorities in this matter.

The secular courts, in other words, have generally taken a position related to the liberal conception of religion and marriage to be found in most Western countries. According to this conception, religion is only a private matter, and does not enter into consideration in the legal sanctioning of a marriage. But there is one instance, intimately bound up with the question of marriage, in regard to which the civil courts in Israel are regularly obliged to participate in the formulation of a juridical category applying to individuals which is at least quasi-religious in character. This is the question, often arousing stormy controversy in Israel, of "Who is a Jew?" It is obvious why this question is an important one to the religious authorities, especially when they are about to perform marriages, and they furthermore have their well-established criteria for answering it. But the question is also germane to certain constitutional matters, particularly those relating to the Law of Return, passed in 1950. This is one of the fundamental laws of the state, a fulfillment of one of the central purposes of the Zionist ideal. It gives to every Jew in the world—with only certain exceptions, such as escaping criminals—the right to enter Israel immediately as an immigrant; it is furthermore implemented by the Nationality Law of 1951, which gives automatic Israeli citizenship to every Jewish immigrant who desires it. These laws have made the state of Israel into one of the greatest rescue operations in history;

but they also make it necessary for the civil authorities to establish a definition of the Jew for legal purposes.

This problem of definition goes back to one of the unique paradoxes of Jewish history: that of a community dispersed among other communities in the world, whose identity is at once religious and national in character. The historic foundation of the Jewish identity is, as we have seen, inextricably bound up with religious elements; and yet, a Jewish individual can be utterly nonreligious and still be considered Jewish, both by himself and by the most orthodox religious authorities. This is quite simply a matter of inheritance: the child of Jewish parents is a Jew. From the point of view of the individual, it is also often a matter of feeling, especially among those who suffered under the Nazis in the name of their Jewish identity; for such persons, there is often a religious passion about their Jewishness no less profound than that of an orthodox person, but completely different from it in traditional terms. Such persons understand their Jewish identity in historic terms—terms more appropriate than any other to the secular religiosity of the twentieth-century spirit—rather than in traditional ones of Jewish law, but their own conception of their Jewish identity does not conflict with the very different conception of the rabbis so long as they are the children of two Jewish parents. Where a conflict—and a great moral problem— has arisen is in the case of children of only one Jewish parent, who have nevertheless lived and suffered as Jews. In this matter, the grounds for a definition which prevail among the rabbinical authorities are somewhat restricted: a child's Jewish identity is defined according to its mother. In other words, the child of a Jewish mother is Jewish, even if the father is not; but the child of a Jewish father and a non-Jewish mother is not considered Jewish, and if he wanted to be so, he would have to undergo a religious conversion like any Gentile. But a man living today, more or less secular in his outlook, who has experienced imprisonment in a concentration camp because he is the son of a Jewish father, can hardly be expected to be willing to validate his claim to Jewish identity by undergoing a religious conversion.

For this reason, the civil authorities have consistently sought to liberalize the definition of a Jew. For the purposes of the Law of Return and the Nationality Law, which apply to matters in which the religious authorities have no jurisdiction, this aim has been fairly easy to achieve. The practical criterion simply has been:

A person who declares in good faith that he is a Jew, and he is not a member of some other religious faith, will be registered as a Jew.

This definition is a vigorous endorsement of a modern ethical-historical conception of Jewish identity, as opposed to the traditional religious-legal one. But it is still severely limited in its jurisdiction. The son of a Jewish father and a Gentile mother, who considers himself a Jew and has suffered for this identification, is allowed to enter Israel and obtain automatic citizenship, but in principle he still may not marry a Jewish woman unless he converts. Some of the secular leaders of the state of Israel have therefore ardently advocated, not merely the liberal definition of the Jew that now exists in the civil realm, but a revision in the religious definition itself. Supreme Court Justice Haim Cohen, who himself received rabbinical ordination in his youth, argues that there are Talmudic precedents for defining a Jew religiously in just the way that the state does today.

Clearly the time has come when a widespread religious reform is needed in Israel. The narrow and monolithic clericalism which currently stands unrivaled in Israel is intolerable, not only to the modern secularist outlook but also to the spirit of many participants in the revived religious mood that has emerged in the country since statehood. Israel shows signs of becoming, true to her ancient traditions, a remarkable center of religious creativity in the world. This is due not only to the religious passions inherent in Zionism and the poetic stimulus provided by the land itself, but also to the fact that the great German-Jewish tradition of creative religious thought was, as it were, physically transferred to Israel with the emigration there of Martin Buber and his circle. This tradition could flower once again in an atmosphere more liberal than that which presently exists in Israel, closer to that of nineteenth-century German and twentieth-century American Judaism, or to the "nonnormative" spirit of the Second Commonwealth. The Israeli rabbinate of today, although it in no way partakes of anything like the spirit of assimilationism which often prevailed among the priesthood of the Second Commonwealth, is nevertheless in a situation somewhat analogous to it: a powerful establishment, rigidly adhering to practices and attitudes no longer seen as relevant by the community at large.

Any religious reform made in Israel could not, of course, take place without reference to the Diaspora. Now that the first flush of Zionist

enthusiasm is over, it is fully understood in Israel that not all the
Jews in the world are going to settle there in the foreseeable future. A
certain Diasporic appetite remains in Judaism, felt, in fact, even by
Israelis themselves to some extent, as we have seen. Both Israelis and
Jews in other parts of the world have come to see that Judaism is not
yet to be understood solely in terms of a contiguous national community living within a single state, and was indeed never to be
understood in precisely that way. The restoration of a Jewish state
was needed to recover the moral health of Judaism, but the universalist appetite remains in Judaism as well. Therefore, the Judaism of
the next historical epoch will consist of a spiritual collaboration
between the state of Israel and the Jewish communities throughout
the world. In fact, Orthodox rabbis in America, for example, have
already had considerable influence upon the internal religious life of
Israel; but this influence has naturally served to strengthen the
orthodox religious establishment there. On the other hand, American
Conservative and Reform rabbis have not enjoyed influence enough
in Israel as yet. An infusion of their kind of liberal clericalism into
Israeli life could produce great stirrings in religious thought. Among
the large majority of Israelis who cannot in good conscience conform
to traditional Jewish orthodoxy, there are many who feel pious
stirrings enough within themselves that they would be quite amenable to some kind of modernized religious institutional life. Furthermore, such a liberalization would break through the still predominantly Eastern European framework of religion in Israel and enable
the Oriental Jewish spirit to make itself felt more significantly. The
results of such a distillation could in turn redound upon the Jewish
communities of the Diaspora, giving greater vigor, for example, to
American Reform and Conservative Judaism, which often tend to
have a too pallidly middle-class character. In this way, a truly
"ecumenical" reform in Judaism could take place, which would surely
have reverberations within the religious and moral climate of whatever nations Jews are to be found in throughout the world.

This would be a return to the universalist impulse which has
always resided in Judaism, that impulse which, among other things,
gave rise both to Christianity and to Islam. Israel was created out of
an ardent revival of the national spirit, a return to the uncompromising zeal of the defenders of Masada, and their refusal to be separated
from the Land. Some Zionists dreamed for a while that virtually

every last Jew in the world would come to settle in a reborn state of Israel. But now, as we have seen, Israelis are recovering a sense of the Diaspora, and are coming to perceive that the universalist impulse in Judaism is not reconcilable with the kind of exclusive nation-state that predominated in the late-nineteenth-century Europe in which Zionism originated. Indeed, there are signs that the European states themselves, which once represented the spirit of exclusive nationalism at its height, are moving on to a new ideal of internationalism. Cultural distinctness no longer has to imply a rigid and often aggressive political exclusiveness. This can be as true of the Middle East as it is of Europe. Israel, far from being a latter-day formulation of the old-style European nation-state, is a unique creation: a political state which is also the spiritual center for a people and for a religion represented throughout the nations of the world. It is the local habitation of a universalist ideal. As such, perhaps the combination of its legacy from the West and its presence in the Middle East could make it one day into the medium through which East and West might come together and discover the spiritual rewards of harmony and real understanding of one another. Here is the possibility of a unique and infinitely rewarding historic experiment; is it to be cheaply traded in for worn-out old patterns of strife and mutual destruction?

Index

Abdullah, King, 126, 170, 175
Abraham, 15, 18
Abramovich, Shalom Jacob, 89
Abulafia, Abraham, 68–69, 70
Acre, Palestine, 152, 166, 167
Aden, 127
Adrianople, Turkey, 78
Agnon, Shmuel Yoseph, 275–80, 285
Agudat Israel (Society of Israel), 292, 293
Ahavat Zion (Love of Zion) (Mapu), 92
Ahdut Ha'avodad (Unity of Labor), 234, 235, 236, 240–41
Aleichem, Sholom, 91, 271, 272–73, 277
Aleppo, Syria, 127
Alexander II, Tsar, 90
Alexander III, Tsar, 90
Aliens Act (1905), 122
Ali, Prince, 126
Aliyah, see Fifth Aliyah; First Aliyah; Fourth Aliyah; Second Aliyah; Third Aliyah
Aliya Bet, see Illegal immigration
Al-Kawukji, Fawzi, 169, 176
Allenby, General Edmund, 152
Alliance Israélite Universelle, 95, 96, 111, 183, 261
Allon, Colonel Yigal, 176, 237
Altalena, S.S., 174, 244
Alterman, Nathan, 280
Amenia, New York, 112, 113
America and the Americans, 91–92, 117, 121, 147, 160–61, 164, 166, 168, 172, 195, 197, 245
American Jewry, 123, 160–61, 197, 291
American Judaism, 297
Amihai, Yehuda, 284–85
Amman, 127
Amoraim, the, 13
Amsterdam, Holland, 68, 80
Anatolia, 119
Anglo-American Committee of Inquiry, 163, 164–65, 166
Anilewitz, Mordechai, 145
Antiochus Epiphanes, King, 12

Anti-Semitism, 27, 36, 37, 38, 39–40, 44–45, 48–49, 54, 63, 107, 108, 111, 117, 121, 126, 165, 234
Apocalypse, the, 79
Aqaba, Transjordan, 128
Arabic language, 253, 255
Arab-Israeli War, 168–76
Arab League, 172, 175
Arab Legion, 173, 175
Arab nationalism, 123, 125–36
Arab riots, 133, 134–35, 152, 154, 168, 179, 227
Arabs, the, 105, 109, 123, 125–36, 148, 153, 154, 156–57, 164, 165, 167, 168, 169–76, 184, 187, 200–01, 227, 228, 255
Aramaic language, 249, 250, 253
Archaelogical excavation, 16–20
Arms and munitions, 168–69, 174
Ashkenazi Jewry and Ashkenazim, 195, 198, 199, 200, 201, 202, 203, 204, 224, 290, 293
Asquith, Herbert, 121
Atlantic, S.S., 150
Auschwitz death camp, 137, 142, 145, 146, 147, 159
Austria, 81, 88
Auto-Emancipation (Pincker), 55, 94, 95, 96
Avriel, Ehud, 168

Baal, worship of, 8
Baal Shem, 83
Baal Shem Tov, 82–85, 99
Babel, Isaac, 155
Bab-el-Wad, Palestine, 170
Babylonia and the Babylonians, 9, 179, 181, 249, 250
Babylonian Exile, 9–10, 11, 12, 15, 249, 250, 289
Bacher, Eduard, 56, 57
Baden, Grand Duke of, 54
Baer, Rabbi Dov, 85
Baghdad, Iraq, 181
Balfour, Arthur James, 121–22, 123
Balfour Declaration (1917), 53, 115, 117, 122, 123–25, 129, 130, 133, 161

301

Index